MILITARY H

OF

THE CAMPAIGN OF 1882

IN

EGYPT.

PREPARED IN THE INTELLIGENCE BRANCH OF THE WAR OFFICE

BY

COLONEL J. F. MAURICE, ROYAL ARTILLERY.

Originally printed and published in 1887

AUTHOR'S PREFACE.

IN the course of the following narrative frequent references will be found to the opinions and views of Arabi Pasha and of the chief leaders of the Egyptian forces employed against us. For these I am indebted to the most skilful and careful cross-questioning of the Egyptian State prisoners in Ceylon by Colonel Duncan, at present Deputy Quartermaster-General in Dublin. It seemed advisable to compare the views of what took place, presented by the official documents, and by the numerous letters from officers of all branches of the force engaged, with which I have been favoured, with such statements as could be obtained from the other side. By the kind permission of the Governor of Ceylon, and with the assistance of Sir John McLeod, then the Commander-in-Chief in the island, this was done in such a way as to assure the prisoners that the sole motive for the inquiries was to ascertain the truth. I think it will be found that considerable light is thrown upon some parts of the History by the evidence so supplied.

J. MAURICE, *Colonel, R.A.*

May 10, 1887.

NOTE.

The Official History of the 1882 Campaign was completed in manuscript by Colonel Maurice some time prior to the Nile Expedition of 1884-85. On his departure for that Expedition it was left to be edited and brought out by an officer who was himself interrupted in the work by being sent on active service to South Africa. It was again resumed by Colonel Maurice on his return from the Sudan, and the subsequent time has been occupied in circulating the work in proof among the most important actors in the campaign, in order as far as possible to correct the work by criticism from those who could assist in making it a true report of what took place.

H. BRACKENBURY.
D.Q.M.G.

TABLE OF CONTENTS.

MILITARY HISTORY

OF

THE CAMPAIGN OF 1882

IN

EGYPT.

CHAPTER I.

EVENTS IN EGYPT PRIOR TO THE CAMPAIGN.—PRELIMINARY ARRANGE-
MENTS IN ENGLAND.—MEMORANDUM OF THE 3RD JULY ON THE
PLAN OF CAMPAIGN.—MOTIVES DETERMINING THE CHOICE OF THE
LINE OF ADVANCE ON CAIRO IN THE EVENT OF HOSTILITIES.

By the middle of May, 1882, a series of military demonstrations
had placed Arabi, a Colonel of the Egyptian army, in virtual
possession of the executive power in Egypt. Thewfik, who had, on
the deposition of Ismail in June, 1879, been appointed by the
Sultan, at the instance of the European Powers, Khedive of Egypt,
retained little more than the title. The armed power was in the
hands of Arabi, and it had become evident that, whatever Ministers
were appointed, they would be virtually puppets in Arabi's hands.

Ninety thousand Europeans, of whom the majority were English
and French subjects, were engaged in business in Egypt. The
English and French Governments had, on the 6th January, 1882,
given to the Khedive an assurance of their support in an "identic
declaration," since known as the "dual note," in which they
declared to him "that the English and French Governments consider the maintenance of His Highness on the throne, on the
terms laid down by the Sultan's Firmans and officially recognized
by the two Governments, as alone able to guarantee for the present
and the future good order and general prosperity in Egypt, in
which England and France are equally interested . . . . . . ; they
are convinced that His Highness will draw from this assurance the
confidence and strength which he requires to direct the destinies of
Egypt and its people."*

On the 20th May, 1882, the allied English and French fleet

entered Alexandria Harbour to watch over the threatened interests, and to offer an earnest of the promised support.

On the 7th June, 1882, Dervish Pasha, with full powers from the Porte, arrived in Alexandria to restore order in Egypt. For a few days it remained uncertain what the result of Dervish Pasha's action might be, but on the 11th June, whilst he, the Khedive, and Arabi were in Cairo, riots of a serious character broke out in Alexandria between the Mahometan and Christian population. The effect was immediately to awaken throughout the country a religious excitement which had long been smouldering among the Mahometans, and in the course of the next few weeks it is calculated that fully two-thirds of the European population had fled the country, the whole course of business was thrown out of gear, and large numbers of Arab employés were clamouring for bread.

On the 23rd June a Conference of six of the European Powers assembled for the first time at Constantinople to deal with the affairs of Egypt. Turkey refused to send a Representative.

On the 24th June the English and French Controllers, who till then had held decisive authority as Representatives of the protecting Powers, received a notice that they would no longer be allowed to sit in Council with the Egyptian Ministry; Arabi announced his intention of resisting by arms any attempt to restore order by landing troops; earthworks were begun by the Egyptians between Ramleh and Abukir.

At about the same time it was announced that the Sultan had conferred upon Arabi the First Class of the Order of the Medjidie.

Great alarm as to the safety of the Suez Canal began to prevail in consequence of the general disorder and religious excitement. Bedouins were reported as frequently appearing in threatening groups along the banks.

Various indications showed that, even if Arabi could be trusted to do his utmost to preserve order, his power to do so depended upon the temper of the Egyptian soldiery, which was daily more and more passing beyond control.

It soon became clear that no mere occupation of the Suez Canal alone could be more than a temporary expedient. The danger lay in the disorder existing in Egypt. That disorder could only be dealt with at its head-quarters in Cairo. This conclusion, which on general grounds was hardly open to dispute, was enforced by the consideration that the whole supply of fresh water, both of Alexandria and of the stations on the Suez Canal, was under the control of those who held Cairo and the interior of the country.

The Suez Canal Company had found it indispensable to construct, at great cost, the "Ismailia Canal," which, drawn off from the Nile at Cairo, branched at Nefisha, sending one arm to Suez and one to Ismailia, whence the water for Port Said was conveyed in pipes. Thus the only security for the continued maintenance of the salt-water canal depended on the friendliness of the holders of Cairo.

Nor was this all; for, as a military problem, it is scarcely possible to exaggerate the contrast between the rapidity and certainty with which it was possible to deal with the question at Cairo, and the danger, the loss, the difficulty, and the expense of a long occupation of the Canal. A force detailed to hold the Canal would be exposed throughout the entire length of that highway of commerce to the attacks of an enemy holding the Delta. The railway running direct from Zagazig to Ismailia and Es-Salihiyeh, nearly at right angles to the course of the Canal, would offer to such an enemy the greatest possible facilities for moving and supplying his troops. The whole of the Egyptian army could thus be, at any moment chosen by its Commander, directed against a fraction of the force defending the Canal. The weariness, and consequent loss of health, spirits, and efficiency, entailed by such an occupation, when protracted, would become a serious element of weakness for the protecting troops.

The danger of attack from the Bedouin tribes on the eastern side would continually increase as they became better and better aware of the fact that we had not ventured to disturb the hostile power of Arabi in Egypt, and that he was seriously threatening our position. Our troops holding the narrow strip of the shores of the Canal, receiving all their supplies along that very line, would thus find the desert along which all the water-traffic must pass occupied by hostile tribes; and the successful attack upon any isolated post or ship would enable the Egyptians to block the whole course of the Canal, and to destroy the means of communication and supply throughout.

The very occupation of the Canal itself would give such warning of our intentions to use force in Egypt, that if, instead of being the immediate prelude to a march upon Cairo, it were simply an act of passive tenure, the result would be that we should be deprived of the opportunity of converting it into anything else; for the Egyptians, so warned, would be able, whilst utilizing the railways and Fresh-water Canal for the purpose of striking at our hold on the Maritime Canal, to prepare the means of rapidly destroying them, if we should subsequently, in consequence of the failure of our effort to gain our ends by the mere occupation of the latter, attempt to dictate terms at Cairo. Nothing would then be easier for Arabi than to provide means for emptying the Fresh-water Canal at his leisure, and for destroying the railways, whilst yet he used them as long as we held to the Maritime Canal. Hence, not only was it necessary from a military point of view to prepare for a march upon Cairo, but it was necessary that that march should follow rapidly upon the first seizure of the Canal, and that no attempt merely to hold the Canal should, as a half-measure, be adopted in the first instance.

It is necessary very clearly to distinguish between the aspect which this question presented as a purely military problem, and the determination on the matter which Her Majesty's Government, taking the whole political situation into account, were able as yet to arrive at.

Not for a long time yet, as will be seen in the sequel (*vide infra*, p. 19), was any decision for the dispatch of an expedition arrived at, but it became the duty of the military authorities, from this time forward, to place clearly before Her Majesty's Government the nature of the military problem involved, and by the end of June it had become obvious that, under certain circumstances, an expedition might become necessary to restore order in Egypt. The possibility of such an event had been for many months taken into account by the War Office as a military problem. Various papers with a view to it had been prepared, under the directions of the Adjutant-General. But events had not arrived at a stage for definite preparation, even on paper, until the 28th June, when what may be considered the first official step was taken.

A Return called for by the Adjutant-General was furnished by the Commissary-General, showing the number of horses, mules, carts, &c., which were on the transport establishment at Gibraltar, Malta, and Cyprus, the strength of the different companies at home, and the amount of transport that would be required for the first line of a corps of about 24,000 men, should such a force be dispatched from England.

On the 29th June the Secretary of State for War, in consultation with His Royal Highness the Commander-in-chief, decided to take other preliminary steps, such as determining what would be necessary in case an expedition should start, collecting detailed information, making arrangements and organization on paper, &c., so far as this could be done without attracting attention and without exceptional expenditure.

A Committee formed of the various Heads of Departments held its first consultation on Egyptian affairs on the 30th June. On that day the future Commander-in-chief of the expedition laid before the Committee the broad outlines of the plan of campaign.

The scheme then verbally explained is embodied in an official Memorandum addressed by the Adjutant-General to the Surveyor-General of the Ordnance, dated the 3rd July, 1882.

As the whole subsequent working out of the campaign turns upon the points mentioned in this Memorandum, the following extracts from it will be found to be of interest, especially the two last sentences, which are here given in italics. In the latter part of the paper detailed arrangements were made for providing at once seven battalions, then in the Mediterranean stations, with the necessary transport.

Extracts from Memorandum by Sir G. Wolseley.

" With a view to rendering mobile the two divisions of infantry and the brigade of cavalry which it is contemplated we may have to send to Ismailia, it is essential that each regiment of cavalry, battalion of infantry, battery of artillery, and company of engineers should embark complete with their regimental transport.

"Egypt is a country where, in ordinary times, a very large amount of camels and pack animals can be obtained; but if we have to undertake military operations there, we cannot expect to obtain any in the country until we have defeated the Egyptian army in the field.

" I think I may assume that our operations in the first instance would consist of an advance from Ismailia upon Cairo. A railway passing through Zagazig connects those two places. We may or may not be able to seize some useful amount of rolling-stock on that railway, but we should at least make arrangements to be independent, by taking with us 5 locomotives, with large separate tenders, 5 brake-vans, 100 open goods wagons, with tarpaulin covers, and 5 breakdown wagons, with ample supply of tools for repairs; also at least 10 miles of steel rails, with bowl sleepers, bolts, nuts, fish-plates, keys, points, and crossings in proportion.

" A *personnel* to work this limited amount of rolling-stock can be supplied by the Royal Engineers, and should accompany the *matériel*, together with a sufficient number of engine-fitters to put the engines together when landed. I can furnish the detail o this *personnel*.

" We can thus count upon the aid of four trains working on the railroad (it is a single line as far as Zagazig, from thence to Cairo it is double), which will carry provisions, tents, firewood, and reserves of ammunition, and will enable us to send our sick daily to the hospital ships at Ismailia.

" *This will enable us to cut down our transport very much, especially as it may be expected that the Egyptian army would make its stand somewhere in the neighbourhood of Tel el-Kebir.*

" *If the action comes off there no serious fighting may be anticipated until Cairo is reached; indeed, although it is possible that some attempt might be made to hold that city, if the Egyptian army is well defeated in the field, any further resistance would be insignificant.*

" (Signed)   G. J. WOLSELEY.

" *July* 3, 1882."

On the same day (3rd July) proposals were put forward for the purchase of 1,000 mules in America, to be brought to England at once; for the purchase at Malta of ninety pack-mules, and the dispatch to Gibraltar, Malta, and Cyprus of the necessary pack-saddles; for the distribution to battalions going from home of such proportion of pack-saddles, water-carts, two-wheeled carts, horses, &c., as could be supplied by the Army Service Corps or Royal Artillery; for the immediate examination, repair, and distribution of carts, &c. Many of these arrangements were necessarily post-poned on grounds of international political expediency; but on the following day (4th July) secret instructions were issued to the officers commanding the regiments of cavalry, battalions of infantry, and batteries of artillery included in the force to be sent out, directing them to be prepared to move at the shortest notice, giving them the numbers with which they were to embark, and stating from what sources those numbers were to be made up. Instructions were also given that from this time the battalions should be solely employed on work adapted to prepare them for the possible campaign. A considerable force had been detailed for peace manœuvres. This made it possible to order the cavalry regiments to organize "*for the manœuvres*" the regimental transport that would be necessary for the campaign.

Already (3rd July) the details necessary for a campaign across the desert had been settled. It had been determined what baggage should be left at Ismailia, to be sent forward afterwards by rail, what was to be carried with the troops. The intention then was that the men should carry seventy rounds of ammunition in their pouches, and thirty rounds per man as a first reserve on mules. Forty-three small-arm ammunition-carts were to be provided to carry the second reserve of the force, and 1,000 boxes were to follow on a special train (seven trucks). The men were to carry one day's rations. Their great coats, two days' rations, and, if possible, 2 lbs. of fuel per man, were to move with the regiments in carts ; five days' rations, including fuel, were to follow by train.

All further details were now worked out day by day. The number of these was necessarily very great in the case of a special expedition which involved, in the first place, the sudden seizure of a hostile shore, to be reached through a narrow channel, then the almost as sudden seizure of a line of railway and canal which could be reached only by a march across a desert, and at all times provision for the exceptional conditions of nearly tropical and desert life.

On the 7th July it was decided that the autumn manœuvres should be abandoned, but for some time the decision was kept secret.

The following statement will give some idea of the questions that had at this time to be settled. Arrangements were made to provide tents, wood as fuel for 20,000 men for sixty days from Cyprus, and to be ready to purchase mules. The formation of a railway-construction company of engineers, the organization of a corps of military police, regulations as to newspaper correspondents, were determined on. The establishment of hospitals at Gozo (Malta) and Cyprus, water supply, revolvers, carts, the extension of service of men then serving with regiments from six years to seven years, had to be considered. Every measure which would reduce the number of horses to be taken with the force had to be resolutely enforced. The formation of a Postal Corps was determined on and a scheme for it devised. It was decided to arrange with the Indian Government as to the dispatch of troops from thence. All these points had been settled, and the details departmentally worked out, by the 10th July.

It had further been decided, when the plan of campaign was first discussed, that an advanced force should be sent forward from the Mediterranean garrisons ; that it should rendezvous in Cyprus, and be ready to seize the Suez Canal twenty-four hours after receiving orders for action.

On the 6th July, in consequence of an application to that effect made by the Adjutant-General on the 2nd July, Sir Archibald Alison had left England to take command of this force, and travelling viâ Brindisi, he reached Cyprus in Her Majesty's ship "Salamis" on the 14th July. The 1st Battalion South Stafford, the 3rd Battalion King's Royal Rifles, and the 17th Company Royal Engineers, arrived at Cyprus about the same time, having left Malta on the 8th July.

It has seemed advisable to report these particulars without comment, because it will be seen from them that the line of advance upon Cairo which was ultimately adopted had been decided on early in July as that which was to be followed if an expedition were sent ; that all arrangements for the campaign were fixed by the determination to make the advance across the desert between Ismailia and Zagazig ; and that an advance from Alexandria upon Cairo had never been proposed.

The choice of the line of operations was determined by the following considerations :—

In the first place, it was more convenient, as a joint expedition was to start from Europe and from India, that the Indian forces should occupy Suez, and those from the Mediterranean Port Said ; Ismailia, lying midway on the Canal, was in point of mere position, therefore, the natural point of junction of the whole army.

In the second place, the distance from Ismailia to Cairo was only 75 miles, while that from Alexandria was 120 miles. These advantages were independent of the time of year, and were so obvious that in the beginning of 1882 Major Tulloch had been dispatched to report upon the line of advance from Ismailia upon Cairo, and had brought back much detailed information.

But there were other considerations which, weighty at all seasons, were for the months of August, September, and October so decisive as to leave little choice as to the route to be adopted.

Since the period of Napoleon's campaigns in Egypt the country has undergone great changes. The Nile has been much more completely brought under control, and the whole of the Delta is now irrigated by a vast system of artificial canals. There are no roads whatever for wheeled vehicles, all the transport of the country being conducted either by railway, by boat along the canals, or on pack animals.

During August, September, and October, the period of "high Nile," the whole Delta is laid under water by means of the irrigating works. The advance of an army must necessarily be exceedingly slow over such a country ; artillery can hardly travel over it at all, and cavalry cannot manœuvre in it.

It has very frequently been assumed, in references to "the desert," that desert ground is all of one character, and that to move over it implies always that men can only march "ankle deep in sand." In fact, there are two kinds of desert, the "hard desert," a firm smooth gravel, and the "soft desert," a loose heavy sand.

Now the desert which lies between Ismailia and Cairo is throughout almost its entire length "hard." There are in the course of it sandy mounds and sandy patches which have to be crossed; these are very trying both to man and beast, but speaking generally this desert presents a very fair marching-ground both for infantry and cavalry, and though wheeled transport and artillery have in many places much difficulty, because of the necessity of passing over the sandy patches, yet movement for artillery is at least possible everywhere to an extent which does not exist in the irrigated country at all, and, throughout much of the desert, artillery manœuvres are more easy than they are on average ground in Europe.

Under these circumstances, not only was a march across a short desert to be preferred to an attempt to pass an army along the slippery and narrow banks of the small irrigating canals, but it was most desirable, if possible, to induce the enemy to fight a decisive action in the desert, where the full power of a better organized army could be employed against him.

It was known that, in all the schemes for the defence of the Delta, it had been taken as a point of honour that, on the Ismailia side, the works of defence should be so constructed as to keep the assailant away from the cultivated ground, and it was certain that this feeling would operate more, not less, strongly in the case of a man like Arabi Pasha, who was anxious in every way to conciliate the fellaheen and to appear as their champion. There was every reason, therefore, to expect that Arabi, if assailed from Ismailia, would choose his fighting-ground somewhere in the neighbourhood of the barracks that were known to have been constructed at Tel el-Kebir, a station of which he had himself been formerly Commandant, and where, according to the schemes of defence, entrenchments had long been planned to cover the approach to the several railway and canal junctions in the neighbourhood of Zagazig.

Further, from the first, the seizure of Cairo was the object of the campaign. It was of the last importance that wherever a blow was struck it should not only be a decisive one, but that the cavalry, the arm whose duty it is to reap the fruits of victory, should be able, if possible, to appear at the gates of Cairo whilst its inhabitants were still stupefied by the failure in his first battle of the military leader of revolt. So only was there a reasonable prospect of saving from destruction the "Pearl of the East," and the historical treasures of Bulak; so only could the first great blow be made to end the war.

Now there is on only one side of Cairo, as an inspection of the Map will show better than a long discussion, any approach which will permit a rapid cavalry advance from ground which would admit of the fighting of a decisive action. By skirting the hard desert along the line of the Ismailia Canal, such an advance may be made into the very heart of the city. In any other direction works of irrigation and the absence of roads prohibit rapid movement, and, in general, the advancing troops would find themselves on the wrong side of the river on their arrival in the neighbourhood of Cairo.

Included, therefore, in the earliest plans of the campaign which were decided on by Sir Garnet Wolseley, and approved by the Government, from the time that he was appointed to conduct the operations, was a cavalry advance upon Cairo along the desert.

The advantages of a canal flowing beside the whole course of the proposed march, both for the purposes of transport and of water, need not be enlarged upon. The facilities afforded by the railway are discussed in the Minute of the 3rd July (p. 5).

It is only necessary to add that as, in England, we have not hitherto maintained during peace-time any transport adequate to supply even a small army, it is only in a case where we are able to seize, within the assailed country, internal communications which reduce to a minimum the additional transport needed in the field, that a rapid blow can be struck shortly after a cause of hostilities has arisen.

Of the other possible routes, that by the Western Desert was forbidden by the fact that the sand is nearly throughout "soft;" while a river expedition by one of the arms of the Nile, which, in many respects, promised advantages, was threatened with difficulties by the bars at each of the mouths. An advance from Ismailia would directly cover and protect the Suez Canal, which would have been completely exposed during an advance upon Cairo from Alexandria. Lake Timsa would furnish an admirable basin for the gathering of the transports.

For all these reasons, therefore, there could be no doubt that the route by Ismailia must be selected.

It was necessary that the decision should be promptly made, and should, unless a change were absolutely forced by circumstances, be subsequently adhered to ; for the nature of the preparations required depended on the route selected. It was almost equally necessary that the decision should be kept secret ; for at the time everything that was known in London was regularly telegraphed, by way of Constantinople, to Cairo, since the Syrian lines remained open. As far as possible, therefore, Alexandria was always referred to in London as the future base of operations, though, from the first, all arrangements as to landing-stages, transport, commissariat, &c., were made on the understanding that Ismailia was to be the place of landing.

CHAPTER II.

THE BOMBARDMENT AND OCCUPATION OF ALEXANDRIA. — THE
WORK OF CAPTAIN FISHER AND OF SIR A. ALISON UP TO
THE 31ST JULY IN PROTECTING THE TOWN AND SECURING
ORDER.

Whilst these plans and arrangements were being made in
London, events had been rapidly moving forward at Alexandria.

The Egyptians, under Arabi's orders, ignoring alike the Khedive
and Dervish Pasha, continually worked at the fortifications, mount-
ing guns, strengthening the parapets, and endeavouring at night to
drop stones in such a manner as to block up the entrance of the
outer harbour. The naval authorities reported that the safety
of the fleet was seriously threatened by these proceedings. It
was impossible not to compare the situation with that which
had occurred at the Dardanelles in 1807, when the Turks,
whilst professedly carrying on for weeks peaceful negotiations
with Admiral Duckworth, and promising always to yield to his
demands, employed the time in so strengthening the outer
defences that the fleet had great difficulty in forcing its way out
again, and did not escape without heavy loss. In the present
instance the Egyptians accurately repeated the Turkish tactics, and
whilst always promising compliance with Sir Beauchamp Seymour's demands, invariably took advantage of night to carry on the
work again. There is a quaint Report, which afterwards fell into
our hands, from one of the Egyptian officers in charge of a battery,
addressed to one of the superior officers of the army; in it the
officer complains of the very improper conduct of the English fleet
in that, whilst his men were at work in the battery at night, suddenly a blaze of electric light was thrown upon them so that what
they were doing could be seen as if it were day—a proceeding
which, as the officer avers, was distinctly discourteous on the part
of the English.

By electric light and other means it was ascertained that the
promises of the Egyptians to stop work upon the batteries were
merely deceptive, and that the fortifications were being daily made
stronger.

At length it became evident that there could be no security
against these doings unless a portion of the fortifications were
handed over to our men. It was necessary however, great as the
risk might be, to give time, if possible, for the escape of Europeans.

On the 10th July Sir B. Seymour, after having ascertained that
the last of the probable fugitives had embarked, addressed a final
demand announcing that he should begin a bombardment within
twenty-four hours if certain forts were not given up to him within
twelve hours.

At 7 A.M. on the 11th July the bombardment began, and continued
all day, the forts being silenced by night time. On the 13th July
El-Meks and the adjacent forts were found to be evacuated. The

city had been set on fire, and the greater part of the European quarter destroyed. The city was in the hands of pillagers. It became necessary to organize police protection.

It will be seen that these events, though they materially affected the subsequent military operations, in no way determined the arrangements for the campaign, which had been settled in principle before a shot had been fired by our ships at Alexandria. The bombardment was precisely what it was asserted to be at the time—a measure for the protection of the fleet from threatened and imminent danger. All the discussions which have been raised on the assumption that the bombardment was a deliberate beginning of the campaign are beside the mark, simply because that was not the case. The naval authorities reported that the risk to the fleet was too serious to admit of any delay or of any other action. In so far as the military operations were concerned, it would have been much more convenient not to occupy Alexandria at all. Its occupation was forced upon us by the disorder existing in the town. When the numbers for the campaign were originally fixed, the intention was that the whole corps, with both divisions complete, should move by Ismailia; it was by no means intended, as happened in the sequel, that a fine brigade should be left eating their hearts out in Alexandria whilst the campaign was being carried through the Eastern Desert.

The whole series of events which had led up to the bombardment had taken place between the 6th July, when Sir A. Alison left England, and the 14th instant, when he arrived at Cyprus. No information, therefore, of the details or circumstances of those events had reached him. It appeared as if the decisive moment had arrived when, hostilities having begun, the advanced force ought to seize the Canal. Telegraphic communication was at the moment interrupted, and therefore, fearing to miss the very purpose for which he was sent out, Sir A. Alison moved with his troops to Port Said to be ready for eventualities.

At Port Said further information of the facts was received; the need of troops at Alexandria was evident; Sir A. Alison at once sailed thither, and arrived on the 17th July.

The situation at Alexandria was in many ways peculiar. The sole necessity which forced an occupation was actually and literally what it at the time was declared to be—one of police. It was impossible, after what had taken place, that we could allow the town to be given up to incendiaries and pillagers. Under every other aspect the occupation was, for our purposes at the time, an unmixed disadvantage. It was completely outside of the scope of the proposed military operations; it occurred at a period when negotiations with foreign Powers, especially with Turkey, had not reached a stage sufficiently definite to permit of our actually entering upon a serious campaign; yet Arabi's army, excited by the recent events, but unbeaten, lay within 14 miles. It was therefore necessary that the English force on shore, which so far as its status was concerned was merely a police, should nevertheless be in a condition to resist any hostile attempt against the town which might be made by Arabi. The news of the plunder of Alexandria had spread among the whole Egyptian population. The people received only such reports as it suited Arabi's policy to issue. The whole machinery of government was in his hands, and it was not surprising, therefore, that a people, always accustomed to submit to the ruling power, should be easily persuaded to aid in every way the fellah General so long as he was believed to be successful. The force under Arabi was therefore continually gaining strength, large numbers of the natives worked at entrenchments for him; the Bedouins gathered to his standard; the position at Kafr ed-Dauar was becoming each day more formidable.

On the 17th July, the day of Sir A. Alison's arrival, the Stafford Regiment and the 17th Company Royal Engineers were disembarked at Alexandria. A battalion of the Royal Marines had also arrived in the "Tamar" from Cyprus and disembarked.

On the 18th the King's Royal Rifles landed.

The seamen and marines who, under Captain Fisher, had been hitherto engaged on most exhausting work as firemen and custodians of the town, were now relieved.

The services which had been rendered by Captain Fisher and the officers and men under him cannot be passed without notice, though the description of them in detail does not fall within the scope of this history. The small force available, the variety of the work to be accomplished, the size of the town, and the wild disorder which prevailed at first, made the task one of exceptional difficulty.

On the evening of the first day of landing (the 17th) a body of mounted infantry—two officers and thirty men—was formed, under the orders of Captain Hutton. The Khedive supplied his private horses for the purpose. They were of an excellent breed, and proved invaluable. The men were taken by careful selection from the battalions landed (Stafford and King's Royal Rifles). Both these battalions had served in South Africa, and the men selected had been there employed as mounted riflemen, those of the King's Royal Rifles having belonged to Captain Hutton's corps of mounted infantry in South Africa; no doubt much of their efficiency depended on that fact.

On the 18th a party of the mounted infantry patrolled 10 miles towards the enemy, and from this time onward daily rendered most valuable service.

The strength of the force now in Alexandria was 3,755, including seamen and marines. There were seven 9-pr., two 7-pr. guns, six Gatlings, and four rocket-tubes. In the event of attack it was possible for Sir B. Seymour to reinforce this body by 1,200 men. The full number available for defence in an extreme emergency was therefore nearly 5,000.

Major Ardagh, R.E., was employed in completing the defensive works, and by the 19th had made the place practically secure against any attack likely to be at that time attempted.

On the 22nd July the railway in front of the Mallaha junction on the enemy's side was destroyed by a force under

Captain Hutton, while some companies of the Rifles and four naval guns formed a support upon the high ground above Ramleh under Colonel Ashburnham. The work was carried out without loss. An inspection of the Map will show that as long as the beds of Lake Mariut and Lake Abukir are impassable there are only three narrow lines by which Alexandria can be approached: one along the sea-coast from the town of Abukir, one between the two lakes direct from the Delta, and a third by way of El-Meks from the Western Desert. Of these, the middle approach, which was the most important, because it was the direct communication with the position taken up by Arabi's army, consists in fact merely of the railway embankment and of the two banks of the Mahmudieh Canal, for the Lake Mariut at that time extended on both sides of the railway bank up to the banks of the Canal.

The bed of Lake Abukir was not covered with water, but parts of it were quicksand, part marsh. It was impassable everywhere for artillery, though passable almost everywhere for cavalry and infantry. Lake Mariut receives the drainage of the small canals of the country, which are in this neighbourhood drawn off chiefly for irrigation purposes from the Mahmudieh Canal.

A large dam across the canal was almost immediately begun under Arabi's orders, and two cuttings were made in the bank of the canal on the side of the dam nearest to the position which his army had taken up at Kafr ed-Dauar.* This had the double effect of cutting off the supply of water from Alexandria and of making an artificial inundation covering nearly the whole front of his works. Incidentally also, as the hot weather came on, it tended to cause the drying up of the bed of Lake Mariut, and to change the character of the defensive works at Alexandria. This, however, only took place gradually, and at the time of Sir A. Alison's occupation a strong ridge above the suburb of Ramleh completely commanded the only available ground by which Arabi could advance direct from his lines upon Alexandria; that is to say, works placed upon it would be able to sweep both the canal and the railway embankment.†

On the side of Abukir the line of approach was completely commanded by the guns of the fleet. The works at Gabbari closed the approach from the side of El-Meks.

An occupation of the ridge at Ramleh would therefore complete the defences, and as many villas, and the all-important waterworks, were within the area thus inclosed, Sir A. Alison decided to push forward his line of defence to that point, and on the arrival of reinforcements in the harbour, viz., the Duke of Cornwall's Light Infantry and the half-battalion Sussex Regiment, he at daylight on the 24th moved out a force‡ under the command of Colonel Thackwell, which seized the position without opposition, and·threw up entrenchments.

<hr>

* More exactly Kafr ed-Dauar el-Gidid.
† From Ramleh to Rosetta Gate 3½ to 4 miles.
‡ 1st Battalion Stafford, 2nd Battalion King's Royal Rifles, Mounted Infantry, 2 naval 9-prs. and their crews, 2 naval 7-prs. and their crews.

The original intention had been to protect the right flank by floating rafts or flat-bottomed boats, but the shallowness of the water and the rapid fall of Lake Mariut made this impossible. It was, therefore, to meet this difficulty that Captain Fisher devised and worked out an armoured train, which proved most serviceable. This train consisted, at first, of two trucks fitted with iron plating and sand-bags as protecting cover, with a Nordenfelt and two Gatling guns. A 9-pr. was also placed on one of the trucks, with a crane, by means of which it could be lowered out immediately; 200 blue-jackets, with small arms, in other trucks protected by sand-bags and boiler-plating, bullet-proof, completed the fighting force of the train.

On the 29th July, on the Alexandria side of the Mallaha junction, the railway line which had been destroyed by Arabi's outposts was repaired. To accomplish this a small force consisting of the mounted infantry, two companies of marines, and one company of infantry, assisted by the armoured train, were pushed forward sufficiently close to Arabi's outposts to cause the deployment of the whole force there stationed. It consisted at first of a battalion of infantry and two squadrons of cavalry, subsequently reinforced by two more battalions and some cavalry. A gun and a rocket-frame were brought up by the Egyptians, and fired some innocuous shots over the train. The object of the advance was secured in the completion of the line, which enabled sufficient rolling-stock to be run round on the main line between Moharam Bey of the Cairo-Alexandria line and the advance position at Ramleh. The position at Ramleh was thus connected with Alexandria by a second line of railway, the local narrow-gauge Alexandria-Ramleh Railway having been in operation several days previously, thanks to the energy and devotion of its Manager. A regular service of trains was established connecting Ramleh with Alexandria on both lines.

The armoured train, having been found so useful, was now further improved by putting one or two empty pioneer-wagons in front of it, and placing a 40-pr. gun upon a truck, protected by an iron mantlet. The locomotive was placed in the middle of the train, and was protected by slung sand-bags and railway iron.

CHAPTER III.

So far all that had been done at Alexandria had consisted
of measures necessary to secure the safety of the town from the
enemy and from marauders. Meantime, events had been taking
place which finally determined the character of the interven-
tion.

On the 15th July an "identic note" had been presented at
Constantinople by the European Powers, requiring the Porte to
send troops to Egypt to suppress disorder. To this the Porte did
not reply till after a debate in the French Chambers, on the
18th July, had disclosed the purpose of the French and English
Governments to act in the event of the Porte's declining to
do so.

On the 19th July the Porte, late at night, replied *by consenting to
send a Delegate to the Conference.* As this implied further delay,
on the 20th July the two Cabinets resolved to send a joint
expedition.

On the 21st the Secretary of State for War, in consultation
with the Commander-in-chief, decided to call out that portion of
the reserves which had left the colours in the previous two years.
The preliminary notices warning the men of the coming call were
sent out at once.

A telegram was sent on the same day telling Sir A. Alison that
two Divisions were to be sent from England to Cyprus and Malta.
It was known that Arabi was preparing to destroy the Suez Canal,
and on the 24th July orders were sent to Sir B. Seymour and
Sir A. Alison warning them to be ready, in case of necessity, to
seize Port Said, Ismailia, and Nefisha.

As, however, there was every reason to avoid any indication of
the direction of the intended advance up to the last moment,
action was not to be taken till specific orders were sent.

On the 25th July the part of the reserves already warned was
called out.

On the 27th July the House of Commons, by a majority of
275 to 19, voted a credit of 2,300,000*l.*

On the 29th July the French Chambers, by a majority of
416 to 75, refused any credit for the expedition.

It was now clear that England alone would act in Egypt. It
was at once determined that the campaign should be carried out on
the lines laid down in the Memorandum of the 3rd July

(see p. 9), in accordance with which all paper arrangements had been made. But of the force proposed in the Memorandum, a large brigade was already engaged in the defence of Alexandria. The necessity had arisen since the programme had been drawn up. Inconvenient as this fact in itself was, it appeared to be advisable to take advantage of it to induce Arabi to believe that the whole force now to be sent out, of the approach of which to the coast of Egypt he was sure ere long to be informed, was designed to reinforce the troops in Alexandria, and that the scheme of campaign involved a direct attack on his position at Kafr ed-Dauar.

Orders were therefore, on the 31st July, telegraphed in these words : " Keep Arabi constantly alarmed."

From this time, therefore, Sir Archibald's operations were designed to make Arabi believe that the troops at Alexandria were preparing the way for a serious attack upon Kafr ed-Dauar. This result was the more easy to bring about that by this time Alexandria was filled with the special correspondents of newspapers of all nations ; that though there were brilliant exceptions among those so employed, many of them felt themselves fully competent to criticize every military operation ; that the one thing which many of them thought that they could not afford to do was to allow their readers to suppose that there was anything which they did not know, or that it was possible that a movement should take place of which they did not understand the motives. In order to have something to write about, they were sure to exaggerate the importance of all that was done, and, in particular, they were sure to describe every reconnaissance or feint upon Arabi's position as a serious attack, and to proclaim to the four corners of the earth its hopeless failure. In a town with a population like that of Alexandria it was certain that the impressions of these gentlemen would be conveyed to the enemy's camp, and would tend to assure Arabi of the gravity of the attempts made against him, of the triumphant success that had attended his defence, and of the secret discouragement of his enemies. Already, when Sir Archibald had on the 28th secured his double railway communication with Ramleh, it had been reported as an " aimless skirmish." Not now only, but throughout the campaign, these reports served our purposes very admirably, by tending to instil into the minds of the population, and so into that of the hostile Generals, a false impression as to the aspect of affairs.

To this result M. de Lesseps contributed in a very important degree. As soon as he heard of the rebel General's intention to destroy the Canal, he hastened to Arabi's camp and assured him that if he would not touch the Canal neither France nor Italy would intervene, and that the English forces would not venture to invade territory which he regarded as personally his own.

The Khedive having on the 16th July issued an order dismissing Arabi from his post as Minister of War, Arabi, on the 21st, replied by a Proclamation denouncing the Khedive. From that time forward action was taken in Egypt by us in the Khedive's name. On the 27th July, the day of the Vote of Credit in the House of Commons, Her Majesty's ship "Orion" passed into the Suez Canal, and moved towards Ismailia, the Khedive having issued express authority for the Canal to be occupied by England. M. de Lesseps protested against the proceeding. On the 30th July Admiral Hewett arrived off Suez. Admiral Hoskins lay off Port Said with three ships. From this time, therefore, we had in our hands the means of seizing the Suez Canal simultaneously at all the most important points. On the 31st July all the French war-vessels, till then remaining at Alexandria, withdrew, with the exception of one gun-boat.

Sir Archibald at once began to act in accordance with his new instructions, and almost daily reconnaissances of Arabi's position were carried out. Such affairs are not matters of much interest in detail.

On the 2nd August a sudden advance of Egyptian cavalry during the night upon an outpost to some extent surprised a picket, which they compelled to fall back a certain distance.

Mr. De Chair, a Midshipman, sent with despatches, had been captured on the 29th July, and being sent to Cairo, was paraded through the streets with an announcement that it was Sir B. Seymour who had been made prisoner. Both these events tended greatly to raise the enthusiasm of Arabi's followers, but also to concentrate attention on Alexandria.

On the 5th August Sir Archibald, to give more emphasis to the daily skirmishes, to test the truth of native reports that Arabi was intending to retire from Kafr ed-Dauar, and to keep up the impression that the real offensive movement was to be made from Alexandria, undertook a reconnaissance in person. His own force being greatly inferior to the enemy in numbers, it was very unadvisable to begin to move very early in the day, lest the force should be too seriously engaged, and lest the deliberate intention of retreating at an early stage should be too evident.

Accordingly, the troops were ordered to be in position by 4·30 P.M. The force moved in two columns.

The left column, under Lieutenant-Colonel Thackwell, consisted of—

    1st Battalion Stafford (half-battalion).
    2nd Battalion Duke of Cornwall's Light Infantry (half-battalion).
    3rd Battalion King's Royal Rifles.
    Mounted infantry.
    Two 9-pr. naval guns.
    In all, about 1,000 men.

The right column, under the personal direction of Sir A. Alison, was composed of—

    Royal Marine Artillery.
    Royal Marine Light Infantry.
    The armoured train (with its 40-pr. gun).
    Two 9-pr. naval guns.

This column also was about 1,000 strong.

The left column advanced along the banks of the Canal, the right along the railway.

Each column in turn threatened the flanks of the enemy's outposts as it advanced.

The most interesting incident of the engagement was the good service done by the 40-pr. from the armoured train. The enemy only yielded successive positions as the artillery fire became too much for him, or as his flanks were turned. The Egyptian troops were quite disposed to fight, and it was evident that they had every intention of holding their advanced posts. Reinforcements were rapidly pushed up from their main position. Sir Archibald's object had been secured, and the rapid coming on of darkness made the withdrawal from the position to which the enemy had been driven appear natural, so that it could be carried out without diminishing the confidence which the men had gathered from their successful advance in the first engagement that had taken place. This was obviously the matter of most importance, for, as the troops could not be informed of the purpose for which they were being employed, and were likely to read the comments of those who understood it as little as themselves, it was right to avoid all risk of discouraging them in the delicate work of " keeping Arabi alarmed " by movements which were intended to have no other result. Their object could not be mentioned even in the official reports of the officer in command, published, as these necessarily were, upon their receipt in London. A congratulatory telegram from Her Majesty had in all ways an excellent effect, as tending both to encourage the men and to assign importance to these operations.

It is difficult to judge how far any of Arabi's reports at this time represented his own belief, and how far they were only intended to leave a certain impression in Egypt; but as he reported officially in a despatch which was sent to Cairo, and thence to Constantinople, that the left wing of the English consisted of three battalions of infantry and three squadrons of cavalry, together with four guns, and the right of three battalions of infantry and one battery of artillery, while the centre consisted of one regiment of cavalry, it is, perhaps, not unfair to infer that the object of imposing upon him the belief that a considerable force had been engaged against him was fully attained.

Not a single cavalry soldier and not a single horsed gun had been landed. The four guns were moved by hand, the 40-pr. in the armoured train. The *amour-propre* of Englishmen at home was much hurt at the time by the comments of Continental journals, which, ignorant alike of the intended plan of campaign and of the inexorable conditions of ground which determined the choice of the Ismailia route, assumed always that a direct advance from Alexandria upon Cairo was to be carried out, and that these "aimless skirmishes" showed only that the English Generals did not know what they were about, and were without any definite plan. It will be, perhaps, a sufficient compensation now to know that these very comments, reaching the Egyptians through numerous sources, were the most valuable assistance which these journals could have rendered. They helped to form an admirable screen, under which the plan which had been consistently kept in view, at least since the 3rd July, was being developed and put in execution.

CHAPTER IV.

THE EXPEDITION LEAVES ENGLAND.—DETAILS OF THE FORCE, AND
THE EGYPTIAN ARMY AS FAR AS THEN KNOWN.—SIR G.
WOLSELEY ARRIVES IN ALEXANDRIA AT NIGHT-TIME ON THE
15TH AUGUST.

The expedition in the meantime had begun to leave England.
The "Orient," with His Royal Highness the Duke of Connaught,
commanding the 1st Brigade, and General Willis, commanding
the 1st Division, their Staffs, and the 1st Battalion Scots Guards,
was the first ship to sail with troops of the expeditionary force.
The "Orient" left the Royal Albert Dock, North Woolwich, at
12 o'clock on Sunday, the 30th July.
From that date till the 11th August the various ships conveying the force cleared daily from the several ports of the
kingdom. The transports were to call at Malta for orders, and
were there directed to proceed to Alexandria.
It had been originally intended that Sir Garnet Wolseley, with
his Staff, should go overland, viâ Brindisi, but a sharp chill,
caught in returning from Osborne, whither he had gone to receive
Her Majesty's commands prior to his departure for Egypt, prostrated him with an attack of erysipelas. The doctors recom-
mended a sea-voyage as the only means of making him fit to take
up the command on his arrival in Egypt, and he sailed on the
2nd August, in the "Calabria," with General Drury Lowe and the
head-quarters of the Cavalry Brigade.
On the 10th August the "Orient" arrived in Alexandria.
General Willis assumed the command. In the evening General
Sir John Adye, who had travelled overland to Alexandria, arrived
with Sir E. Malet, and took over the command.
On the same day Sir Garnet Wolseley, perfectly recovered,
touched at Gibraltar, and thence sent the following secret telegram
to Sir John Adye.
It may be as well to premise that a railway from Limasol to
the hospital in Cyprus had been for some time in contemplation.
A bombardment of the Abukir forts had been a subject of discussion at Alexandria and of orders from England, but had, for various
reasons, been postponed.

"Sir Garnet Wolseley to Sir John Adye, Alexandria.

"I hope to reach Alexandria 15th instant. Do not move troops
to Canal until I arrive, but have everything ready for the movement. Attract Arabi's attention to Alexandria by daily reconnaissance towards flank of his position. Can you approach him by
steam-launches? If Abukir has not been bombarded, prevent it
being so for the present. Tell Khedive and people that we mean

to lay down a railway in Cyprus upon existing roads from Limasol to hospital in mountain, and embark, nominally for this purpose, four engines and eighty light carriages in a ship that can go to Ismailia; at all events embarking six light carriages which we can use on railway with horses at first. Arrange with Admiral to transport five battalions, one regiment of cavalry, and one battery from Port Said up Canal."

A Civil Intelligence Department, under Sir F. Goldsmid, had been established in Alexandria from the commencement of the occupation. Lieutenant-Colonel Tulloch, who had been dispatched to Alexandria, and attached to the Staff of Sir B. Seymour, prior to the bombardment, had been employed in collecting military information. Through these sources it was known that Arabi had moved troops down towards Suez and to Nefisha, the point at which the Canal and railway branch off towards Suez and Ismailia; that he had established a force at Es-Salihiyeh, the terminus of one branch of railway from Zagazig, a point equi-distant from Ismailia and Kantara* (20 miles from each); and that he was entrenching the old military station of Tel el-Kebir, the barracks at which place were filled with soldiers.

On the 2nd August Admiral Hewett had occupied Suez with a force of marines without resistance. On the 9th August, seven transports, with the Indian Contingent, had sailed from Bombay. As yet there was nothing to lead Arabi to suppose that any movement from the direction of Suez would be other than a diversion effected by the Indian Contingent; all his preparations along that line were, in fact, as is now known, merely intended to prevent such forces as might be detached for an advance, independent of the main attack, from entering the Delta.

It was especially necessary to keep up this illusion, but the presence of so considerable a body of hostile troops in the vicinity of the Canal made Sir John Adye anxious lest a move towards the Canal should be attempted, and he replied to Sir G. Wolseley's telegram by one to Malta, informing him of the Egyptian forces which were now gathering on the eastern side of the Delta, and assuring him that he would make no movement towards the Canal unless it became indispensable for the security of that communication itself.

Sir Garnet replied from Malta by the following secret telegram:—

"Sir Garnet Wolseley to Sir John Adye.

"Malta, August 12, 1882.

"Except very emergent, do not go to Ismailia until I arrive, as field artillery and cavalry are essential to make first engagement there fully successful."

The "Holland," with the first body of cavalry, the detachments of the 1st Life Guards and Royal Horse Guards, reached

---

* More exactly El-Kantara el-Khazneh.

Alexandria on the 14*th August*, and the men and horses were disembarked. It was a great advantage for the condition of the horses to have even a couple of days on shore.

The first field battery to arrive, A | 1, R.A., reached Alexandria on the same day, and the horses were landed the following day.

On the night of the 15th August Sir G. Wolseley himself reached Alexandria.

Since the reconnaissance of the 5th August the only material changes which had taken place in the situation had been the successive arrival of troops at Alexandria. The Guards Brigade had disembarked on the 12th August, and had moved out to Ramleh. The electric light was now used nightly, with the effect of exposing to view the whole ground in front of the position up to Arabi's lines. The naval force in the Canal had been increased on the 14th August by the entry of Her Majesty's gun-boat " Ready " from Port Said.

CHAPTER V.

THE DETAILED PLAN OF CAMPAIGN. DIFFICULTIES TO BE OVERCOME AND INTENDED MODE OF MEETING THEM.

The moment had now arrived for putting into execution the first part of the programme of the campaign. It will be convenient here to set forth in order the nature of the whole scheme as it was designed to be carried out.

To effect the purpose of marching upon Cairo it was necessary—

1. To obtain possession of the Maritime Canal, so as to insure the safe passage of the expedition.

2. To move to Ismailia, in such successive order as the conditions permitted, the force to be employed.

3. To keep the enemy by every artifice under the impression that the attack would be made from other points than Ismailia until force had arrived there sufficient to insure its safe possession.

4. To seize and secure the line of railway and the Sweet-water Canal to within striking distance of the position in which it was known that the enemy was preparing to place his main force for the defence of the eastern side of the Delta, that is to say, within striking distance of Tel el-Kebir.

5. After these lines of communication had been seized, to put in order such parts of either railway or Canal as the enemy had obstructed or damaged, and to place upon them such rolling-stock and store-boats as would render them available for the supply of the army in the field.

6. To accumulate at an advanced post, under an adequate guard, stores and ammunition sufficient to make the army, when it moved forward, independent, except for the purposes of distribution, of all other modes of transport; but in order to hasten this accumulation, and to provide against contingencies, to secure as auxiliary to the railway and Canal such animal transport for general purposes as time permitted.

7. To engage the enemy in a general action when, and not before, the accumulation of stores, or their regular daily transmission along the line, permitted the concentration of the army for the delivery of an effective—if possible a final blow.

8. To follow up this action with the greatest rapidity, in order: (*a*) both for political, military, and other reasons, to secure possession of Cairo; and (*b*) to seize the points of concentration by which alone, after the defeat of the army at Tel el-Kebir, the numerous Egyptian forces stationed at Kafr ed-Dauar, Cairo, Damietta, Rosetta, and Es-Salihiyeh could unite so as to become a formidable force, effective for acting in the field.

Some of these points require a little elucidation in order to show how far the course of the campaign could be, and how far it was, foreseen, and what elements in it remained to be determined by the course of events. The execution of its several parts had to be intrusted to various hands, but the co-operation of these as the campaign developed will show the working out of an orderly and prearranged plan consistently prosecuted from the first.

The ordinary rate of movement of ships in the Suez Canal during peace-time is determined by special considerations.

The narrowness of the channel and the character of the banks make it impossible for a large ship to pass down at a rapid rate. The effect of any attempt to move quickly with large steamships is to cause such a wash upon the banks, and such a consequent back-water, as are not merely destructive of the Canal itself, but actually impede the working of the engines of steamships.

It is clear, therefore, that even if in an extreme military emergency it were right to be indifferent to temporary injury inflicted upon the property of the Company, no advantage could be secured by attempting to drive the ships at a rate more rapid than usual. In fact, there were conditions which tended to make the proposed passage of the expedition more than ordinarily slow.

Even in a country possessed of so vast a mercantile marine as England, it is necessary, when the ships for so great an undertaking have to be chartered within a very short time, to engage many vessels which have not been specially built for a single route. Many, therefore, of the transports employed had never been through the Canal before. Special steering gear is fitted upon all ships which are employed regularly on this route, and the passage through the short reaches and rapid bends of the Canal can only be effected with perfect security by ships so prepared, and by officers accustomed to this special work. Many of the ships' officers necessarily employed for the Egyptian expedition had, like the ships, never before travelled from Port Said to Suez.

The deep part of the Canal is much more narrow than the actual water-space between the banks, and the smallest error of direction results in grounding, which, in the case of a long column of vessels following one another at short intervals, not only causes long delay to the grounding steamer, but also checks the whole column behind it. The hostility of M. de Lesseps, who had in his employ every special Canal pilot, must also be taken into account as causing an impediment to rapid movement.

It does not lie within the scope of the present history to detail the admirable forethought on the part of the naval authorities by which these difficulties were provided against. It will be sufficient to say that it was arranged that a naval officer should be placed in authority over every transport; that the whole detailed working and organization should be placed in the hands of Captain Fisher, under the supreme direction of Admiral Hoskins; and that the Thornycroft torpedo-boats, which, drawing little water, were able to pass through the shallows near the banks at a startling speed (about 20 statute miles an hour), furnished the agency by which communication was established throughout the length of the passage, so that as soon as a vessel should ground, assistance could be brought to it, and either enable it to proceed, or in a more serious case to move it off to the sides of the Canal so as to allow others to pass.

What however it is of direct importance to point out here is that the facts above mentioned had to be allowed for as part of the military problem. Nothing was to be gained by moving to the mouth of the Canal at Port Said the entire expedition simultaneously, because, even with the force required to transport one Division, many vessels must remain outside the Canal for more than a day waiting their turn to take their places in the slow procession. On the other hand, delay in the gathering of vessels at the destined base at Lake Timsa was not the unmixed disadvantage that it might at first sight appear.

An inspection of the accompanying plan of Ismailia as it was at this time will show that only one small pier then existed there. Ships did not at first anchor nearer than about half-a-mile from the shore. Every man of the force, every horse, and every gun, as well as all the ammunition and stores for the supply of the army, had first to be transhipped from the transports into barges and small boats, rowed or tugged to shore, and then landed on the small pier. Thence they had to proceed up the narrow road leading to the single small bridge over the Canal across which at first everything must necessarily pass.

To judge by the comments which were made in Europe subsequently, no conception of the nature of such an operation exists on the Continent at all. This is not surprising. It is a class of work that has rarely been undertaken by any Continental army, but it is an operation very characteristic of ordinary English expeditions beyond sea. In this particular case the difficulties were somewhat greater than usual, or, what is the same thing, the necessary time that would be required to effect a landing and to enable the force to move forward were somewhat longer than is generally the case, because Ismailia is a station which in ordinary times has very little traffic passing through it, and because of the consequent want of landing-stages, &c. The railway brings very few people from Cairo to meet the boats through the Canal, and very little merchandize finds its way through the same route ; in no sense are the conditions for the rapid landing of a large number of troops and of a vast quantity of stores in existence there. It is true that this state of things could ultimately be changed by our engineers. But this also would be a question of time. Every tool, every scrap of material, all the bridging stores, and all the means of constructing other piers, for laying down tramways and increasing the pier accommodation, must, by an inexorable necessity, be first landed under the conditions actually existing. Materials for all these purposes, including landing-stages expressly made for Ismailia, had been prepared in England before the expedition sailed, but it would not be possible to send them forward in the most advanced vessels of the fleet, for those ships must be otherwise filled. In order to secure the all-important lines of communication—the railway and Sweet-water Canal—for the advance from Ismailia, it was essential that the first vessels of the fleet should be occupied by the troops which would be sent forward to seize them. Those troops, once sent forward, must be supplied with food and ammunition, so that a considerable force, with all its guns and equipment, tons of supplies, ordnance stores, and ammunition, and the means of local transport for these, both by railway and Canal, as well as baggage animals, must be sent on in the most advanced ships before any engineering materials for the improvement of the means of landing and for additional bridging over the Canal could be put on shore.

It was not difficult, therefore, to foresee that, however effective and rapid the first movement to Ismailia might be, and however successfully the first seizure of the lines of communication for the advance were carried out, these actions must be followed by long periods of hard, uninteresting work, very little likely to be understood or appreciated at a distance.

These considerations determined alike the most suitable moment for the movement on Ismailia, and the order of disposition of the ships for the Canal passage.

At the time of Sir Garnet Wolseley's arrival at Alexandria on August 15 the reports of vessels passing Malta, received by telegraph, showed that by the 19th of August nearly the whole of the infantry of General Willis', the 1st Division, would have reached Alexandria. The Household Cavalry had arrived, one battery of Horse Artillery was due on the 16th, and one battery on the 19th, while the remainder of the cavalry and artillery were at sea, but could be directed to follow so as to reach Ismailia as soon as it was possible for them to disembark.

It is necessary to explain another feature of an expedition of this kind which habitually determines the mode of arranging troops on the line of advance. Looking forward to the period subsequent to the intended seizure of the Fresh-water Canal and railway in advance of Ismailia, to the period during which the accumulation of stores would be made preparatory to the general advance, it will be seen that the one method of hastening the final movement would be to shorten the time spent in collecting stores at the front. But out of the stores sent forward a certain proportion would necessarily be required for the daily consumption of the force actually at the front, engaged in protecting the accumulation. That amount of daily consumption, whatever it might be, would necessarily be deducted from the progressive accumulation at the advanced depôt. It is obvious, therefore, that the fewer troops sent forward the smaller would be the daily deduction from the accumulating stores, and therefore the more rapid would be the rate of accumulation. Now, it will not be difficult even for a non-military reader to understand that the force which, when adequately entrenched behind defensive works at an advanced post, is sufficient to guard the station with all its stores, may be much less than the army which is required to engage in a general action, especially if that general action involves the attack upon an army elaborately entrenched in a well-chosen position. These considerations apply with peculiar force to the case of a campaign against an army like the Egyptian, which, though it was known to be very effective behind entrenchments, was by no means likely to make a very determined attack upon English troops when in an entrenched position.

It follows that the most rapid way of carrying out the campaign would be, as soon as possible after an adequate force had been landed at Ismailia, to push it forward so as to seize the line of railway and canal, and then to keep at the advanced station, within striking distance of Tel el-Kebir, a protecting force just sufficient to hold that station, but no larger than would just be sufficient for this work. Hence, as a first deduction from all that has been said, it follows that it was advisable to leave at Alexandria all the infantry that would not be required for the first movements from Ismailia. As only a small proportion of the artillery had arrived, and as the disembarkation of that arm is a very slow operation, it would, on the other hand, be advisable to send all the remaining batteries forward to Ismailia, but not beyond it, as soon as the ships reached Alexandria, because their movement to Ismailia and their disembarkation could take place whilst the preliminary operations in the front were being carried on. The same remark applies to the remainder of the cavalry also, with this addition, that the earlier movements were sure to demand the services of that arm. Moreover, the larger the force for the time being in Alexandria, the more easy was it to continue to keep the Egyptian General uncertain as to the true line of attack.

Before returning to the steps taken to put into practice the military movements determined by these motives, it may be well to illustrate the nature of the whole operation by one other remark.

During a certain period of the campaign, when the hardest work that fell to the lot of the little army throughout the whole course of it was going on, but when nothing brilliant could be recorded of a kind likely to tickle the ears of readers at home—in fact during that very period of dull preparation which, as has been seen, could be fully anticipated when the scheme was first worked out—a comparison was made between the six weeks within which the Prussian army in 1866 conquered Austria and the eighteen days which elapsed between the earlier operations of the advance and the actual movement on Tel el-Kebir. It was assumed to be a kind of Rule of Three sum, the working out of which was greatly to the disadvantage of the little force in Egypt. It is necessary to point out that to make such a comparison is not *merely* to compare great things with small, but to institute a comparison absolutely irrelevant. Supposing that the army which fought at Sadowa could by any mercantile marine in the world have been transported to Port Said, it must thence have moved under the conditions which have been here described. So moving, supposing its stores could have been transported across the desert and by the line of railway and Sweet-water Canal at all, it could not have carried

CE-C

out the operation under many months. The larger the force the slower would have been the movement. The force which was just sufficient to capture the lines of Tel el-Kebir, and there crush the Egyptian army, was the force which could most rapidly effect the conquest of Egypt.

For this reason, and for no other, that force was fixed upon; it was not for want of other resources in England.

Indeed, whilst Sir Garnet Wolseley was still at sea, the question of preparing a 3rd Division as a reasonable precaution had been entertained at the War Office, and soon after his arrival at Alexandria the following two secret telegrams were exchanged between him and the Secretary of State for War, the dates of which will remove a misunderstanding subsequently common as to the cause and circumstances of the preparation of this reinforcement. It will be seen that it was suggested from home, and accepted as a prudent step, before the campaign proper had begun :—

" *The War Secretary to Sir Garnet Wolseley.*

" *August* 17, 4·25 P.M.

" We are discussing preparing for another Division, though hoping you will not require it. We are preparing regimental transport. We are also considering making up establishment of men and horses for Departmental Corps. Shall be glad of your opinion whether there is probability of either a brigade or whole Division being called for."

" *Sir Garnet Wolseley to the War Secretary.*

" *August* 18.

" I do not believe we shall require more troops after depôts have been fully made up and formed here, but this should be done at once. I think formation of a 3rd Division a wise precaution. Regimental transport should be on the scale laid down in Regulations, not according to Special Scale."

Exact calculation as to the forces needed for a particular work does not justify the absence of provision for possible chances. Precisely the same remark applies to the preparation of a siege train. The reason of its preparation was by no means that it was supposed that it would certainly be required, but that in a country containing strongly fortified works it would have been very rash not to have the means at hand for reducing them. Though the campaign was to be decided in the open field, it was certain that the surrender of the fortresses would be hastened by the knowledge that the invading army possessed a powerful siege train.

CHAPTER VI.

The Seizure of the Maritime Canal by Admirals Hoskins and Hewett.

On the first day which Sir Garnet Wolseley spent in Alexandria, 16th August, the whole of the arrangements for seizing the Canal, and for the movement to Ismailia, were worked out between him and Sir B. Seymour.*

On the evening of that day Admiral Hoskins left in the "Iris" for Port Said, to communicate through the Canal the plan of operations to Admiral Hewett, commanding at Suez, and to make arrangements with him for the preliminary operation of seizing and clearing, throughout its entire length, the Suez Canal on the destined morning of Sunday, the 20th August.

Since the beginning of August Admiral Hoskins had been in possession of the following mandate from the Khedive, authorizing him to seize and occupy, in the Khedive's name, all necessary points along the Suez Canal :—

" M. le Contre-Amiral,   " *Alexandrie, le 1ᵉʳ Août*, 1882.

"Vous êtes autorisé à occuper tels points de l'Isthme de Suez que vous jugerez utiles pour assurer le libre trafic par le Canal, la protection des villes et populations situées sur son parcours, et repousser toute force qui ne reconnaîtrait pas mon autorité.

"Vous êtes également autorisé, M. le Contre-Amiral, à prendre les mesures nécessaires pour enlever aux rebelles la voie ferrée entre Suez et Ismaïliah.

" (Signé)   Méhémet Thewfik.

"Sir A. H. Hoskins, C.B., Contre-Amiral
     Commandant les Forces Navales
     Britanniques à Port-Saïd."

It will be convenient to follow through the preliminary operations, carried out by Admiral Hoskins, before detailing the movement of the troops, which were to pass down the Canal under the security provided by him. As the Canal does not admit, throughout its general course, of the passage of large ships going both ways at the same time, this difficulty is met by the construction, at certain points, of stations or "gares," where the Canal is widened out to a considerable extent, so as to allow ships to lie out of the course of the Canal whilst others pass. No ship is allowed to move between "gare" and "gare" till the passage is announced by telegraph to be clear from vessels moving in the opposite direction. These conditions made it necessary to provide beforehand that no ships should be moving northward whilst the expedition passed south.

At 10 A.M. on the 17th August Admiral Hoskins reached Port Said. Captain Fitzroy had been in the Canal in Her Majesty's ship " Orion " since the 27th July (*vide* p. 21, *ante*).

The small squadron at Ismailia, consisting of the " Orion," " Carysfort," and " Coquette," had had an anxious duty for nearly a ' month in watching over the security of the Canal. On Friday morning, 18th August, Captain Fitzroy visited Admiral Hoskins at Port Said, and received, personally, instructions for seizing Ismailia before daybreak on the morning of the 20th August. Captain Fairfax, of Her Majesty's ship " Monarch," was ordered to seize Port Said, at the same hour. Commander Edwards, of Her Majesty's ship " Ready," started at 8 o'clock on Saturday evening, the 19th, to occupy all barges, dredges, &c., along the line to Ismailia, to seize the Kantara telegraph station, and restore telegraph communication throughout the line from Port Said to Ismailia, to cut Arabi's telegraphic line of communication with Syria, and to require all ships in the Canal between Port Said and Ismailia, bound for Port Said, to move into the " gares " and there remain.

The " Nyanza," a condensing steam-ship, was sent early on the 17th to Ismailia with tents, provisions, and an extra 100 men as a reinforcement to the squadron there. The " Ready " and " Dee' gun-boats, with three companies of marines, were also sent as a reinforcement.

Admiral. Hewett, on his side, was to allow no ship to enter the Canal at Suez on the 19th, to drive the enemy out of Shaluf on the morning of the 20th, and, as soon as possible, to capture Serapeum. In this way the whole length of the Canal was to be seized and cleared from Port Said to Suez, so as to be ready soon after daybreak on the 20th August for the passage of the expedition from Alexandria.

With the exception of the seizure of Serapeum, which did not take place till the 21st, all these operations were simultaneously and successfully carried out soon after 3 A.M. on the morning of the named day.

No difficulty was found in occupying the various dredges and other boats, each with an officer and fifteen men. Nearly all the ships passing through the Canal were safely retained in the " gares." One vessel, the " Melbourne," of the Messageries Maritimes Company, claimed the right of a French mail-boat to pass. As a matter of international courtesy, the " Melbourne " was allowed to continue her journey.

The captains of two English steamers, the " Ross-shire " and " Counsellor," intent upon the profit of their owners, and it is to be hoped not realizing the mischief they might very possibly have occasioned to a national undertaking, in which their owners had more than the ordinary interest of Englishmen, failed to remain in the "gare," and directly the gun-boat "Iris" was out of sight followed in the wake of the "Melbourne." They thus reached a part of the Canal in which it was useless to stop them. With the exception of these three ships, the whole of the vessels in the Canal were cleared out of the way of the coming expedition soon after dawn on the 20th August.

The seizure of Port Said by Captain Fairfax was equally successful. In order to distract attention from the attack there the "Falcon" had been sent, just after sunset on the 19th, to anchor off the coast midway between Port Said and Fort Gemil. The "Northumberland" anchored off Fort Gemil during the night.

At Port Said, before the attacking parties left the ships, the sentries were surprised and seized by Lieutenant-Colonel Tulloch, who landed from an open boat with six marines.

By an ingeniously-constructed floating bridge, formed of a lighter planked over and of the launch of the "Monarch," the men from that vessel were able to land on a broad front.

From the "Iris," also, in the Canal, there was landed, under Lieutenant Cook, R.N., a party which, meeting two companies of seamen from the "Monarch," under Commander Hammill, formed with them a chain of sentries, which, stretching across the neck of land between Lake Menzaleh and the sea, effectually cut off all retreat from the town, and thus prevented any information from being conveyed elsewhere of what was going on. Meantime, a company of the Royal Marines, under Captain Coffin, from the "Iris," with a Gatling, moved straight upon the barracks, while from the "Monarch" a company of the Marine Battalion, under Captain Eden, Royal Marines, and a Gatling from the "Monarch," moved to meet them on the other side of the barracks. The soldiers in the barracks, taken before they could be roused, laid down their arms. The Khedive's Governor, who had been expelled by the rebels, landed with the English troops, and assumed at once the local authority.

Kantara was occupied without resistance.

At Ismailia the force given below* landed at 3 A.M., and surrounded the lock guard before they were discovered. The guard fired off their rifles, but only wounded an officer, Commander Kane. The guard over the Governor's house laid down their arms.

A small native village just outside Ismailia, known as "Arab's-town," was occupied by the enemy; but they were easily dislodged by the seamen and marines, who advanced under a covering fire from the ships.

By 4 A.M. the whole place was occupied.

As soon as the telegraph office had been seized, it was ascer-

---

* From "Orion:"—40 marines, 1 9-pr. gun's crew, 1 Gatling, a torpedo engineer party, 12 riflemen. From "Northumberland" and "Coquette:"—1 Gatling, a rifle company, 1 7-pr. gun, 21 Royal Marine Artillery under Captain Stephenson, C.B., a company of marines under Captain Gore. From "Nyanza" troop-ship:—100 seamen and marines. In all, 565 officers and men.

tained from the messages found there that the enemy, who had about 2,000 men in Nefisha, were intending to reinforce that station by train, in order to attack Ismailia and the ships. Her Majesty's ship "Orion" and Her Majesty's ship "Carysfort" were therefore ordered by Captain Fitzroy to shell the railway station, and, though the distance was about 4,000 yards, a train was wrecked by a shell, and the camp so much injured that the enemy abandoned the place.

Telegrams were found to be still arriving from Cairo to the traffic manager at Ismailia. A reply was sent, in the traffic manager's name, to the War Office in Cairo, to the effect that 5,000 English troops had landed, and that any attempt to relieve the place was too late. The War Minister acknowledged the receipt, and said he had informed all concerned. The position of Ismailia was immediately strengthened.

Meantime, a very successful operation had been carried out by a force of the Seaforth Highlanders and the seamen and marines of Her Majesty's ships "Seagull" and "Mosquito," sent by Admiral Hewett from Suez to Shaluf.

It was important to seize Shaluf, not only because it gave possession of the part of the Suez Canal between Suez and the Bitter Lakes, but also because there is at that point a lock of the Fresh-water Canal permitting the water to be emptied into the Suez Canal. The lock-gates had been opened, and the town of Suez would soon have been deprived of its supply of fresh water.

The lock was at once seized by a company of the Seaforth Highlanders, under Captain Lendrum, and the lock-gates closed.

The enemy opened fire, and showed in some force on the further side of the Fresh-water Canal. Two Highlanders were drowned in attempting to pass; but Lieutenant Lang, Seaforth Highlanders, having swum across under fire and procured a boat from the further side, the men crossed the Canal, and, with the assistance of a well-directed fire of small arms, Gatlings, and a 7-pr. from the tops of the "Seagull" and "Mosquito," the Highlanders and ships' landing companies easily drove back and dispersed the Egyptians.

The enemy showed no want of courage, but their shooting was so bad that only two sailors were wounded. In this skirmish sixty-two Egyptians were made prisoners, and a considerable quantity of stores and ammunition captured.

Everything was thus prepared for the passage down the Canal, the landing at Ismailia, and secure communication by the Canal with the Indian Contingent on its arrival at Suez.

CHAPTER VII.

THE MOVEMENT TO ISMAILIA.—THE DISEMBARKATION BEGINS:
19TH AUGUST TO 23RD AUGUST.—NECESSITY FOR THE ADVANCE
OF A SMALL FORCE TO SAVE THE FAILING WATER.

To return to Alexandria: everything having been on the 16th
August arranged for the movement on the 19th, so that the fleet
might arrive at Port Said by early dawn on the 20th August, that
which chiefly remained to be done was to embark the troops in
such a way as not to convey information to the enemy of the
destined point of attack. To this end it was essential not merely
to spread rumours of a destination other than that actually intended,
but to leave almost every one under the impression that, for the
moment at all events, something was to be done which was in fact
not contemplated at all. It was so certain that what was believed
by the troops and correspondents to be about to take place would
be reported to Arabi that it became very important that every one
in Alexandria should believe that we were not moving to the
Canal. As the purpose of attacking the Abukir forts had been for
a long time seriously entertained, and as it was at least probable
that some hint of this intention had reached the rebel forces, that
fact made deception the more easy. It was easy to issue actual
orders for the attack upon the forts at Abukir, to move thither, and
to make every preparation as if for this end, because the movement
and the preparations would all serve for the purpose really intended.
Accordingly orders were issued to the fleet to prepare for the long
contemplated bombardment of Abukir, and elaborate arrangements
were made for supporting this by a combined movement of the
whole of the forces to be left in Alexandria under the orders of
Sir Edward Hamley, who had arrived from England, a few hours
before Sir G. Wolseley, to command the 2nd Division. Sir E.
Hamley was instructed to make arrangements for advancing upon
Arabi's works to co-operate with a supposed advance of the rest
of the army from Abukir Bay, and worked out all the details of
that operation, issuing orders to his two Brigadiers, Sir A. Alison
and Sir E. Wood, on the evening of the 18th, after all his
proposals had received the full approval of Sir G. Wolseley. Sir
Edward, who was not in the secret as to the operations that were
really intended, was not a little incommoded in his plans by the
fact that, for the reasons already given, no field artillery was left to
him, but after having clearly pointed out his weakness in this
respect, he did his best to compensate the defect by his general
arrangements.

On the 18th the whole of the Brigade of Guards was re-em-
barked, as were also the cavalry and artillery which had been
landed. One of the first points to which Sir Garnet's attention
had been directed on his arrival at Alexandria was the embarkation

of the four locomotives and eighty carriages, which up to that time had not, unfortunately, been put on board ship. In his telegram of 10th August from Gibraltar (see p. 21) he had ordered them to be embarked. Immediate arrangements were now made for their being dispatched to Ismailia.

On the evening of the 18th all the fleet anchored outside the outer harbour of Alexandria with the exception of the "Salamis" and "Helicon," dispatch-boats, the first containing Sir Garnet Wolseley and the Chief of the Staff, the second Sir Beauchamp Seymour.

At noon on the 19th the fleet of eight iron-clads and seventeen transports was joined by the two dispatch-boats, and Sir B. Seymour immediately gave the signal for weighing anchor. Each iron-clad had two transports detailed to accompany it and to work as a small division under the orders of the Naval Captain.

In moving off the twenty-five ships formed in five lines, sweeping eastwards towards Abukir. About 4 P.M. the ships anchored in Abukir Bay. There they remained till night-fall, when the small craft were sent close in shore and opened fire, whilst the rest of the fleet steamed off towards Port Said, which was reached soon after sunrise.

It was not possible at once to enter the Canal, because the "Melbourne" and the two English steamers had not cleared out (vide p. 30). It was necessary, however, to provide an immediate reinforcement, in case of accident, for the holders of Ismailia, and Major-General Graham, with a wing of the West Kent, was therefore transhipped into a torpedo-boat, which, for the reasons already explained, was able to pass through the Canal, though no larger vessel could have done so. After the torpedo-boat had passed the three steamers which blocked the way, General Graham's party was transhipped into the gun-boat "Falcon" and landed at Ismailia at 10 P.M.

As soon as the three ships moving north had cleared out of the Canal, the expedition entered it in the following order:—

Names of Ships.	Troops, &c., carried.
Penelope	500 Marines and lighters.
Helicon	Naval Commander-in-chief.
Thalia	Six lighters and working parties.
Salamis	Commander-in-chief.
Rhosina	570 Marines and forage.
Nerissa	380 Marines and Engineers; coal and railway stock.
Euphrates	2nd Battalion Duke of Cornwall's Light Infantry; 3rd Battalion King's Royal Rifle Corps.
Catalonia	1st Battalion West Kent; 2nd Brigade Staff.
Nevada	2nd Battalion York and Lancaster.
Orient	Scots Guards; 1st Division Staff; 1st Brigade Staff; 19th Hussars (detachment).
Iberia	Coldstream Guards.
Batavia	Grenadier Guards; ½ battery Garrison Artillery.
Capella	Staff, Head-quarters.
Osprey	Commissariat and Mounted Infantry.*
Marathon	½ Bearer Company and two Field Hospitals.
Calabria	} Household Cavalry and Mounted Infantry.*
Holland	
Italy	~~Household Cavalry.~~ 7 *D.G. Wing*
Egyptian Monarch ..	Wing of 7th Dragoon Guards. *H-Qr.*
Tower Hill	Battery Royal Horse Artillery. N | A.
Palmyra	,, Royal Artillery.
Champion Tug . ..	Four lighters with railway plant.
Tug .. ⟨ ..	,, ,, staff.
Gun-boats	

On the 20th the vessels in front of the "Catalonia" reached Kantara by dusk. The "Catalonia" at sunset grounded 8 miles from Port Said. All the ships forming part of the expedition from Alexandria anchored in the Canal.

The eleven transports, conveying the remainder of the artillery, the 4th Dragoon Guards, the Royal Irish, and Royal Irish Fusiliers, which had not reached Alexandria by the 19th, were still at sea from 24 to 48 hours from Port Said.

At 9 A.M. on the 21st Sir Garnet Wolseley reached Ismailia, and at 10 A.M. sent forward General Graham, with his half-battalion of the West Kent and a naval Gatling gun, to occupy Nefisha, reinforcing him with the battalion of marines as soon as these could be landed.

The vessels in front of the "Batavia" reached Ismailia by dusk. The "Batavia" repeatedly grounded, so that those astern of her only accomplished 20 miles by night-fall.

The Indian Contingent had begun to arrive at Suez on the evening of the 20th August.

The action at Shaluf, on the 20th, was followed up on the 21st by the occupation of Serapeum by the Seaforth Highlanders, under Lieutenant-Colonel Stockwell. The lock from the Sweet-

---

* The Mounted Infantry, 70 men and horses, were under command of Captain Parr, 1st Somersetshire Regiment.

water into the Salt-water Canal was, like that at Shaluf, found to have been opened, and was closed. The enemy, who had retreated from Shaluf, were not aware of the occupation of Serapeum, and attempted to reach the lock, but were easily driven off. From prisoners it was ascertained that all the parties of the enemy stationed between Nefisha and Suez were retreating northwards across the desert.

The lock at Geneffeh had been occupied in the passage northwards of the " Seagull " and " Mosquito " with the Seaforth Highlanders for Serapeum.

Thus, by the 22nd, the whole line of railway and Fresh-water Canal between Suez and Ismailia was in our hands, and communication by land with the Indian Contingent had been secured. In several places, however, the line of railway had been injured, and it could not be repaired till engineer stores had been landed for the purpose. The railway had been also injured, though to no great extent, beyond Nefisha.

The disembarkation was now carried on as rapidly as the conditions permitted, but it is necessary to observe, first, that it was not till late on the evening of the 23rd that even one division of two guns of N | A Royal Horse Artillery, the first battery to be landed, had completed their disembarkation ; and not till the afternoon of that day that the Household Cavalry, the leading troops of that arm, were on shore. It is necessary to press attention to this question of the time required for the work of disembarkation, because from the comments, made by even professional critics, it might be supposed that the movement and disembarkation of an army are precisely the same thing as the movement and disembarkation of a single traveller.

By the evening of the 23rd, that is, four days after the expedition had sailed from Alexandria, about 9,000 men, nearly the whole of the *personnel* contained in the ships forming the first part of the expedition, were on shore ; but the disembarkation, as a military force, of even that fraction of the whole army was by no means complete. The narrow roadway between the landing-stage and the bridge still teemed with men and animals, moving backwards and forwards in the transport of materials. The whole of the space nearest to the landing-stage was piled with stores of all kinds awaiting removal, and only a small number of the transports had been cleared.

By the evening of the 23rd August the 7th Dragoon Guards had arrived, but had not completed their disembarkation. The 4th Dragoon Guards had arrived in harbour, in the " Greece " and " City of New York," but were not disembarked. The greater part of the artillery which had not sailed from Alexandria with the expedition had just arrived, and could not complete their disembarkation for some days. The " City of Paris," with the Royal Irish, and the " Arab," with the Royal Irish Fusiliers, came into Ismailia on the 23rd.

So far as the small supply of engineering materials yet landed made it possible, work had already been begun for the purpose of joining the railway-station, by a tram-line, with the landing-stage, but progress was as yet very slow.

In order to get rolling-stock on to the line it was necessary to send round to Suez the engines which had been brought from Alexandria, and before they could be brought up from thence the line of railway had to be repaired. A train of carriages, but no engine, had been captured at Nefisha, and no rolling-stock of any kind, except two broken-down carriages, used for local purposes, had been taken at Suez.

The water in the Sweet-water Canal was rapidly falling, and, from local information, it was ascertained that the part of the canal where the most serious injury could be inflicted upon it by the enemy lay within a few miles of Ismailia. Sir Garnet Wolseley, therefore, resolved to push on a small force in order to occupy the canal as far as Magfar, a point at which it was known that the enemy had constructed a dam, stopping the flow of the canal. Beyond Magfar the ground rises steadily towards Tel el-Maskhuta. Around Magfar the land is flat, and is irrigated by numerous small canals drawn off from the main one. If, therefore, in rear of this dam the enemy broke through the sides of the Ismailia Canal, they could easily draw off all the water that would flow down to Ismailia and Suez; whereas if this part of the canal were held by us, though they could still *dam* it higher up, it would be by no means so easy for them to break down the much higher banks where the canal flowed through the more elevated land beyond Tel el-Maskhuta. Moreover, in drawing off the water at Magfar, the injury inflicted on the fellaheen would be very small, whereas any attempt to empty the canal higher up in its course to such an extent as to deprive us of water would occasion an injury to the crops which it was probable that the Egyptians would be very unwilling to inflict.

An immediate movement, therefore, as far as Magfar was imperatively necessary for the safety of the army. As far as the dam at Magfar stores could be pushed up by boat, and a system for supply by this means was at once organized.

Before detailing the operations consequent upon the determination to advance to Magfar, it will be well to notice the effect which the seizure of Ismailia had had upon the movements and actions of the enemy, and what had happened elsewhere.

CHAPTER VIII.

ALEXANDRIA FROM THE 19TH AUGUST TO THE 23RD AUGUST.—
EFFECT ON THE ENEMY OF THE MOVEMENT TO ISMAILIA.

When Sir Garnet left Alexandria on the 19th August, the
Chief of the Staff put into Sir Edward Hamley's hands a sealed
packet, to be opened early on the morning of the 20th August. The
packet contained this private letter from Sir Garnet to Sir
Edward :—

"*Alexandria, August* 18, 1882.

" My dear Hamley,
" I do not mean to land at Abukir; my real destination
is Ismailia. I hope to reach that place about 4 P.M. on Sunday
next. We make our demonstration all the same at Abukir to·
morrow, and I hope it may have the desired effect of imposing
upon 'Arabi and his friend Lesseps. A French ship is now
aground near Lake Timsa, and if this has been done purposely, it
may somewhat retard my passage down the Canal.
" When you open this, keep the news to yourself, *tell no one*,
and do nothing beyond showing as many men as you can con-
veniently in Arabi's front, and giving him as many shell from any
of your guns of position that can reach him in his works. I do not
even telegraph the news of my intended movements home until I
have reached Port Said myself, which I hope to do before daybreak on Sunday morning.
" I shall bring you on as soon as I can, as I shall want every
available man I can get for my fight near Tel el-Kebir, if Arabi
will only in kindness stay to fight me there.
" Good-bye for the present.
" Sincerely yours,
(Signed) " G. J. WOLSELEY.
" Sir E. B. Hamley."

It is to be noted that the ground, over which troops could
advance, between Arabi's front at Kafr ed-Dauar and our front from
Ramleh to Alexandria, was no longer at this time, as was at first
the case (see *ante,* p. 13), restricted to the strip in which lay the
Canal and railway embankment. Lake Mariut was receding every
day, and left a large margin of dry strand and of shallow water
towards the town wall of Alexandria ; and, on the other side,
Lake Abukir had dried up so far that from the whole front of the
town of Ramleh up to and beyond the whole extent of Arabi's
works was a level space of hard sand along which infantry and
horses could advance everywhere, though a marshy strip outside
the Palm Grove of Ramleh prevented guns from going far into the
plain. Consequently, Arabi's force on the one side, or our troops
at Ramleh on the other, were perfectly free to manœuvre across
the wide space now left between the two lakes.

A reconnaissance had been carried out on afternoon of the 19th by Sir E. Wood with half a battalion of the 1st Berkshire, in which one man had been severely wounded.

On opening Sir Garnet's letter Sir E. Hamley dismissed the troops who had, according to orders of the previous night, turned out at daybreak for the attack on Kafr ed-Dauar. He ordered a fresh parade for 4 P.M., the afternoon being, for the same reasons which determined Sir A. Alison's choice of hour in the reconnaissance of the 5th August, more suitable than the morning for a demonstration not intended to be pressed home. But, meantime, he placed four companies at points of the edge of the Palm Grove to look like the heads of columns and rode into the plain with some of his officers as if reconnoitring Arabi's works, which were kept fully manned by the enemy. At 4 P.M. Sir E. Wood's troops as below* advanced along the Mahmudiyeh Canal towards the enemy's position at Kafr ed-Dauar, while Sir A. Alison's moved out from the Palm Grove, under the personal direction of Sir E. Hamley, and advanced across the dry bed of the lake towards the enemy's works, manœuvring there as if to attack the main front. The enemy opened fire from one very large gun, and apparently from three smaller ones, and also firing many rockets, which, as well as the shells from the large gun, passed over the troops, exploding mostly behind them. The enemy having developed his full force, our troops fell back without casualties and retired within the lines.

The Highland Brigade was this day completed by the arrival of the 2nd Highland Light Infantry and the Black Watch (1st Royal Highlanders). Reconnaissances were at first carried out daily, but by the 23rd August they were discontinued; it being judged no longer possible to deceive the enemy by mere repetition.

On the 22nd August Sir E. Hamley received a telegram from Ismailia informing him that it was proposed to leave for the garrison of Alexandria the Manchester and Derbyshire Regiments, and 1,000 men of depôts from England. It was hoped that if two regiments of Sir E. Hamley's force were, in addition to the above, detained in Alexandria, as well as one battery of Garrison Artillery and the Malta Fencibles, the remainder of the 2nd Division might be brought round to Ismailia as soon as the place was clear enough for their disembarkation. Major-General Harman had already been ordered out from England to take up the command at Alexandria.

It was necessary, however, to consider not only the military, but also the political situation, and Sir E. Hamley was directed to consult on this subject Sir E. Malet, the British Minister. Sir E. Malet expressed a strong sense of the political importance of retaining a powerful force in Alexandria.

---

* 3rd Brigade, Sir A. Alison : 1st Gordon Highlanders, the Cameron Highlanders. 4th Brigade, Sir E. Wood : 1st South Stafford, 1st Berkshire, with two guns drawn by mules.

In order, therefore, to provide for the reduction of the garrison and to hasten the transfer of his Division to Ismailia, Sir E. Hamley proceeded vigorously with the entrenchments of Ramleh. Under his directions, Colonel Maitland, the Commanding Royal Engineer of the 2nd Division, converted the place therefore virtually into an entrenched camp, with a strong interior redoubt on the signal hill. Powerful guns were removed from the sea front of Alexandria, and mounted on the works of Ramleh. He also provided for the defence of El-Meks and of the walls of Alexandria, and redistributed the two regiments forming its garrison in posts for the better maintenance of internal order, and protection of the town in case of assault.

According to the information which we now possess, the ruse employed to deceive the Egyptians as to the destined movement to the Canal was entirely successful. At the time when Arabi fell back from Alexandria after the bombardment, and was dismissed by the Khedive from the Ministry of War, he very prudently appealed to a Council of Notables in Cairo. Uncertainty as to the exact scope of the power and responsibility attached to particular offices is characteristic of revolutionary Governments. It appears that from this time onwards a Military Committee, selected from among the Notables, exercised, in their own belief, all authority over the army, and regarded Arabi simply as one of the Generals under their orders. He, on the other hand, continued to regard himself as the Commander-in-chief and Ruler of the country.

His great influence, however, depended not upon any military knowledge or capacity, but upon his being able to excite the enthusiasm and fanaticism of the soldiers and people. All the communications of the country by rail, water, and telegraph centred in Cairo, while his services were most valuable in presence of the enemy. It was therefore almost inevitable, since information of what was going on from all parts of the country went to the War Office in Cairo, that the direction of the larger movements should practically come thence.

Yakoub Sawmy Pasha was President of the Council in Cairo, and at all events believed himself, and was considered by the Council, to have the direction of affairs in his hands. A body of twenty-five Notables formed the Council under him. Arabi, whilst at Kafr ed-Dauar, received information daily of all that took place in Alexandria, partly from inhabitants, partly from men paid to obtain news. He heard of all orders issued to our troops ; all the town rumours were reported to him. As, however, the action taken on our side had been based on the assumption that this would certainly be the case, he found himself much more often deceived than aided by the news he so obtained.

At the date of the bombardment the Egyptian army consisted in all of about 9,000 men, 48 batteries of 6 guns each (288 field guns), but they had only 750 horses ; 5,000 of these troops were in Alexandria, the remainder being distributed over the country. The Egyptians say that, up to ten days after the bombardment, the force at Kafr ed-Dauar did not exceed 6,500 regulars, and that

Bedouins did not begin to come in till twenty-five days after the bombardment. By calling in to the colours the old reserve men, some of them over 50 years of age, the army was at once raised to 60,000 men.

At the time of the seizure of Ismailia their army was thus distributed. In round numbers:—

15,000 at Kafr ed-Dauar.
15,000 at Abukir, Rosetta, and Burlus.
7,000 at Damietta.
12,000 at Tel el-Kebir and on the eastern side
        of the Delta.
11,000 at Cairo.
—————
60,000 in all.

The Bedouins had then begun to come in, and there were about 3,000 of them at Kafr ed-Dauar and about 3,000 at Tel el-Kebir, in addition to the above.

The Egyptian Council had been completely convinced by the assurances of M. Lesseps that the Canal could not be occupied by us. The occupation of Suez had, however, so far alarmed them that they had thought it prudent to have a considerable force at Tel el-Kebir, though they did not expect any movement from Alexandria by the Canal till it actually took place.

The reports of the threatened attack upon Abukir reached Cairo, and a bombardment of that place was so fully expected that on the 19th, the day on which the fleet sailed, 3,000 men were sent to Abukir from Cairo. When the fleet sailed no news of that event reached the Council. The first intelligence they received of the movement of the fleet was from Abukir, whence a report of the threatened bombardment arrived as soon as the fleet appeared, and it was then fully expected that a general advance would be made from both Abukir and Alexandria. Later news from Abukir informed the Council that some of the ships had anchored, and that others had gone on, probably to Damietta. It was then thought that Damietta would also be seized, and an attack made from thence simultaneously with one from Kafr ed-Dauar. The news that we had seized Port Said and Ismailia reached Cairo through our own telegrams as soon as those events took place, though the information was conveyed in a form designed to impose upon them, and to induce them not to attempt to disturb our possession.

Strange as it may appear, it seems now to be certain that the great transfer of force on the 19th August from Alexandria to Ismailia remained unknown to Arabi till he heard of it with evident astonishment in Ceylon about a year later. All that was known to him or to the Council at the time was that English forces had appeared at the different points on the Canal.

As soon as it was known that we had seized Ismailia the Council resolved to increase the army. By the enlistment of recruits, who had had no previous training, the numbers were raised to 100,000 men. After a few days' drill the men were drafted into the ranks and took their place with the trained soldiers. When the war broke out 150,000 rifles were in store, so that they were able at once efficiently to arm the whole force, but they had equipment and clothing for only 40,000 men. By working day and night, however, they soon succeeded in completing the clothing and equipment for the whole 100,000; 11,000 transport animals were obtained from the " free-will offerings "* of the people, and all the field guns were horsed by the same means, though with untrained horses.

The Bedouins wore their own clothing, and were provided with old muskets and whatever equipment could be given them.

One other element of strength on the side of the Egyptians must be taken into account. The whole mass of the people are labourers trained in one particular class of work. Their living depends upon their skill in constructing embankments for the damming of water both in the direct course of the canals and also on dry land, to prepare for the proper flooding of their fields as soon as the water is turned on to them. Thus the ruling Council had at its command, in the then excited condition of the peasantry, an unlimited supply of skilled labour which they resolved to turn to the utmost account. The works which they proposed to undertake would in any other country appear incredible. That they would construct a series of dams across the Ismailia Sweet-water Canal to prevent our troops from obtaining water, and that they would embank the railway to interfere with our using it for purposes of transport, was from the first to be expected; but the scheme of entrenchment which they proposed to carry out for barring our progress, though it would certainly have failed from its very extent, is probably without a parallel in improvised fortification. The design formed, as soon as it was known that the line of our advance would be from Ismailia upon Cairo, was to erect, in addition to fortifications at Tel el-Maskhuta, Mahsama, and Kassassin, a series of continuous entrenchments, first from Es-Salihiyeh to Tel el-Kebir, a distance of over 20 miles, and thence to have continued it southwards to Dar el-Beida, a further distance of 30 miles across the desert. Dar el-Beida lies just off the old overland route which ran direct from Suez to Cairo, and the extension thither was intended to provide against a possible attempt to advance simultaneously from Suez and Ismailia. The design will at least give an idea of the amount of labour at the command of the Egyptians.

---

* It should be observed that Mr. Wallace, who has travelled much among the fellaheen since the war, and used great skill in eliciting facts, doubts whether the aid furnished was really obtained without a rigorous application of the kourbash.

CHAPTER IX.

The Seizure of the Lines of Railway and Canal as far as Kassassin Lock.

Advance Guard Action of the 24th August.—Flight of Enemy's Advanced Force from Tel el-Maskhuta on the 25th August.—The Cavalry capture Mahsama, 25th August.—General Graham is pushed on to Kassassin, 26th August.

At the end of Chapter VII (page 37) it was stated that on the 23rd August an advance upon Magfar had been determined on, for reasons there explained. The orders issued on the 23rd were as follows :—

"The following movements will take place : — The three squadrons of Household Cavalry, two guns of N Battery, A Brigade, Royal Horse Artillery, the detachment of the 19th Hussars, and the Mounted Infantry, will march independently to-morrow morning at 4 A.M. for Nefisha, and will place themselves under the orders of Major-General Graham.

"As soon as Major-General Graham has been joined by the above troops he will proceed, together with those now under his command, to Magfar, and take up a position there. The Duke of Cornwall's Light Infantry will also proceed at the same time to Nefisha, and on arrival will remain there and protect the station, the bridge, and the canal, their camp equipage being sent by rail.

"The camp equipage of the troops moving from here will be taken by rail, and also that of the force now at Nefisha, to Magfar."*

The battery of artillery had been working late into the night of the 23rd August at the disembarkation ; the division of two guns ordered to move forward was the whole artillery force as yet ready, and officers and men had been so worn out by the continuous labour of disembarking that, in the darkness of the morning of the 24th, it was impossible for even this division to be horsed and moved off punctually at the appointed hour.

Though the desert on the eastern side of the Delta is generally "hard" and excellent marching ground, it happens that that

---

* Detail of troops ordered to move :—
    From Ismailia : 3 squadrons Household Cavalry, detachment 19th Hussars, the Mounted Infantry, 2 guns N | A—R.H.A.
    From Nefisha : 2nd Battalion York and Lancaster, Royal Marine Artillery.
    To Nefisha : Duke of Cornwall's Light Infantry.

CE-D

portion of it which lies immediately between Ismailia and Magfar is relatively " soft," bad marching ground. Moreover, banks of exceedingly heavy sand must be crossed, and there are about 2 miles of very heavy and soft desert, so that this part of the route is peculiarly trying for all arms. For artillery almost the only practicable route is by way of Nefisha, along the railway embankment ; even there the soil is sandy, and difficult for wheeled carriages.

There had not yet been time for any engine to arrive from Suez, so that the trucks sent by the railway had to be drawn by mules and Commissariat horses.

The men had received their rations for the 24th. Two days' rations in addition had been issued to regiments, of which the meat and most of the groceries and fuel were carried in the regimental carts, while the men carried the two days' biscuit.

Sir Garnet, with a certain portion of his Staff, and General Willis, with his Staff, accompanied the cavalry to Magfar, in advance of the infantry.

The cavalry, with Sir Drury Lowe himself in command, moved along the desert on the right of the railway ; the infantry and guns followed on the railway embankment.

To the east of Magfar our cavalry found the enemy's outposts, and easily drove them in. The cavalry advanced to a point nearly half-way between Tel el-Maskhuta and Magfar. The enemy then began to show infantry in force, and to threaten an attack.

A few prisoners were captured, from whom it was ascertained that the Egyptians had constructed a second dam at Tel el-Maskhuta, and that his infantry were there in force behind entrenchments.

In order to appreciate the nature of the decision at which Sir Garnet now arrived, it is necessary to recall one or two points. In a general sense, the object of this period of the campaign was to obtain a secure hold of the railway and canal as far as Kassassin. This was necessary in order to prevent the enemy from doing these lines of communication any further damage, to remove the dams and any other obstruction he might have made, to get rolling-stock upon the railway, and to begin to accumulate supplies. The quicker this could be done the shorter would be the length of the whole campaign, the greater would be its political effect, and the less the loss of life and the privations entailed upon the troops.

But the special advance on the morning of the 24th August to Magfar had not been made with the immediate view of securing by it the communications as far as Kassassin ; it had been made solely for the sake of seizing the low-lying country around Magfar, in which the first dam had been constructed, and where the facilities for emptying the canal and depriving Ismailia and Suez of water were exceptionally great.

.The apparent determination of the Egyptians to hold on to Tel el-Maskhuta offered a new prospect. For about half-an-hour or more the General carefully watched the enemy. He saw trains arriving at the railway station; he saw formed bodies of Egyptians show beyond the line of entrenchment. Everything indicated that they intended to make a serious stand. Few as were the troops then available, and long as the march would be for any additional infantry and guns, he saw that that very smallness of force was likely to tempt the Egyptian Commander to remain where he was, and therefore to give the English troops from Ismailia time to come up, with the result of inflicting upon this outlying body of the enemy a defeat which, if vigorously followed up, would probably enable us to secure the very line of railway and canal as far as Kassassin, which it was at this time all-important for us to get into our hands.

Omelets are not to be made, however, without breaking eggs; and it was certain that to call upon cavalry just landed from shipboard, with their horses in no condition for severe exertion, would place a great strain upon that arm. Moreover, there was considerable risk that the troops pushed forward to hold the railway and canal would have for a day or two to undergo some privations whilst the dam on the canal was being removed. But it was certain that, by straining every nerve for their supply, the privations would be discomforts only, not dangerous to life, and that, on the whole, the troops would gain by the sacrifice from the shortening of the period of the campaign. The moral advantage of so great a first success, and the serious encouragement to the enemy which would be a consequence if we then fell back when he was showing a disposition to hold his own, were also important elements in the question.

Whilst Sir Garnet Wolseley had been examining the enemy's position, the advanced troops of General Graham's force had reached Magfar. About 7·30 A.M. orders were sent for the infantry to continue their march, and for the two guns to move on with all possible rapidity. About 8·30 A.M. Lieutenant Childers was dispatched to Ismailia with orders for the Guards Brigade and all cavalry and artillery that might be by the time of the receipt of the order ready, to push on to the front. Colonel Harrison returned to Ismailia to make arrangements for the supply of the force now ordered up. Orders were at the same time sent to the 2nd Battalion Duke of Cornwall's Light Infantry, which had been left at Nefisha, to move on to the front.

On the arrival of General Graham's infantry half a battalion of the York and Lancaster Regiment were placed between the canal and railway, the left resting on the canal at the point where the nearer dam had been constructed 3,200 yards from the enemy's position on the Tel el-Maskhuta dam. This was the most advanced body of our troops, the remainder of the force being écheloned from it to the right. A place was selected for the two guns under the shoulder of a sand-hill 500 yards to the rear of the near dam, 600 yards from the canal. The guns were, however, not able to reach it till nearly 9 o'clock. The right half-battalion York and Lancaster were in line with the guns extending from the canal on their left. The marines were still further to the right. On making up his mind that he would now have an opportunity for fighting an action of some importance to the campaign, Sir Garnet had ordered General Willis to take command of all the troops, and to take up a position, pointing out the sand-hills as a place for the guns.

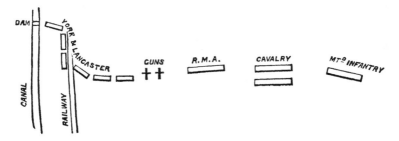

The above was at first the formation. General Willis gave orders that all were to lie down under cover of the scrub, bushes, and sand-drifts, and not show or fire without special orders.

The cavalry and Mounted Infantry were considerably further to the right, about a mile from the canal, watching any attempt of the enemy to turn our right. At 9 A.M. the enemy opened upon the cavalry a distant but heavy musketry fire.

The position now held by the enemy was a range of hills which, in its general relation to the ground occupied by our guns and infantry, was somewhat like that of the upper seats in a lecture theatre to the place of the lecturer, the enemy actually holding chiefly the ground represented by the seats from the lecturer's left front round to his right, whilst our cavalry manœuvred on the same high ground on the enemy's left, threatening and opposing any attempt to extend further round us on that side.

The position held by our infantry and by the two guns had, however, the great advantage that it lay amidst sandy hillocks, which gave a very effective protection from the enemy's fire, and made it difficult for the enemy to estimate our strength. Both in front and rear of our line, throughout that part of it which looked directly towards Tel el-Maskhuta, the ground was so soft, in part from deep sand, and in part from marsh, that any shells from the enemy were sure at once to bury themselves on striking. The ground, on the other hand, near Tel el-Maskhuta, and from thence along the line of hills occupied by the enemy, and in part by our cavalry, was hard gravel, on which shells produced much greater effect.

The enemy had extended his extreme right beyond the canal, and soon after 9 A.M. advanced both cavalry, infantry, and artillery in our immediate front to within less than 2,000 yards of the gun hillock. This brought him to pretty close quarters with our left, where stood the York and Lancaster half-battalion, but the steady fire of these men from a well-protected position checked him at once ; he did not venture to close, and soon retired on that side, continuing, however, to extend and advance his left. For nearly an hour the cavalry and Mounted Infantry continued holding in check the enemy's left on the hard gravelly flats on the hill-tops. The reports from the cavalry were that as soon as any of the enemy more bold than the rest ventured to attempt an advance they were instantly picked off by the men of the Mounted Infantry, who, being all chosen marksmen, had dismounted, and by their effective shooting for the time entirely stopped all movement on that side. From the encircling position occupied by the enemy, the cavalry and Mounted Infantry were throughout nearly the whole day in much closer contact with the enemy than any other portion of the force except the extreme left detachment.

Sir Garnet with his Staff had been standing upon the top of the hillock above the position occupied by our two guns. At 9·40 A.M. the enemy opened four guns upon this hillock. They had obtained the range with so much accuracy that the first shot struck immediately at the foot of the hillock in front ; the second passed a few feet over the General's head exactly in the right line ; a third followed, with as good an aim, breaking a horse's leg just behind the hill. For a few shots they continued to fire in the same direction, but as soon as the horses had been all led behind the hill, so that no conspicuous object was presented to them, they turned the guns upon the Mounted Infantry and cavalry. Soon after 10 they added two more guns to the four already in action ; their practice was so accurate that the cavalry and Mounted Infantry were ordered to fall back. The wide plain afforded them little shelter, but fortunately, despite the accuracy of laying of the enemy's guns, their shells were very inefficient. Their shrapnel, of which they did not appear to have many, fitted with time fuses, burst high in air, and were nearly harmless. Most of the shells, fitted only with percussion fuses, were intended to burst on touching the ground, but, always on the sandy soil and on the irrigated ground, usually even on the gravelly desert, these buried themselves before bursting, so that unless they actually struck man or horse on their first impact, they produced no effect. Our losses would have been serious but for this fact.

Hitherto no reply had been made to the Egyptian artillery by our two guns. Sir Garnet had been anxious to reserve them till the enemy ventured upon a nearer approach. The one duty of the small force now engaged was to retain the enemy until reinforcements could arrive, and it was therefore most unadvisable to expend on distant fire any strength which could be kept for the decisive moment in case the enemy should venture to close.

But the reports from the cavalry showed that the extreme accuracy of the enemy's artillery on that open plain might, despite the inefficiency of their shells, inflict serious loss unless some relief were obtained.

Our range-finders gave a reading* of the distance of the enemy's

---

* 2,900 yards instead of 1,750 yards. The mirage no doubt made it difficult to use the range-finders. Subsequently a range taken at the nearest guns gave 1,800 yards. A trial shot showed this distance to be under 1,400 yards.

guns from our own which exaggerated it by more than 1,000 yards, but a couple of trial shots proved that this part of the Egyptian line was within effective range. At 10·30 A.M. two rounds of shrapnel, which burst exactly over the enemy's artillery, at once caused them to withdraw some of their nearer guns beyond the crest of the hill. They then turned all the fire they could bring to bear upon our artillery. At first six guns were directed against our two from that part of the range of hills which fronted us towards Tel el-Maskhuta.

As their troops arrived by train they gradually worked round behind the crest on to our extreme right, and at 12 o'clock opened six fresh guns* from this side, enfilading and in part taking in reverse the main position held by our infantry and guns. As this fresh battery was supported by both infantry and cavalry in considerable numbers, it was impossible for our cavalry any longer to prevent their holding this ground, but the cavalry and Mounted Infantry continued to threaten and check them. Shortly before this new development had taken place, two Gatlings and a party of sailors from Her Majesty's ship "Orion" arrived. Some low-lying sand-hills at right angles to the position of our infantry gave capital shelter for a new line to be formed by the sailors and Gatlings fronting the new fire.

General Willis carried out the new dispositions. One of the Gatlings was placed in the line now formed, and a shelter-pit was made for it. One of the two Horse Artillery guns was brought up to a shoulder of the gun hillock, from which it was able to reply to the flanking battery. The same hillock furnished protection for the wagons and limbers, which were at first directly exposed to the fire of the enemy's new battery. Thanks to this and to the fact of the shells burying themselves before bursting, the result was that, despite the accuracy of the enemy's artillery, which continued to cover all exposed places with a heavy shell-fire, the losses were small.

The second Gatling† was sent to the assistance of the part of the York and Lancashire Regiment on the left flank, between the canal and railway. It had hardly been placed in position before a new forward movement of the enemy on that side gave occasion for its employment. The extreme heat of the day, to which one man after another succumbed, and the severe labour entailed upon the gunners in keeping up a constant fire against a very superior force of artillery in very favourable positions, were the greatest dangers to which the troops were exposed. For there could be little doubt that if our guns had been even for a time silenced,

---

* These new guns were Krupps. The first battery consisted of bronze rifled muzzle-loaders.

† Each Gatling was so placed that it could both fire to the front and also flank the general front of the position. It may be noted as an indication of the difficulties of the march from Ismailia that both of these Gatlings had been unable to move through the sand, and that General Willis had sent back two pairs of artillery horses with lasso harness to drag them up for the last two miles.

either because one of the shells which were constantly passing from both directions just over the heads of gunners, drivers, and horses, every now and then killing a horse or breaking a leg, had exploded in a wagon, or if the labour of pushing up the guns after each recoil through the heavy sand had so exhausted the men as to prevent their replying promptly to the Egyptian artillery, the enemy would have acquired a confidence which would have induced him to try his greatly superior numbers in a close attack, which we had barely sufficient numbers to meet. That he did not, under such favourable circumstances as were presented to him, venture to attack us was an element to be taken into account throughout the future progress of the campaign. It was clear that a small defensive force in an entrenched position might, from this time onward, be safely intrusted with the guardianship of any position where it was for other reasons not advisable to accumulate many men.

Meantime, on this day, the longer the enemy delayed the less was the risk. At 1 o'clock, an hour after the development of the enemy's encircling movement on our right, the Duke of Cornwall's Light Infantry from Nefisha made their appearance, and at 2 P.M. were in position as a reserve. At about a quarter to 3 two shells in succession took effect in the little battery, killing on the spot two men and several horses. General Willis then sent some of the Marine Artillery to the assistance of the division of Horse Artillery, which had now for five hours sustained the duel against six times their own number of guns. It would hardly have been possible for the gunners alone to have borne the strain so long, but the drivers had volunteered to work at the mechanical labour of pushing up the guns through the heavy sand, and by a well-arranged system of bringing from the canal water, which was poured over the heads of exhausted men, by keeping as many as possible under the shade of the wagons, and employing only those that were indispensable, the work had been carried on with cheery alacrity, and it was not very willingly that the men submitted to accept the indispensable help of the Marine Artillery, who, from this time, shared with the Horse Artillery the severest labours of the day.* The Mounted Infantry also suffered much from want of water. General Willis sent his Aide-de-camp, Captain James, to them with water and also with reserve ammunition.

Meantime, a scarcely less trying task had fallen to the lot of the Brigade of Guards. A march over the 2 miles of heavy road between Ismailia and Nefisha, difficult at any time, was, during the burning hours of the midday sun of an exceptionally hot day, a very serious task indeed. Throughout all the rest of the campaign, both before and after this, troops were ordered to march in the cool hours of the early morning or of the late afternoon and evening. The sudden necessity for taking advantage of the enemy's stand at Tel el-Maskhuta alone made this severe task imperative. Even for the troops in presence of the Egyptians the direst enemies all that

---

* Lieutenant S. C. Hickman was in command of the two guns.

day were the sun and the parching glare of the desert sand. But at least they had the excitement of actual fighting, and were able at times to take advantage of any shade that wagons or hillocks afforded, and they had not during those hours of fierce heat the additional labour of plodding over sand, burning to the feet and ankle-deep. Man after man during the march was knocked down by the severity of the strain, and by stroke of the sun. All who were physically able pushed on with honest pride and steady discipline, but it was not till 6·20 P.M. that the march was over, and that His Royal Highness the Duke of Connaught was able to bring up his brigade to the support of the troops engaged.

The four remaining guns of N | A R.H.A. arrived with the Guards, and relieved the two which had been in action all day.

An hour earlier Sir Baker Russell, with 350 sabres of the 4th and 7th Dragoon Guards, just disembarked, had joined the cavalry, as the enemy was threatening a fresh advance. About 5·15 P.M. the enemy's guns and cavalry came well down the slope on our right, but whether the troops could not be induced to close, or whether the appearance of our fresh cavalry, whose approach could be clearly seen, caused a change in the orders for their advance, they did not come within infantry fire.

By the time that the Guards had reached the ground the sun had set. The troops bivouacked for the night. The enemy, at 7·30 P.M., threatened a late attack on the left, probably only intended to cover their own withdrawal into camp. At all events it was not seriously pressed.

Sir Garnet returned for the night to Ismailia, leaving General Willis orders " to hold his own during the night and to attack the enemy " at daybreak the following morning.

After midnight A | 1 Battery R.A. (16-prs.) joined the force. It relieved the four guns of N | A on the sand-hill at daylight.

The Division had left the bivouac and were advancing against the enemy's position when Sir Garnet, with his Staff, reached them on the following morning, the 25th August, at 5·30 A.M.

General Graham's brigade moved along the canal in attack formation. The Foot Guards were, with a considerable interval, on the right of General Graham's brigade, in direct échelon of battalions from the right. The cavalry, Mounted Infantry, and N | A Battery R.H.A. to the extreme right front advanced over the ground which had on the previous day been held by the enemy's extreme left. The King's Royal Rifles and Marine Light Infantry, who had joined in the early morning, were in second line. Two guns of A | 1 were on the right of the Guards ; four guns of A | 1, starting at 6·15 A.M. from the "gun-hillock" of the previous day, moved between the two brigades. As soon as our outposts came within sight of the enemy's position it was evident that he had altogether abandoned the works. Our infantry advanced towards Tel el-Maskhuta, while Sir Garnet sent orders to the cavalry and Horse Artillery to push on at once, "to work well round the enemy's left and cut off his retreat, if possible."

The cavalry horses were scarcely fit for such severe exertion so recently after landing from ship-board. The small Egyptian horses on which the infantry were mounted, well bred and accustomed to the country, enabled that little force to cover the ground with greater ease.

The cavalry manœuvred according to Sir Garnet's order, but no formed body of the enemy was seen until the heights over Mahsama were reached. Then Sir Drury Lowe found himself opposed by a large force of infantry, with guns in position, and eight or ten squadrons of cavalry. The artillery had been reinforced by the two guns from A | 1, at first on the right of the Guards. The shrapnel proved extremely effective, as did also the fire from the Mounted Infantry, employed strictly in their proper function of galloping up into effective positions, dismounting, and bringing close and well-aimed infantry fire to bear. The enemy successively fell back, and at last the camp at Mahsama was captured, the Mounted Infantry joining in a final cavalry charge. Seven Krupp guns, large numbers of Remington rifles, a great quantity of ammunition, stores, camp equipment, and a provision and ammunition train of seventy-five railway wagons thus fell into our possession.

At 8 A.M. the infantry had reached Tel el-Maskhuta, and as it was found that the village on the south side of the canal would afford shade and cover for the Brigade of Guards, Sir Garnet decided to encamp them there, sending on General Graham's brigade, as soon as there had been time for it to rest, towards Mahsama. The order for this was, however, provisional; it was to depend on the possibility of supplying the troops at Mahsama before the two dams at Tel el-Maskhuta and Magfar had been cut through, and before the great embankment which it was found that the enemy had constructed across the railway could be removed. The first order sent to Sir Drury Lowe on his reporting the capture of Mahsama had been to destroy what he could and fall back on Tel el-Maskhuta, as infantry could not be sent. But, on receiving the full report of the supplies that had been captured, General Willis sent on, at 5 P.M., the battalion of marines and Marine Artillery to support the cavalry. General Willis' orders had been to bring back the cavalry, but as he was well aware that this was solely because of the difficulty of feeding them, he, on his own responsibility, made the new dispositions, thus anticipating an order dispatched on the 26th from Head-quarters, as soon as the news of the captures was received, to keep the cavalry at Mahsama. An order to occupy Kassassin Lock with General Graham's brigade, and to entrench it, was sent from Head-quarters at 8 P.M. on the 25th and received by General Willis at 1·30 A.M.* on the 26th August. General Willis, therefore, sent forward this order to General Graham, who had already left the camp with the Royal Marines and Marine Artillery. At the same time the two other regiments of his brigade were sent forward to him in accordance with the order. At dawn, therefore, on the 26th August, General Graham, with the York and Lancaster Regiment, the Duke of

---

* According to endorsement on the original order.

Cornwall's Light Infantry, and the Royal Marines, marched to the cavalry camp at Mahsama. Lieutenant-Colonel Herbert Stewart had, before General Graham's arrival, reconnoitred the position around the canal lock at Kassassin, and found it evacuated by the enemy. It was occupied by a detachment of the 4th Dragoon Guards at daylight on the 26th, and later in the day General Graham, with his brigade, moved forward and occupied the position at the lock.

Thus, by the morning of the 26th August, the whole of the canal and railway as far as Kassassin were in our hands.

On the 25th an important prisoner had been captured in the person of Mahmoud Fehmi Pasha. Arabi subsequently attributed his not having made more serious efforts to dislodge our small advance-post at Kassassin to the fact, that in consequence of Mahmoud Fehmi Pasha's capture he could not ascertain what our forces were. Fehmi had been especially endeavouring to ascertain this at the moment of his capture.

CHAPTER X.

The Fulfilment of a Prophecy of Sir Arthur Wellesley.—Removal of the two Dams on the Sweet-water Canal and of the great Embankment on the Railway.—Accumulation of Rolling-stock on Railway.—Accumulation of Supplies at Kassassin.—Telegraphic Orders of the 26th and 28th August to Sir E. Hamley for Transfer of Highland Brigade to Ismailia.—Advance Guard Action of the 28th August.—Twelve more days of Preparation.

In the year 1807 the greatest of English Commanders was engaged on an expedition the most daring that had ever been undertaken by an English Cabinet.* In the result that enterprise, unfettered by any nice regard for punctilio, secured and brought back the largest capture ever drawn into English harbours. The work was accomplished within a time so short that the conqueror of the Continent, in the zenith of his power, was staggered by the vigour and rapidity of the stroke. But in England, the "delay" and "sloth" which attended the military movements were so severely commented on during the course of the contest that the criticism drew from Sir Arthur Wellesley these words :—"I don't doubt their impatience in England ; but I don't think they ever form in England an accurate estimate of the difficulties attending ANY military enterprise which they undertake."†

It would have been surprising if the Egyptian expedition had escaped the fate thus foretold, which has attended with unbroken regularity every expedition which has left England from 1807 to this day.

The rapidity of the operations which had hitherto taken place left at once an impression in many quarters in England that "the army" had arrived at Kassassin, that the Egyptian "army" had been expelled from all that country, and that the moment was immediately at hand when a final forward movement upon Cairo was to take place. What had happened was, however, very different from this, and for the understanding of the campaign it is necessary to show clearly what had been gained up to this time, and what remained to be done.

As a result of the events recorded in the last chapter, the objects of the fourth stage of the operations of the campaign, as explained in Chapter V (page 23), had been secured. We were now able to work at the *fifth* stage, that of removing the obstacles from canal and railway, repairing the railway, and accumulating stores.

---

* The seizure of Copenhagen and the Danish fleet.
† Supplementary Despatches, vol. vi, p. 20.

A favourable opportunity had allowed this result to be obtained by a fraction of the force before the earlier stages were completed.

The disembarkation at Ismailia was by no means finished. All the troop-ships which left Alexandria on the 19th August were not, on the 26th August, yet cleared. Of the artillery which was on the 19th August at sea, and had not then passed Alexandria, only a portion had been disembarked. General Hamley's Division was still at Alexandria. The greater portion of the Indian Contingent was still at Suez. Brigadier-General Wilkinson, commanding the Indian cavalry, with one troop 6th Bengal Cavalry and the 13th Bengal Lancers, had, on the 25th August, marched to Shaluf from Suez, *en route* to Ismailia, and on the 26th to a lock on the Fresh-water Canal 6 miles north of Geneffeh. The remainder of the Indian cavalry partly landed at Suez on that day, partly came round by the Canal to Ismailia. The bulk of the Indian force was ordered to come round to Ismailia through the Suez Canal, and arrived there on the 27th and 28th August. The repair of the railway between Suez and Ismailia was not completed till the 27th August, on which day the first engine brought from Alexandria came up from Suez, reaching Ismailia in the evening. All the engines from Alexandria had been sent for disembarkation to Suez, it being impossible to land them at Ismailia.

It will be seen, therefore, that, rapid as the earlier movements had been, what had taken place had been by no means an advance *of the army* to within striking distance of the position at Tel el-Kebir, where from the first Sir G. Wolseley had believed that the decisive action of the war would take place; but that the way had been made clear for the collection of such rolling-stock on the railway, and of such transport on the Canal, as would, within a given time, make it possible to accumulate supplies at Kassassin sufficient for the final advance of the army.

The Head-quarters of the army were still at Ismailia, which was the centre of all the work that was going on, and whence telegrams to England, Alexandria, Cyprus, Suez, Port Said, and India were continually being sent, and where replies were daily received. Telegraphic communication was established as far as Tel el-Maskhuta, so that in case the forces at the front, and those placed for their reinforcement, should prove inadequate to the defence of the line, it was possible at once to increase their number.

Once more it is necessary to recall to memory the fact, explained in Chapter V, that the more the mass of the force—the greater number of eating mouths—could be kept back from the front, the more rapid would be the accumulation of supplies, and the quicker, therefore, the final advance. These considerations, and the necessity of providing working parties for the clearing of the railway and canal and a defence for the line, determined the distribution of the troops along the line of railway. The stores, and in particular the large quantities of forage and fuel captured at Mahsama and Tel el-Maskhuta, made it possible for the cavalry to be maintained at the former station, and for the Guards to be left at Tel el-Maskhuta. Thus, there were forces left within supporting distance of the small body which, under General Graham, had been pushed on to hold the head of the advance.

Large working parties taken from the troops at Tel el-Maskhuta were now employed in the unpleasant work of clearing away the large embankment across the railway, and in removing the dams at Tel el-Maskhuta and Magfar. This last proved to be an even more serious task than might have been expected, for the skilful dam-makers by whom the works had been constructed had so wattled in reeds, telegraph wire, and other binding material into the mass of the earthwork that our men, standing in the muddy canal without any convenient foothold, had the greatest difficulty in removing the obstacles. It was several days before either dam could be cut through; and any attack upon the front, which made it necessary to withdraw the soldiers, to be ready either to reinforce General Graham or to prepare for a possible attempt upon Tel el-Maskhuta itself, still further delayed the work.

Meantime, all stores had to be transhipped at the dam, and at first, till the dams were cut through, the stores had to be unloaded at Magfar, the boats lifted across the dam by hand, and reloaded on the further side.

The whole of the arrangements for supply in the field up to the advanced depôt were in the hands of General Earle, the "General Officer Commanding the line of communications and base." On the 24th he had sent Colonel Harrison with the force which advanced to Magfar. When Sir Garnet determined to hold the position, which he occupied on that morning, Colonel Harrison returned at once to Ismailia, having received authority from Sir Garnet to ask Sir Beauchamp Seymour to place upon the canal steam-launches and towing-cutters. This was immediately done; so that by the afternoon of the 24th a steam-launch towing three boats, containing 1,500 rations of preserved meat and biscuit, and a ton of oats, had been unloaded at Magfar, which were made available for the troops at the bivouac that night.

On the morning of the 24th the troops had started from Ismailia with one day's rations (with the exception of meat) in the men's haversacks, in addition to what remained of the proper ration for the 24th. Two days' rations—properly those for the 26th and 27th—were carried by the regimental transport, which accompanied the march. But the character of this particular portion of ground had made the work of drawing the regimental wheeled carts very difficult for the animals; indeed, wheeled transport could not here be depended on at all.

In the attempt to enable the draught animals to draw the carts up to the troops by night time on the 24th, provisions of all sorts, ammunition, &c., had been thrown out, and were strewn upon the course of the march. Many of the carts had broken down, and were lying helpless on the ground. It was necessary, therefore, to issue fresh supplies, irrespective of the rations that had been given out, and to push up stores, not only for the regular feeding of the troops, but for the deficiency occasioned by the loss on the march.

It was this necessity which had made it indispensable to get some steam-launches at once on to the canal; otherwise, as every opening of the lock-gates allowed a certain amount of the water to flow out, and as it was most important by all means to husband the canal water, it would have been better, and was at first intended, to trust chiefly to the railway. A line of railway, 200 yards long, had been broken in front of Magfar, so that till that part was repaired no goods could be pushed up by rail further than to Magfar. Up to that point, however, wagon-loads of stores were dragged along the rail by mules. As soon as the wheeled transport had been put in order after the march, it had to be employed in conveying the stores as they reached Magfar to the regiments. An intermediate depôt was thus necessarily formed at Magfar. The mules were not powerful enough to drag the wagons satisfactorily, so that their use on the railway was only a temporary expedient till the engines could be brought up. Still, by 1·30 A.M. on the morning of the 25th, that is, some hours before the troops left the bivouac in advance of Magfar, three trucks loaded with provisions, forage, and camp equipage, and two trucks loaded with provisions and a field hospital, reached Magfar.

The transport with regiments, in struggling through the deep sand between Ismailia and Magfar, had broken down irregularly; some battalions were completely supplied, while others had lost the greater part of the provisions that had been issued to them; there were, as a result, during the early days of the occupation of Tel el-Maskhuta, deficiencies of supply in particular instances, but these deficiencies were rather due to the difficulty of providing beforehand, from a distance, the particular parts of the rations that had been lost, and supplying the precise thing that was wanted, than at any time to a general shortness of supply. To put it another way, the Commissariat supplies available on the spot were at all times in excess of the general wants of the troops, so that such privations as the troops at Tel el-Maskhuta during these days underwent were almost entirely due to the loss of the services of a certain number of carts belonging to regiments, making it difficult for them to draw from the depôt on the spot the precise stores of which they had need, and for the Commissariat to judge on what class of stores there would be a particular call in consequence of the loss of provisions already supplied. At most the want of such things as were short amounted to inconveniences and discomforts only, and were no more than such as are inevitably incident to any rapid operations in the field. The case illustrated the extreme importance and value of a thoroughly effective regimental transport, and the loss which is entailed upon an army by the regimental transport being even temporarily unadapted to the conditions under which it is placed.

Practically, however, as a result, the supplies for men and horses were for several days very short, and, as has been explained, very often when large quantities arrived there was an excess of one kind and a deficit of others.

But the most trying circumstance which the rapid movement had entailed was the absence of tents and camp equipage. These were pushed on by rail and canal as rapidly as the condition of both permitted, but for some days the necessity of depending for chance shade upon the shelter of the trees and village under that glaring sun called for much endurance on the part of the troops so employed. It was the price paid for the rapid successes of the 24th and 25th. The tents reached the troops at Tel el-Maskhuta on the 28th. The valises of the men reached them on the following day.

Dead men and dead animals of the Egyptian army had fallen into the canal near Mahsama. There was no remedy for the impure condition of the water, except that of boiling and filtering, but, fortunately, the supply of fuel at each station was considerable ; and additional fuel obtained from the ships was pushed up daily, both by canal and rail, so that the chief danger from the bad water lay in the desire which the great heat produced to drink directly from the canal.

The disembarkation had so far advanced by the 26th that, in view of the progress towards the front already made, Sir Garnet decided that the time had come when General Hamley's Division might be brought forward from Alexandria. There was a very great amount of work to be done at Ismailia in disembarking stores of all kinds. It was as easy to provision them at Ismailia as in Alexandria. Now, therefore, that a sufficient number of the ships already arrived had been cleared, it was advisable on every account to bring round to Ismailia all troops that could be spared from the defence of Alexandria. At Ismailia they would be immediately available for the future advance as soon as the time had arrived for making it.

A telegram from Sir Edward Hamley was received on this day, which showed that at Alexandria everything was ready and Sir Edward anxiously awaiting orders for the move :—

" Sir E. Hamley to Chief of the Staff.

"August 26, 1882.
" Can you not tell me what you wish me to do ? This place will be in good state of defence this evening, ammunition on the works placed in magazines, two 7-in. guns ready. Will open fire with them to-morrow with view of making the enemy show what guns he has. He is still throwing up new works, as if he expected to be besieged there. Our inner line of defence, excluding village of Ramleh, is about 1 mile in length, but not continuous, and well armed with artillery. I could, therefore, leave three and a-half battalions for this line, and bring you four, or, if sailors take the police duties, could bring you five. Shall I take any steps for embarkation ?

" HAMLEY."

A reply to Sir E. Hamley was accordingly sent in the following terms :—

" Chief of Staff to Sir E. Hamley.

"August 26, 1882.

" It is proposed that you embark for Ismailia with Alison and Highland Brigade (four battalions), and for the present that Wood with his brigade (three and a-half battalions), the Derbyshire and Manchester, two garrison batteries Royal Artillery, and Malta Fencibles remain as garrison of Alexandria. This, with assistance of navy, is deemed sufficient, but before order is given state concisely your views after consultation with Malet. The police duties will be performed by the soldiers, and any marines or sailors landed to be sent to the front. Sir B. Seymour concurs in this. General Harman is coming to command at Alexandria, and a depôt of 1,830 men will reach Alexandria about 16th September. We hope shortly to bring on Wood and his brigade. Use War Office cypher."

The telegram was delayed in transmission by the telegraph clerks at Alexandria, but on the 28th Sir E. Hamley, having satisfied Sir E. Malet as to the safety of Alexandria, replied that he was ready to start. He was on the same day ordered to come round to Ismailia.

On the 26th Sir E. Hamley opened fire from his two 7-in. guns, to force the enemy to show his strength in artillery. The first shell dispersed a large working party. The enemy did not reply at the time, but the following day he began firing from his large gun, and was silenced by our fire.

There were some occasional skirmishes with marauders, one on the 24th at Ramleh, one on the 27th at El-Meks.

Sir E. Hamley had received news from the Khedive of the arrival of considerable numbers of Arabi's troops opposite to El-Meks: and, as the drying up of the ground already mentioned had left this side open to attack, he wished, before leaving Alexandria, to utilize the Highland Brigade by an attack on the enemy's forces opposite El-Meks, moving it thither on the night of the 30th, and attacking just before dawn. On telegraphing to Sir Garnet Wolseley for permission to do this, he received the following reply :—

"No; embark as soon as all ready ; desire Sir E. W. to remain on defensive and risk nothing."

On the 28th, the Indian Cavalry Brigade having arrived at Ismailia, a new organization* of the cavalry was made, the whole cavalry of the force being formed into a Division, of which the English regiments constituted the 1st Brigade under Sir Baker Russell, the Indian Cavalry the 2nd Brigade under General Wilkinson, the whole being under the orders of General Drury Lowe, with Colonel Herbert Stewart as Assistant Adjutant-General. On the same day at the front the enemy made their first attempt to disturb our posts

---

* See Appendix II, p. 113.

The position at the Lock of Kassassin which General Graham had been ordered to occupy and entrench was in some respects unfavourable for defensive purposes by a small force. It was indispensable to hold it because of the importance of securing the lock, and thereby the supply of water in the canal and the means of transport. The lock occurred at a point where the ground on either bank was low-lying, so that here, as at Magfar, the canal, if in the hands of the enemy, could have been easily emptied. From this point there rose from the canal towards the north, and in the direction of Tel el-Kebir westwards, at a distance of from 2,000 to 3,000 yards, a series of hills from 100 to 160 feet high, forming on this side round the lock an amphitheatre from which the enemy's artillery could play upon the camp without being seriously exposed themselves.

In the rapid previous movements it had been impossible to drag the artillery wagons through the heavy sand. On the 25th, during the attack upon Mahsama, N | A Battery R.H.A., in particular, which had been chiefly engaged, had been obliged to leave four wagons behind in the desert. The additional horses were required to assist the guns themselves over the ground. Immediate steps had been taken at Ismailia to remedy this difficulty as far as possible. All the available horses from other batteries that had been landed were sent out into the desert to restore to the batteries in front their wagons, but it was not till the 31st August that the last of the wagons was brought in. Reserve artillery ammunition to replace the ammunition expended, and to compensate the deficiencies due to the absence of wagons, had been at once pushed up from Ismailia by canal, but by the 28th August this ammunition had only reached Mahsama, progress for heavily-loaded boats being very slow because of the two dams not yet removed, and because of the shallowness of the water in the canal.

Hence it happened that on the morning of the 28th August the two guns with General Graham's force had with them only the ammunition in their limbers.*

At 9·30 A.M. (28th) the enemy's cavalry were reported as appearing on the right front on the hills to the north. General Graham at once signalled to the cavalry at Mahsama placed there for his support. The Cavalry Brigade turned out, and remained in communication with General Graham by signal, but

---

* The force available at the beginning of the day was—

At Kassassin, R.H.A. (40 officers and men and 2 guns of N | A), 4th Dragoon Guards (15 officers and men), 7th Dragoon Guards (42 officers and men), Duke of Cornwall's Light Infantry (611 officers and men), York and Lancaster (690 officers and men), Mounted Infantry (70 officers and men), Royal Marine Artillery (427 officers and men).

At Mahsama, under General Drury Lowe, 1st Cavalry Brigade, under Sir Baker Russell, Household Cavalry (3 squadrons), 7th Dragoon Guards, 4 guns N | A Battery R.H.A., 2 guns G | B Battery R.H.A., Royal Marine Light Infantry.

At Tel el-Maskhuta, the 4th Dragoon Guards, 19th Hussars (2 squadrons), 4 guns D | I Battery R.A., Brigade of Guards, 3rd Battalion King's Royal Rifles.

Later arrived, West Kent Regiment, I | 2 and N | 2 Batteries R.A.

only an ineffectual and distant artillery fire was attempted by the Egyptians, and by 3 P.M. the enemy was reported as retiring. The force at Kassassin was therefore withdrawn, having been much exposed to the sun, but not to the enemy, and at 4·30 Major-General Drury Lowe similarly withdrew into camp. On the receipt of the first news of the enemy's threatened attack on Kassassin, General Willis sent out the cavalry from Tel el-Maskhuta to reconnoitre, and Majors Molyneux and Hildyard were dispatched by him to communicate with General Graham, to whom four guns of D | 1 were also sent as a reinforcement. The mirage was so great that no orders or information could be transmitted by flashing signals between Tel el-Maskhuta and Kassassin.

At 4·30 P.M. the enemy at Kassassin began to show signs of threatening a serious attack, advancing a line of skirmishers, supported by a heavy fire of artillery.

The dispositions made to meet this attack were as follows:— The enemy not having any force on the south side of the canal, a small force of our own, disposed under good cover and protected by the canal, would be able to forbid to the enemy any approach on our left along the canal. The low-lying open ground in front of the camp made this defence the more effective. On this side, therefore, and in a very favourable piece of ground, General Graham placed the Marine Artillery, with orders to protect the north and west of their position with a sweeping fire. About 800 yards east of the position of the Royal Marine Artillery were placed the Duke of Cornwall's Light Infantry, at right angles to the Marine Artillery. The York and Lancaster Regiment was écheloned upon the Duke of Cornwall's Light Infantry to the right rear. Three companies only of the Duke of Cornwall's Light Infantry and two and a-half companies of the York and Lancaster Regiment were extended in skirmishing order. The railway embankment afforded cover to the supports and reserves of the Duke of Cornwall's Light Infantry; those of the York and Lancaster, withdrawn still further towards the east, were also placed in favourable ground.

At first both the Duke of Cornwall's and the York and Lancaster fronted in a north-westerly direction; afterwards their right shoulders were brought up so as to place them in a nearly westerly direction.

The left being thus perfectly protected by the formation taken up and by the nature of the position, it only remained to secure the right, which, from the mode in which General Graham had refused it to the enemy, was the nearest part of the whole force towards Mahsama, and would be effectually covered by the advance of the cavalry from that post.

At the same time, as the enemy now evidently threatened a serious attack, it appeared right to inform General Willis, at Tel el-Maskhuta, that it might be necessary to move to the assailed point if the enemy should prolong their attack beyond the few hours of light which now remained to him. When, therefore, the new dispositions were made, Major Molyneux rode back, by way of

Mahsama, to Tel el-Maskhuta, bearing a message to General Lowe, requesting him to move up the cavalry to cover the right flank, which had been placed expressly with a view to tempt the enemy to expose himself to the very effective attack which the cavalry would be able to deliver if the enemy should venture down into the lower ground in hopes of turning this extreme flank. A heliographic message was at the same time sent to the cavalry, desiring them to turn out and be ready for this movement.

Rather more than half-an-hour later, at about 5·20 P.M., General Graham, thinking that the enemy's cavalry were beginning the forward movement, which would fully expose them to the cavalry attack, sent his Aide-de-camp, Lieutenant Pirie, 4th Dragoon Guards, with the following order to General Drury Lowe :—

"Take the cavalry round by our right, under cover of the hill, and attack the left flank of the enemy's skirmishers."

Observing that the enemy were receiving reinforcements by train, General Graham, thinking that the enemy's cavalry might make an attempt upon his extreme right before our cavalry's move could be accomplished, warned the reserve company of the York and Lancaster to be ready to receive the cavalry in line.

Meantime, the shells from the enemy's artillery were chiefly directed upon a Krupp gun which, taken from the enemy at Mahsama, had been mounted on a railway truck, and was worked by a gun detachment of the Marine Artillery, under command of Captain Tucker. Two fresh Horse Artillery guns, belonging to G | B Battery R.H.A., had arrived at 3 o'clock, and were therefore available, as well as the two of N | A Battery R.H.A., when the action began again at 4·30 ; but, like the other two, they had only their limber ammunition, since, though they had started from Mahsama with their wagons, it had been impossible to bring them on with the guns. Their fire became so slow from want of ammunition as scarcely to relieve the marine detachment with the Krupp on the railway line from the enemy's fire.

Somewhat later, as the guns were absolutely without ammunition, it was thought better by the officer commanding them for all these four guns to go back to Mahsama to supply themselves at the nearest point at which it was possible for them to get ammunition. Meantime, the infantry fight had been steadily and fiercely maintained.

About 7·15 P.M. the battalion of Royal Marines under Colonel Jones, and a fresh battery of six 16-prs. A | 1 Battery R.A., Major Taylor, complete with wagons, arrived on the ground. It was already too dark for effective fire, and Major Taylor therefore thought it useless to waste ammunition, and did not fire.

At the same hour, 7·15 P.M., General Graham, now assured of his rear and flank by the arrival of these reinforcements, and thinking that the hour for the cavalry charge, which would of itself secure him on his flank, must have come, began a general advance, in which, as soon as he heard of the actual arrival of the marines, he ordered them to join.

Meantime, Lieutenant Pirie, who had started at 5·20 P.M. to carry the order to General Drury Lowe, had not found the cavalry at the point where General Graham had believed that it was when he dispatched him. The cavalry had returned into camp much later than the infantry from a most exhausting day. It seemed very unadvisable to hurry them out again unless serious danger threatened, and unless their presence was really necessary. Hence the cavalry had not moved up towards Kassassin as early as General Graham had at first expected them. Lieutenant Pirie, missing the cavalry in the darkness, galloped to find them till his charger dropped from fatigue, and then, coming upon one of the batteries which were retiring, obtained a new horse from them. Lieutenant Pirie knew that General Graham's arrangements had been made upon the calculation of the coming cavalry charge. In the course of his ride he had become anxious at not finding the cavalry where he had expected to find them. The breakdown of his horse had still further delayed him. According to all evidence he had been most cool and collected when with his General and under fire, but anxiety to execute his mission had undoubtedly excited him. He became before all things anxious to get up the cavalry to the front as rapidly as possible, and not clearly distinguishing between the precise message which had been delivered to him and the sense of anxiety for his General, due to his not having been able to deliver his message at the hour he had expected, an anxiety which had been increased by his finding that the guns were retiring, he at length met General Lowe, who had in the meantime advanced with the Household Cavalry, the 7th Dragoon Guards, and four guns of N | A R.H.A. (Major Borradaile's battery), to a point 4 miles from Kassassin in a north-westerly direction.· Lieutenant Pirie, under these circumstances, delivered as his message to General Lowe a statement that General Graham "was only just able to hold his own, and wished General Drury Lowe to attack the left of the enemy's infantry skirmishers."

That that *was* the message which reached General Drury Lowe is as certain as that it was *not* the message that was sent by General Graham. The case illustrates the importance of all such messages being written and not verbal.

It is quite certain that at the time that Lieutenant Pirie left General Graham the feeling of the General and his whole Staff was one of the greatest confidence, only looking forward with hope to the enemy's being rash enough to attempt a serious attack; but what is also certain is that there were a few camp-followers, and, as unfortunately must happen in every army, one or two unworthy soldiers, who, when the first burst of artillery fire had fallen upon the little force, being in positions which enabled them at the moment to slip off unobserved, had become panic-stricken, and had carried a false alarm even as far as Tel el-Maskhuta. That the false impressions of men, who have not been under fire before, are not a clear indication of the nature of the actual danger involved is a fact of which London had a year later a pretty sharp lesson. The placards announcing that the dead and wounded were being carried in on stretchers from all parts of Woolwich, in consequence of the rocket bombardment from the explosion of the factory, on September 23, 1883, recorded the impressions of the inhabitants of an incident in which no single person was hurt by a falling rocket.

Nevertheless, it was not with a knowledge of the actual state of things at Kassassin that the cavalry under General Drury Lowe advanced that evening, but under the impression which had been conveyed both by Lieutenant Pirie's message and by soon afterwards meeting the retiring artillery. The sun had set. A bright moon was shining. The flashes from the hostile artillery and infantry afforded some guide to the movement. The advance of the leading regiment, the 7th Dragoon Guards, was directed on the evening star, which, as it happened, was just over the position of the enemy.

The desert haze made the whole outline indistinct. General Drury Lowe took his cavalry round in a wide sweep to turn the enemy's left, and in the haze the brigade arrived unperceived close to the part of the enemy's line which was posted on the high ground above Kassassin Lock, and about 3,000 yards from it.

The Egyptians themselves say that they had been expecting the cavalry movement from Mahsama, and had thrown back a portion of their force to meet it. In any case, they were completely unprepared for the attack actually delivered against them.

The cavalry advance was made with the 7th Dragoon Guards in first line, the guns next, and Household Cavalry in second line right refused.

Suddenly, without being able to gauge the distance, the little force found itself exposed to the combined artillery and infantry fire of the enemy, whose guns were firing over the heads of their infantry. In order to enable the Royal Horse Artillery to fire, General Drury Lowe ordered the 7th Dragoon Guards to wheel outwards, clear the front, and re-form immediately in rear of the guns and Household Cavalry. Orders were at once given by Sir B. Russell, who was in front of the 7th Dragoon Guards, to clear the front of the guns; the 7th Dragoon Guards passed off, in column of troops from both flanks, to the rear of the Household Cavalry. Sir Baker moved across towards the front of the Life Guards, to seize the moment for the brigade to charge. The guns came into action, and fired some effective rounds. The Household Cavalry received from General Drury Lowe the order to charge. Led by Colonel Ewart, the three squadrons took the enemy's infantry in front, but in the direction shown in the sketch, absolutely annihilating, according to the Egyptians' own account, the whole force they struck upon. The enemy's guns lay beyond their infantry, which represented, in fact, the extreme left of the Egyptian line thrown back to meet the attack.

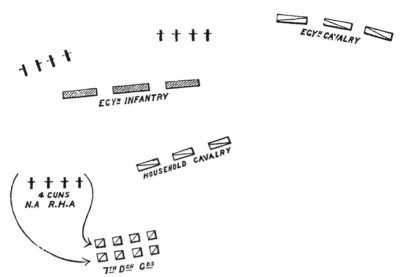

Sir Simon Lockhart, in the charge and darkness, passed on beyond the infantry, and becoming separated from his regiment, on his return saw the Egyptian guns apparently preparing to move off. A few horsemen who had similarly become separated towards the right saw Egyptian cavalry on that side of the infantry. But these cavalry, as soon as our men closed together, threatening to charge, moved off.

The account given by the Egyptians themselves of this part of the affair is that their cavalry and ours were engaged with one another, and that the infantry which had become involved in the cavalry charge were destroyed. As, however, the Egyptian cavalry never attempted any charge, and never even allowed our cavalry to come within charging distance of them, this statement can only be understood in the sense that the attention of the Egyptian cavalry was entirely taken up by the movements of ours, and retired as soon as there was any prospect of a collision.

All evidence, both Egyptian and our own, is concurrent that the Egyptian artillery was never reached by our cavalry. It is, however, probable that, had it not been for the darkness and the impossibility, in an open desert, of obtaining any points to move on after the artillery had ceased firing, our cavalry could and would have captured the guns, whose escort had been destroyed, seeing that the artillery had limbered up and were out of action at the moment the cavalry charge would have reached them, and that the 7th Dragoon Guards, who had followed in support, were an intact body fully in hand and available.

After the charge the Household Cavalry re-formed on the ground over which they had moved.

The night had closed in. According to the Egyptian accounts, the enemy withdrew because of the coming on of night. In any case, an attack not seriously begun till 4·30 P.M. on a day when the sun set at 6 P.M. never had the slightest prospect of success, even if the enemy's troops could have been induced to close.

At 8·15 P.M. an officer of the Life Guards and two troopers, who had been in the cavalry charge, reached General Graham.

At 8·45 P.M. General Graham ordered a general return to camp.

After sunset General Willis moved the Brigade of Guards towards Kassassin in support in case their services should be required. He also sent up ammunition in carts trebly horsed.

The little force at Kassassin, and its supports at Mahsama, had amply fulfilled the trust reposed in them. The only serious inconvenience to which it had been exposed had been a deficiency in the artillery arm, due to the causes already stated, and remedied before night-fall on that day.

Twelve days followed during which there is little of interest to record. They represented the period of hardest work during the campaign. The quay at Ismailia continued to be a scene of busy activity. Gradually the service of steam-boats along the Canal, and of trains along the railway, was put in order.

General Sir E. Hamley, with Sir A. Alison's brigade, in accordance with the arrangements previously made, arrived at Ismailia on 1st September, at 6 P.M. The men, at Sir E. Hamley's suggestion, were kept 'on ship-board, and during the daytime supplied the necessary fatigue parties for disembarking stores, loading trains and boats, &c.

The Indian Cavalry Brigade was pushed up to join the remainder of the cavalry at the front. The Indian Engineers completed the tramway from the wharf to the railway station.

At last, towards the end of the time, with a regular service of trains established, and stores in excess of the daily wants of the troops beginning to accumulate at Kassassin, the period of preparation drew to a close.

Before leaving it, however, it is necessary to remark that, whatever difficulties arose at the front in the matter of supplies, these were in no way due to any defect in the arrangements and work at the base at Ismailia. Usually in a campaign there is ample time before the expedition moves forward to organize the base from which it starts, from which it draws its supplies. In this case, however, from the necessity of seizing the base itself, even Sir Owen Lanyon, the Commandant, was landed some time after the first troops had arrived. Everything had to be organized during the very weeks of pressure. This was aggravated by the fact that as the supplies were shipped in England to accompany the troops, and not, as would usually be the case, sent out on requisitions from the seat of war, stating what supplies were most urgently needed, it happened that, in many instances, the stores most urgently needed were below others, which had to be removed before these could be reached.

The difficulties could only be overcome, and were overcome, by the hearty co-operation of the naval officers on the spot with the officers detailed for work at the base. In addition to the great assistance afforded by the cordial kindness of Sir Beauchamp

Seymour, the army was deeply indebted to the hard work, skill in organization, and brotherly help of Captain Rawson, R.N., Captain Brackenbury, R.N., Commander Thompson, Lieutenant Thompson, Lieutenant Thomson, Lieutenant Hope, and Lieutenant Target. These officers were engaged night and day in assisting Sir Owen Lanyon's Staff, Major MacGregor, Major Sartorius, V.C., and the other officers detailed in the list of that Staff. The absence during the earlier period of any organized gang of labourers was severely felt; the fatigue duties thrown on the soldiers and the necessity for continuously teaching fresh bodies of men represented an inconvenience that requires to be noted for future service. The necessity for these fatigues abstracted from the front a number of men whom it might have been very inconvenient to detain at the base.

It deserves to be recorded that when Ismailia was handed over by the force on its departure no sign of the occupation remained in any damage whatever to the place, except the loss of two trees, necessarily cut down to clear the way for the railway.

CHAPTER XI.

THE CONCENTRATION OF THE ARMY ON KASSASSIN, AND PREPARATIONS FOR ATTACK ON TEL EL-KEBIR.

Orders for Concentration of Army.—Attack of Enemy on the 9th September.—Misapprehension which led to it.—Reasons for not pressing home the beaten Enemy.

By the 7th September various reconnaissances, which had been carried out during the interval which followed the fight on the 28th August, had brought in a fair amount of information as to the nature of the enemy's position. On the 7th September the railway was for the first time reported to be in fair working order, and was able to carry sufficient stores to provide for the whole army, and to allow of some surplus. Accordingly, on that day arrangements were made for the advance to the front of the whole of Sir A. Alison's brigade, of the Indian Contingent, and of the remainder of the artillery, which had hitherto been kept at Ismailia. General Willis' head-quarters were moved up the same day to Kassassin preparatory to the general concentration at that station.

On the 8th the final orders for the march to Kassassin, and the concentration upon it of the whole army, were issued. The march was so arranged that the last troops would arrive at Kassassin in the course of the 12th September. The 9th was fixed as the day of the change of head-quarters from Ismailia to Kassassin. Telephonic as well as telegraphic communication had been established with Kassassin.

At 8 A.M. on the morning of the 9th a telegraphic report of an attempt of the enemy upon Kassassin reached Ismailia, and a little after that hour the telephone clerk at Kassassin, communicating with the clerk at Ismailia, said, "I can hardly hear what you say from the noise of the heavy artillery fire."

At 9·15 A.M., that is, as soon as a train could be made ready, Sir Garnet with his Staff started for the front. At 11 A.M. he reached Kassassin, and had to ride some miles to catch up the troops, which, by the time he reached the front, had already pushed back the enemy to within 5,000 yards of Tel el-Kebir.

This was what had happened. As cattle had been accumulated at the front, the drivers who had charge of them had allowed stray animals to wander at some distance from the camp, where in the "wady" (watered valley) green forage could be obtained; some of these cattle had strayed, and Bedouins prowling round the camp had picked up and driven off a few of them. In order to gain credit with Arabi for activity, they represented to him that Kassassin was only held in very weak force by us, and that they, the Bedouins, had quite cut off all communication between Kassassin and Ismailia. Accordingly, an order was issued that, on the morning of the 9th September, a combined attack should be made from Tel el-Kebir and Es-Salihiyeh, in order to capture the camp at Kassassin, which the Egyptian leader looked upon as quite an easy prey, though at this time, in fact, a force of nearly 8,000 men of all arms was available at the post, without including the Guards, and the remainder of the force at Tel el-Maskhuta,* who were within a long march.

The Indian Cavalry Brigade furnished the outposts during the night of the 8th to 9th September. At 4 A.M. Colonel Pennington, of the 13th Bengal Lancers, the Field Officer of the day, pushed forward with patrols as usual to observe the enemy towards Tel el-Kebir. The reconnoitring party soon observed the enemy advancing in considerable numbers. Reports were sent back to Major-General Graham; these reached him about 6·15 A.M. He sent to General Drury Lowe desiring him to send a cavalry regiment to the front. Somewhat later a report of the general advance of the enemy reached Lieutenant-General Willis. He immediately sent orders to Major-General Graham to turn out the infantry brigade.

Major-General Graham, at about the same time that he received these orders (6·45 A.M.) had had reports sent to him from the cavalry of the enemy's advance in force. Dispositions for the troops, in the event of attack on the camp, had been drawn out by General Willis' orders, and written instructions in conformity with these were now dispatched by Major-General Graham to each of the commanding officers.

The "fall-in" for the infantry was sounded at 6·45 A.M. By 7·10 A.M. the troops were formed in the following order of battle:—

On the south bank of the canal the Royal Marine Artillery and five companies of the West Kent Regiment, with two 25-pr. guns in position, manned by the 5th Battery, Scottish Division, Royal Artillery. At first the Duke of Cornwall's Light Infantry were also placed on this bank, but they were soon afterwards withdrawn to the north bank. On the north bank the King's Royal Rifle Corps had their left resting on the canal. The Royal Marines took up the line from them, the York and Lancaster being on the right of the marines, with the right somewhat thrown back. Two field batteries, 16-prs. (A and D, 1st Brigade R.A.), under Lieutenant-Colonel Schreiber, were at first placed by Lieutenant-Colonel Nairne, who commanded the artillery, in gun-pits which had been previously made to the north of the camp, facing the advance of the enemy from the west. These batteries moved into position at 7 A.M. The Royal Irish were placed by General Willis on the right of the guns, with their right thrown back to show an infantry front against the Salihiyeh force. Immediately after the beginning of the action they were reinforced by the Duke of Cornwall's Light Infantry from the south bank.

At 6·45 A.M. General Drury Lowe ordered the whole of the Indian Cavalry Brigade, of which two troops had been already dispatched to the front, to turn out and delay the enemy.

* 4th Dragoon Guards and a battery R.H.A.

At 7·10 A.M., in consequence of orders from General Willis, the 1st Cavalry Brigade, under Sir Baker Russell, also moved out of camp.

With the Indian Brigade moved G | B Battery R.H.A. With the 1st Brigade was N | A Battery R.H.A.

As the cavalry advanced it became clear that the enemy were moving from two different directions: in fact, from Tel el-Kebir eastwards and from Es-Salihiyeh southwards.

The two brigades of cavalry therefore manœuvred so as to separate these two bodies, and to support one another. Major-General Wilkinson, with the Indian Brigade, was employed in threatening the left of the enemy's force which advanced from Tel el-Kebir. Sir Baker Russell similarly threatened the right flank of the force advancing from Es-Salihiyeh.

The Mounted Infantry under Captain Lawrence was, at 6·45 A.M., pushed up to the support of the Indian Cavalry Brigade, and checked the advance of the enemy's artillery by an effective infantry fire until the arrival of the main body of the infantry relieved them; when the little detachment was sent over by General Drury Lowe to Sir B. Russell's force. The mountain battery was employed with the infantry.

In order more effectually to break up the Es-Salihiyeh force if it should attempt to advance between Mahsamah and Kassassin, General Willis at once telegraphed to His Royal Highness the Duke of Connaught, at Tel el-Maskhuta, to move from that station with the Foot Guards and to endeavour to fall upon the left flank of the Es-Salihiyeh troops. Major Hildyard was sent to guide the Duke along the slope of the high ground between Maskhuta and Kassassin, and to turn north on reaching Mahsama, so as to take the left of the enemy in flank.

With the exception of a cavalry skirmish in the early morning, in which a troop of the Bengal Lancers charged an Egyptian squadron and drove them back, the first shot of the action on our side was fired at 7·15 A.M. from the captured Krupp gun on the railway manned by the R.M.A., under Captain Tucker. This was directed upon a train bringing up some of the Egyptian troops. The enemy's artillery which had already in the early morning fired some distant shots, a few of which fell in the camp, replied at about 7·30 A.M.

At 7·45 A.M. General Willis ordered a general advance of the whole force.

The Egyptians endeavoured at first to overlap the right of the advancing brigade, but the fire from G | B Battery R.H.A. on the extreme right, and from the two field batteries which were withdrawn from the gun-pits, and conformed to the advance of the infantry brigade, drove them back in disorder before the advancing infantry could close with them. The York and Lancaster Regiment were kept back from the front in order to watch any attempt to turn the right of the movement, and the advance was continued with the King's Royal Rifle Corps and marines in the front line, the Royal Irish écheloned on their right rear, and the Duke of Cornwall's and York and Lancaster in support.

The general advance was continued till 10·30 A.M. The marines had one opportunity of coming to close quarters with the enemy, which they seized so effectually, by taking very clever advantage of some under features of the ground in order to cut off a portion of the enemy, that they captured two of the enemy's guns. The King's Royal Rifle Corps at about the same time captured another gun on the left, and the cavalry on the right a gun with limbers and horses complete.

By 10·30 A.M. the enemy had fallen back towards Tel el-Kebir, and the troops had arrived within about 5,000 yards of the fortifications, whence the enemy poured an effective fire from the guns in position there. There was every probability that a close pursuit upon the heels of the retreating troops might have given us —though with very considerable loss, from an enemy armed with breech-loaders behind well constructed cover—possession of Tel el-Kebir itself that day. But such a success would have been useless. Only a fraction of the army would have been available to follow up the victory. Arrangements for provisions and supplies had, of course, not been specially organized for the continued pursuit.

The cavalry could not have advanced directly upon Cairo.

Tel el-Kebir, the desert fortification, might possibly have fallen, and the troops therein might have been dispersed; but the decisive battle of Tel el-Kebir would not have been fought; the army would not have been placed upon the point of junction of the various detached portions of the Egyptian army which were at Kafr ed-Dauar, Es-Salihiyeh, &c. Cairo would not have fallen as a direct consequence of the premature blow, and it would most probably have been burnt before we could have reached it. For it must be noticed that news had reached Sir Garnet of a specific determination on the part of Arabi to burn Cairo in the event of his being defeated in the field. There was therefore now this additional motive for adhering strictly to the plan of campaign originally drawn up (*vide* p. 8, last paragraph). A cavalry pursuit following on the heels of a decisive victory was of the essence of that plan. By that means, and by that only, could Cairo be saved from the fate of Alexandria.

For every reason it was better not to pursue the advantage on that day. Lieutenant-General Willis had therefore, in accordance with the above view and with Sir Garnet's wishes, halted the troops before the arrival of the latter. Sir Garnet remained for some time examining the ground. At 1·30 P.M. the whole of the force returned to camp.

The Es-Salihiyeh portion of the Egyptians had fallen back in a retreat as rapid as that upon Tel el-Kebir, yielding to the fire of the Horse Artillery N] A (Major Borradaile), and to the successive turning movements of the 1st Cavalry Brigade.

The Foot Guards marched into camp by about 4 P.M. after a trying and wearisome march; the rapid retreat of the Egyptians to Es-Salihiyeh having deprived them of the chance of falling with destructive effect upon that body of the enemy.

CHAPTER XII.

TEL EL-KEBIR, 13TH SEPTEMBER.

The few days which followed the action of the 9th September were occupied by the march to the front, and by the successive arrival in camp of those portions of the Army Corps which had not yet been concentrated at Kassassin. The last battalion to arrive was the Royal Irish Fusiliers, which marched into camp on the afternoon of the 12th September, and did not pitch their tents, preferring to bivouac for the afternoon.

Each morning before dawn (5·45 A.M.) Sir Garnet, with a portion of his Staff, was on the undulating ground in front of the enemy's works at Tel el-Kebir. (We had a strong artillery and infantry outpost on the high ground above Kassassin.) He noticed each morning that the outposts and picquets of the enemy were only sent out beyond their entrenchments at daybreak (5·45 A.M.).

This fact confirmed him in his intention of attacking by night. Sir Garnet Wolseley had been always a great believer in night attacks, when possible, as the best means of passing with little loss over that destructive zone of fire that has to be traversed in front of works held by well-drilled soldiers armed with breech-loaders. The ground, unmarked by any disturbing feature, lent itself to the operation; provided only such precautions could be taken as should insure that, over the pathless desert, the troops were properly guided.

Of the advantages of a night march in enabling troops to pass ground over which, in the daytime, they can only advance under breech-loader fire, there had, ever since the introduction of modern weapons, been no question among soldiers. But those advantages were also known to be compensated, under most circumstances, by very great corresponding risks. To seize the advantages and to avoid the risks required a nice adaptation of the means at hand to the particular case to be dealt with.

In the present instance a night march promised advantages other than the ordinary one of carrying the troops in safety over what was, owing to the absence of all cover, an especially dangerous zone of fire. In any case, whether by day or night, some hours of work and of marching must be undertaken. In order to attack the long extended line of Tel el-Kebir it was necessary, for a large portion of the force at least, to be, for many hours, at a great distance from the only supply of water—the canal. In all our movements up to this point we had hugged the canal. To be far distant from it during the hours of the sun's power, and in battle, to move at all during those hours over the burning desert, implied for the troops exhaustion and suffering. The night march offered an escape from these difficulties. Thus it was not the darkness only but the coolness of the night hours that promised advantage. Reconnaissances had shown that the railway and canal had neither of them been seriously injured beyond Kassassin. Therefore the presence of these lines of movement greatly facilitated the arrangement for a desert night march. For, among the necessities of such an operation, one of the first is that the troops shall be able to move with an equipment as light as possible, and shall be able to depend upon receiving necessary supplies promptly after the victory has been won.

One of the first essentials to a successful night attack—a knowledge of the ground up to the enemy's position—had been obtained more perfectly than can often happen in similar cases. Not only had the reconnaissances of the Indian cavalry and Lieutenant-Colonel Tulloch's earlier reports furnished a great deal of information, but, taking advantage of the enemy's flight on the 9th September, Colonel Redvers Buller had ridden in a wide sweep somewhat round the extreme left of the enemy's lines at Tel el-Kebir, and had observed the nature of the works and the general line of their trace. On a previous day he had observed them carefully from the point marked β on the Map to the south of the canal, that being the nearest high ground to the lines on the enemy's right which it was possible to reach. Furthermore, from the front he had taken observations at the point δ. From all these sources and their own observations the distance from the point a on Ninth Hill had been fixed by Lieutenant-Colonel Tulloch and Major Hart, V.C., at 6,660 yards from the work at K, a measurement which will be found to correspond with remarkable exactness to its position as now determined by the triangulated survey. It was therefore possible to estimate with great accuracy the distance which the troops would have to move over in passing from Ninth Hill a towards the works. From previous experience it was calculated that, making all allowances for delays, &c., during the night march, the actual rate of progress to the front over the desert would be about 1 mile per hour, and the time of starting from Ninth Hill was therefore fixed at 1·30 A.M., to allow of the troops arriving just before dawn in front of the enemy's works. Sir Garnet's hope, if everything went well, was that the infantry would actually reach and assault the enemy's works just at the first gleam of dawn.

Such were the local conditions which favoured the movement; but a consideration of the general scheme of the campaign, as it has been dwelt upon throughout this history, will show that there were larger reasons why this particular mode of attack promised advantages not to be secured in any other way. Throughout, Tel el-Kebir had been looked upon as the gateway to Zagazig and Cairo; to Zagazig and a few other places as being the points of concentration for the rebel army dispersed throughout Egypt; to Cairo as the centre and focus of authority.

Now, in order that Tel el-Kebir might thus become the gateway for the final success of our army, it was necessary—

1st. That the Egyptian force within it should not be merely manœuvred out of the position they held, but that that force should be crushed, broken, and dispersed by actual fighting.

2ndly. That this should take place at the earliest hour of the morning, in order to give as much daylight as possible for the cavalry to advance upon Cairo and for the infantry to seize Zagazig. This advance upon Cairo, to save it from its destined fate, was at all times only second in Sir Garnet's mind to the destruction of Arabi's forces in the field, and in every arrangement made by him it counted for much.

Now, any attempt to turn the position at Tel el-Kebir, either by the "wady" to the south or by the desert to the north, could only, even if successful, have resulted in obliging Arabi's army, in greater or less confusion, to fall back upon Zagazig or Cairo. In the cultivated country into which he must thus have retreated it would have been very difficult to have brought him to a decisive action, and in falling back he might expect to be joined by all the other rebel troops throughout Egypt.

The advantages, therefore, on the whole, of this mode of attack, both in the action itself and in the results to be gained from it, were very great. It remained to carry out the purpose in such a way as to minimize the difficulties attendant on such a movement.

In the first place, it was necessary to insure as far as possible a complete surprise. Therefore, it was necessary to strike at the first moment when the whole of the troops were available, and before any knowledge of the completed concentration could have reached the enemy. On this account the time of the march was fixed for the night which followed that day on which the last troops were to arrive in camp. For the same reason no sign of the intended movement was to be given till after dark.

No hint of the intention to carry out any movement at all was published in the camp, on the principle, adopted always by Sir Garnet, that what is known in one camp is sure, sooner or later, by some means or other, to reach the opposing camp. But on the morning of the 12th September, before dawn (5·45 A.M.), Sir Garnet Wolseley himself met the General Officers Commanding Divisions and Brigades, and rode out with them to the high ground outside the camp, from which the most prominent points in the Egyptian works could be seen. He there personally explained to them the nature of the intended movement.

In every night march there is danger of confusion from the darkness, and a possibility of panic. Hardly can even the most experienced troops be altogether trusted to escape these perils under the unwonted conditions and the weird circumstances which night brings with it. On the other hand, all experience has shown that the successful · arrival in the darkness or early dawn of even a comparatively small body of troops within the lines of a suddenly roused enemy is the certain forerunner of victory. It is not merely a question of the actually catching asleep the troops who are immediately assailed, but an army suddenly attacked within the lines which it had reckoned upon to ward off its enemy is in a military sense surprised, even if a large body of the defenders are roused from sleep before actual contact takes place. The advantage of the first collision is nearly always with assailants if they are able to close with their enemy. The *élan* of movement carries them through stationary foes. The time when an assailant has to dread reverse is after the first assault, when his troops, dispersed by the circumstances of action, are met on ground well known to the defenders, are exposed to the close fire of inner works, and are attacked by fresh troops prepared for that purpose. But this counter-attack is precisely that which is impossible to a surprised enemy. The senior officers are not with their troops; no one is at hand to give the necessary orders. The first success of the assailants, instead of only leading to their dispersion and exposing them to the attack of fresh troops, leads them instead on to a complete success.

From these, which are the general experiences of war in such matters, the conclusion to be deduced for the present case was that it was advisable to have as many independent chances of success as could be arranged without unduly weakening the attack delivered at one spot. It was for this reason that, in arranging the plan of attack, the Commander of the expedition determined to assign to each of his two Divisional Generals an entirely independent sphere of operations. Supposing that any confusion supervened in the course of the night, and that one Division failed to deliver its blow at the right moment, then there was every hope that the other, wholly unaffected by this fact, would strike its independent blow, and would secure a success which would give time for the Division, that had so failed, to recover itself, and to serve as a support to the successful wing of the army.

For this reason, then, the two Infantry Divisions were placed at a very considerable interval from one another, and between them was concentrated the whole mass of the artillery of the Army Corps.

The ordinary duty of artillery at the beginning of an action, that of preparing by a distant fire for the approach of infantry, necessarily disappears in a night attack. The whole idea of such an attack is that the infantry approach in the most perfect silence, and unperceived, to the point to which it is usually the duty of the artillery to assist their arrival. But there remained a very important purpose which the artillery might be called upon to serve.

The experience of the campaign had shown throughout the immense effect produced by our guns upon the Egyptians; and it was practically certain that a body of forty-two field-pieces, having arrived by early dawn close upon the entrenchments of Tel el-Kebir, would be able to deliver so overpowering an artillery fire as would cover the rally of either Division if it required such support, or would, in the worst case, break down the resistance of some part of the Egyptian entrenchments, and pave the way for a successful advance, even if the Divisions had not been able to carry the position in front of them by a rush.

The orders for the infantry were in accordance with the well-established usage of night attacks, to move forward up to the works themselves without firing a shot.

In the general aspect of the works of Tel el-Kebir as they

appeared from the desert hills above Kassassin, one part stood out with marked prominence. An observation of the heights, shown on the plan of the ground, will make it clear that that which was thus seen must have been some part of the works marked F to K on the Plan. These stand on ground many feet higher than any of the rest, and represent the southward part of the Egyptian entrenchment, after it reaches the top of the hill which rises from the canal. Observations over the desert are often strangely confused. The mirage throws up an object into prominence at one time, which when next looked at may have disappeared altogether. But there can be no doubt from the various observations taken that it was the part of the work from H to K which was seen by Colonel Buller, and was fixed on by Sir Garnet Wolseley as the most conspicuous object on which to direct the march. On this part of the line it was determined to direct the attack of the 2nd, Sir E. Hamley's, Division, and it was the more easy to do so, because by keeping somewhat to the north of the ridge of the upland ground, and nearly due westward, this part of the works would be reached.

The powerful 8-gun advanced work which lies in front of the Egyptian right had been twice seen, once by Lieutenant-Colonel Tulloch from near the canal, and once by Colonel Buller from the hill at β south of the canal, but on neither occasion had it been possible to distinguish it from the main body of the works, and from the front it could not be seen, being altogether below the crest of the hill. The interior trace of the work was not known, only very incomplete information having been received from prisoners, and no information having been obtained from spies or deserters from within the works. Whether any of the Egyptian Generals or soldiers were secretly loyal to the Khedive or not, a matter which we have now no means of knowing, at any rate we had then no opportunity of ascertaining the fact, or of entering into any negotiations whatever with them; and it may be as well to state here, specifically, that all assertions that any such negotiations had been entered into, or that any bribe had been received by any Egyptian in Tel el-Kebir, are baseless inventions, without a shadow of foundation in fact. All the knowledge we had of the nature of the works was due to reconnaissances, confirmed to some extent by the reports of prisoners.

In order to watch the left of the movement, and to protect it from any counter-attempt of the enemy, the 19th Hussars (two squadrons) were detailed to follow the ridge of the plateau, and to be ready for any movement from the broken ground southwards toward the canal.

The 1st Division was assigned a position on the right, such as would, in its westward march, bring it to a point in the enemy's entrenchment which General Willis had had the opportunity of observing for himself during the course of the fight of the 9th.

He had noticed that the enemy had, in their retreat, chosen, for returning to their works, a certain portion of their line which, as he therefore concluded, must be the weakest, and he proposed to direct the march of his troops upon this point.

That there might in the darkness be no confusion when starting, the lines of direction which, by a due westerly march, would bring the two Divisions to the two required points in the enemy's line, were to be marked by posts, which were ordered to be placed by the Royal Engineers after sunset.

It was obviously necessary to leave very great latitude to each of the Divisional Generals in the carrying out of the details of a plan which was based on the independent action of the two Divisions. The tactical formation which had been intended by Sir Garnet Wolseley was not strictly adhered to in either Division. His idea had been to place the troops in an order of battle which should be adapted to a night movement in this sense, that it should require no manœuvring to pass from the formation of march to the formation of attack. Moreover, in order to avoid, as far as possible, the mixing up of battalions, sure to follow upon the first stage of a successful attack, and liable to be aggravated by the confusion engendered by darkness, he had desired to assign to each battalion its own separate point of attack, and to leave space between it and the next. Thus the formation he had intended for the Highland Brigade, which consisted of the four battalions of Black Watch, Gordon Highlanders, Cameron Highlanders, and Highland Light Infantry, would have been this:—

HIGHLAND LIGHT INFᵀᴿʸ	CAMERON HIGHLANDERS	GORDON HIGHLANDERS	BLACK WATCH
LEFT HALF BATTⁿ	LEFT HALF BATTⁿ	LEFT HALF BATTⁿ	LEFT HALF BATTⁿ
< DEPLOYING INTERVAL >	< DEPLOYING INTERVAL >	< DEPLOYING INTERVAL >	
RIGHT HALF BATTⁿ	RIGHT HALF BATTⁿ	RIGHT HALF BATTⁿ	RIGHT HALF BATTⁿ

Each battalion would thus have had a front of half a battalion to rush in line directly upon the parapet without firing, and a supporting half battalion of its own regiment immediately behind it. Each brigade was thus to have been formed. The brigade in second line of each Division was to act as a reserve for the Division, while the general course of the action would make the 1st Division, which from the beginning was destined to have the most ground to cover before arriving at the Bridge of Tel el-Kebir, and was from the first known to have a somewhat less difficult part of the parapet to cross, into a support for the Division whose course was the most direct.

The cavalry and Horse Artillery, placed on the extreme right with orders to sweep round upon the rear of the position as soon as the enemy was fully engaged in front, had the double function of alarming the enemy, when shaken from his defences, as to his retreat, and thus making a rally impossible, and of being ready for immediate pursuit to reap the fruits of the victory.

The only respect in which this programme was modified during the march and the attack was that, as the formation intended is not one laid down in the drill-book, the Brigadiers found it easier during the difficulties of the night march to adopt established forms, and accordingly they all deviated from this mode of night march and attack.*

The Indian Brigade, under Brigadier-General Macpherson, was to move on the south side of the canal, an hour's march in rear of the rest of the army, because, as it was to pass along the "wady," in which were native villages, it was of great importance that it should not, by startling them too soon, spread news of the coming attack before the main army was ready to deliver its onslaught. Placed as this brigade was, on the line of retreat of the enemy, it was ready to march direct upon Zagazig after the action, and so secure that important junction before the enemy could recover from their disaster. The Naval Brigade, with the 40-pr. gun moving along the railway, was to keep on the same level with and support the Indian Brigade.

It has happened in the past that some night attacks have failed in consequence of the attacking troops meeting on their route cattle, geese, or other animals which have roused the defenders, or roused inhabitants who have given warning to the enemy. By a curiously bad logical deduction, a conclusion has been sometimes drawn from this fact that, therefore, all night attacks are chiefly a

---

* As the question of this formation is of considerable military interest, it may be as well to note the formations adopted by the two leading brigades.

It must be noted that nothing whatever is said about either Division having departed from any "orders" given. It is of the very essence of such a movement that no drill formation can be precisely ordered. All that is mentioned is the certain fact that Sir Garnet contemplated a certain mode of formation as specially adapted to a night march and attack, and that each leading brigade, acting within the full discretion given, adopted a different form. In the case of the Highland Brigade, Sir A. Alison had received orders from Sir E. Hamley to form his brigade "in the order in which it was to attack" at the assigned post 1,000 yards into the desert from "Ninth Hill" along the line of poles. Sir A. Alison had clearly understood Lord Wolseley's wish that each battalion should attack in two lines, and that there should be no change of formation from march to attack formation. With Sir E. Hamley's full approval each battalion was formed in two lines; the first line consisted of two companies of the right and two of the left half-battalion; the second line of the same. Sir Archibald's object was to minimize the mixing up of companies in the attack. By having each half-battalion with two companies in front and two in support, only the companies of each half would be mixed when the supports closed on the front.

The order for each half-battalion "to advance in column of double companies" gave the formation thus sought. Sir Archibald's brigade moved throughout the night and attacked in this formation, Sir Archibald's view being, in accordance with Sir Garnet's, that, in a night attack, any change, even the most trifling, from the order of march to that of attack means confusion, delay, and loss. Hence, in this brigade, orders were issued that no battalion or company officer should give any orders till the parapet had been crossed.

On the other hand, General Willis advanced with the brigades in the drill-book formation of "columns of half-battalions at deploying intervals" until the Division had advanced so far that the leading brigade might have found itself under fire at any moment. Then, as recorded in the text, line was formed, and subsequently the brigade advanced by fours from the right of companies, re-forming line, and ultimately attack formation. These different views and experiences appear to be worth recording in regard to a matter so important to modern war as night attacks, as to which so little modern experience exists.

matter of chance. An examination of the circumstances and of the orders for the night march upon Tel el-Kebir will show that an altogether different conclusion may be drawn, viz., that the possibility of meeting dogs, cattle, geese, &c., is an element that has to be taken into account by a Commander in arranging his plans for a night march. It was almost as certain that on the night of the 12th September the infantry and cavalry, who moved to the north of the canal along the desert, would not meet with cattle, geese, or dogs as that they would not meet with whales. It was absolutely certain that the Indian Brigade, which moved through the " wady " to the south of the canal, would meet with animals of all sorts before reaching the lines ; therefore the hour of the march of the Indian Brigade was fixed accordingly.

The general scheme of the action having been thus explained, the orders issued and the formation of the troops shown on the attached plan will now be intelligible. The orders issued were as follows :—

" *Head-quarters, Kassassin, September* 12, 1882.

" The Army Corps will be prepared to march this evening at 5 P.M.

" The men's valises and blankets, and the officers' light baggage, will be carried to the nearest point of the railway opposite the encampment of each corps and battalion, where they will be stacked alongside the line.

" At 6·15 P.M., but not before that hour, the tents will be struck, packed, and deposited alongside the valises.

" One non-commissioned officer and two men of each corps and battalion will remain with the tents and valises.

" After depositing the tents the men will not return to their camp, but will be formed up by brigades and marched to the ground where they will bivouac.

" After sunset no bugles will be sounded until after broad daylight to-morrow.

" The present camp will be left in charge of one troop 19th Hussars (to be detailed by the General Officer Commanding 2nd Division), the head-quarters and remainder of the 1st West Kent Regiment, except fifty men, the 24th and 26th Companies Royal Engineers, and all details of corps troops.

" These troops will be under the command of Brigadier-General Nugent, C.R.E. ; their tents need not be struck this evening.

" Each soldier will carry 100 rounds of ammunition, all that remains of to-day's rations, and to-morrow's full rations (excepting meat) ; water-bottles will be filled with cold tea if practicable.

" The regimental transport will be packed with cooking utensils, two full days' rations, one day's fuel, butchery, and signalling implements, and as many blankets and great coats as can be carried without overloading.

" The transport will be brigaded at daylight, and follow the army, keeping along the north side of the railway.

" Water-carts and stretchers will accompany battalions when they march out of camp this evening.

" Thirty rounds of ammunition per man carried by the baggage animals will press on at daylight after being brigaded, and will not remain with the rest of the regimental transport.

" The Mounted Infantry will carry seventy rounds per man, and must arrange for the carriage of another seventy rounds on pack animals.

" The Naval Brigade, the Indian Contingent, the cavalry, artillery, and engineers will conform to the above instructions so far as they are applicable and practicable.

" The following alterations will be made to-morrow in the printed ' redistribution ' of troops :—*

" (a.) The Naval Brigade will be detached from the 1st Brigade, and will keep with the 40-pr. gun.

" (b.) The 1st Royal West Kent Regiment will guard the camp, except fifty men, who will be the escort to the ammunition column. The officer commanding this party will report to and receive orders from Major Hebbert, F Battery 1st Brigade Royal Artillery, ammunition column.

" (c.) The Duke of Cornwall's Light Infantry and the 3rd King's Royal Rifle Corps will form the 4th Brigade, under Colonel Ashburnham, King's Royal Rifle Corps, and will belong to the 2nd Division.

" (d.) A Battery 1st Brigade, D Battery 1st Brigade, I Battery 2nd Brigade, N Battery 2nd Brigade, H Battery 1st Brigade, C Battery 3rd Brigade, and J Battery 3rd Brigade, Royal Artillery, will form an artillery brigade under the General Officer Commanding Royal Artillery.

" (e.) G Battery B Brigade and N Battery A Brigade, Royal Horse Artillery, will be attached to the cavalry division.

" 2. The positions which the troops will take up for bivouacking have been pointed out to Generals Commanding.

" Distances will be taken from the 4th Brigade, and the *point d'appui* will be the left of the Duke of Cornwall's Light Infantry, which will rest on Ninth Hill, where the artillery picquet is now posted ; this point is 2,000 yards north of the railway.

" 3. The present outposts, excepting those at Ninth Hill, may be withdrawn, and from sunset this evening all orders and arrangements for the protection of the camp will be made under the direction of the General commanding the lines of communication."

The attached rough plan of attack was distributed to General Officers Commanding Divisions and Brigades..

[*See attached Sketch of Formation for Attack, Tel el-Kebir.*]

---

* *i.e.*, that made on the transfer of Sir E. Hamley with Sir A. Alison's brigade to Ismailia.   It is given in Appendix III, p. 121.

Force available for storming of enemy's position :—

1st *Division (General Willis).*

Guards Brigade (His Royal Highness the Duke of Connaught)—
  2nd Battalion Grenadier Guards.
  2nd Battalion Coldstream Guards.
  1st Battalion Scots Guards.
2nd Brigade (Major-General Graham)—
  2nd Battalion Royal Irish.
  1st Battalion Royal Irish Fusiliers.
  Battalion Royal Marine Light Infantry.
  2nd Battalion York and Lancaster.

2nd *Division (Sir E. Hamley).*

3rd (the Highland) Brigade (Sir A. Alison)—
  1st Battalion Cameron Highlanders.
  2nd Battalion Highland Light Infantry.
  1st Battalion Royal Highlanders (the Black Watch)
  1st Battalion Gordon Highlanders.
4th Brigade (Colonel Ashburnham)—
  2nd Battalion Duke of Cornwall's Light Infantry.
  3rd Battalion King's Royal Rifle Corps.
Naval Brigade.

Royal Artillery (Brigadier-General Goodenough)—

  A Battery 1st Brigade, D Battery 1st Brigade, H Battery 1st Brigade, I Battery 2nd Brigade, N Battery 2nd Brigade, C Battery 3rd Brigade, J Battery 3rd Brigade —42 guns; N Battery A Brigade, and G Battery B Brigade, Royal Horse Artillery.
Royal Marine Artillery.
Cavalry (Major-General D. C. Drury Lowe)—
  3 squadrons Household Cavalry.
  4th Dragoon Guards.
  7th Dragoon Guards.
  19th Hussars (1 squadron).
  2nd Bengal Cavalry.
  6th Bengal Cavalry.
  13th Bengal Lancers.
  Mounted Infantry.
  (F Battery, 1st Brigade, Royal Artillery) Reserve Ammunition Column.
  1 Company West Kent Regiment.

Indian Division.

  1st Battalion Seaforth Highlanders.
  7th Bengal Native Infantry.
  20th Punjaub Native Infantry.
  29th Beloochees Native Infantry.
  (7th Battery, 1st Brigade, Northern Division, Royal Artillery); Mountain Battery.

Total strength :—

Cavalry, 125 officers ; 2,660 non-commissioned officers and men.

Infantry, 422 officers ; 11,702 non-commissioned officers and men.

Artillery, 87 officers ; 2,405 non-commissioned officers and men.

Total, 634 officers ; 16,767 non-commissioned officers and men. Guns, 61 ; Gatlings, 6.

The first stage of the movement of the night, that from the camp to the bivouac on and near " Ninth Hill," began soon after dark.

The difficulty in finding the directing posts, which had been set up by the Engineer officers as guides for the earlier part of the march, was very great. The night was more than usually dark, and it was some time before the troops could be placed in the positions assigned to them. By about 11 P.M. the troops were all in the places shown in the Sketch. About that hour Sir Garnet himself rode on to the ground, and went round the whole of the bivouac. As the sole means of direction depended on the stars, he assigned to Sir E. Hamley, for the direction of the Highland Brigade, Lieutenant Rawson, R.N., his own Naval Aide-de-camp, as a man well accustomed to steer his way by the stars, and familiar with the desert from having accompanied Sir Garnet in his many journeyings to and from Ismailia by night.

The short rest of the troops came to an end at 1·30, when the order to move forward westward was, according to the scheme, given to each part of the force by its leaders. A series of connecting files were, by Sir Garnet's orders, established between the leading brigades of each Division and those behind them, to insure their not losing trace of one another in the dark. The strictest orders were given against smoking, striking lights, or loud giving of orders. Silence was strictly enforced.

The Highland Brigade moved off in half-battalion columns of double companies. The Black Watch on the right, the 1st Battalion Gordon Highlanders next, the 1st Battalion Cameron Highlanders, with the 2nd Battalion Highland Light Infantry, on the left. The right company of the Cameron Highlanders was the company of direction. The guide of that company was therefore placed under the orders of Lieutenant Rawson, R.N. In the observations that had been made, in the early morning reconnaissances, stars had been observed which would stand nearly over the position of Tel el-Kebir, but clouds continually obscured most of the stars at one time or another; the North Star and Little Bear alone remaining, nearly all through the night, visible. It was therefore only possible to take up successive stars, which appeared to be directly in front when the North Star was on the right hand. The artillery moving between the Brigade of Guards and Colonel Ashburnham's brigade with the long front presented

by its forty-two guns,* were constantly through the night aligned
by Colonel Goodenough himself on the North Star. From the
direction shown on the desert by the wheel-tracks, it would seem
(*vide* Plan) that the guns somewhat drifted away northwards from
the Highland Brigade. General Willis himself directed the march
of his own Division, and succeeded in steering them upon the
part of the enemy's position which he had noted as the weakest
during the combat of the 9th September. The march, however, of the 1st Division was in fact slower than that of the 2nd.
It had been originally supposed that they would strike the
trench rather earlier than the 2nd, because the Egyptian line of
entrenchment trends forward towards its left, but in the uncertainty
of night, the delays in the movement of this Division were greater
than in the other.† The leading brigade of the 1st Division
advanced at first in " columns of half-battalions."‡ After advancing
for an hour and a-half the brigade was halted for twenty minutes,
and at an hour, put by General Graham at 3 A.M., and by General
Willis at 4 A.M., it was deployed into line, because General Willis
then calculated that it might be under fire at any moment. It so
advanced, not without great difficulty and many delays. After
some experience of these, and at General Graham's suggestion,
the advance was continued by fours from the right of companies.
Various incidents occurred which illustrated the difficulty of such
a movement, and the consequent necessity of careful management
in detail, and of effective discipline and organization, in order to
accomplish it successfully.
It is impossible adequately to convey an impression of the

---

* The Field Artillery was arranged thus:—

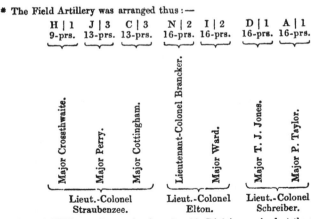

† General Willis attributes the fact that his Division arrived at the trenches later
than the other to this, that the direction taken by the guns, "due west," tended
relatively to the required line to throw the right too much back, so that the 1st Division,
aligned on the guns, was yet further distant from the trenches. As, in fact, the
direction taken was somewhat north of west, this would tend still further to throw back
the right, and, therefore, General Willis' Division.

‡ According to the analogy of the drill of all other armies and of all other arms
of our own Service this should be called, "line of half-battalion columns of companies
at deploying intervals."

absolute silence which prevailed, and of the entire absence of any indication of the existence of a moving army at only a few yards from each of the columns. Staff officers sent with orders to any part of the force had to move into a silent darkness—to steer their way by a general knowledge of the direction of the particular brigade to which they were sent—return again into a silent void and make their way back as best they might by a similar attempt to strike a general direction. Sound or sight at 100 yards from any column there was none, save of the desert and the stars. Hence the tendency to exaggerate the importance of any sounds that suddenly struck upon the ear was great. More than once the movement of a few mounted men of the Head-quarters up to some of the columns was mistaken for an oncoming movement of cavalry, and, in one instance in particular, it was only the careful watchfulness of officers, and the steady discipline of the men, that saved Sir Garnet himself and his whole Staff from being received with a volley by a brigade at the bivouac, roused from sleep by the sudden sound of horses' feet, and prepared for a supposed attack of Bedouins.

Under such circumstances it is not surprising that rumours spread that the movement had been watched throughout the night by Bedouin horsemen, who retired before us, and carried notice of the coming force into the lines of the Egyptians. We now know for certain that nothing of the kind happened. No notice had reached the Egyptians of the movement of the force, or of the coming attack.

During all that night, according to Turkish and Egyptian customs, the portion of the army detailed for the defence of the parapets and for the artillery batteries were lying in the trenches, with their arms beside them, and with an ample store of ammunition disposed ready for use. Bedouins had been detailed to remain outside the entrenchments as an outlook, and some cavalry appear to have been stationed on the ground between the advanced work on the Egyptian right and the main line of entrenchment. But neither of these moved from the near neighbourhood of the entrenchments themselves, and they sent in no report.

After marching for about an hour and three-quarters the Highland Brigade halted and lay down for twenty minutes, in accordance with the orders for the night, in order to refresh the men.

As all orders were given only in a low tone, and passed on from company to company and battalion to battalion, the order to halt did not at once reach the outer flanks. The consequence was that, as the flanks continued to step out, while touch was maintained with the centre, the flanks lost their direction, and circled round so that the brigade halted in a crescent-shape formation. When the order to advance was again given, the flank battalions, supposing themselves to be moving still in the old direction, advanced directly to their front. The result was that the flank battalions almost met in front of the centre. As soon as this was perceived, the brigade was halted, and Sir A. Alison personally placed the company of direction upon the true line with the help of Lieutenant Rawson's observations. The other companies of the Cameron Highlanders were carefully formed upon it, and the other battalions were then gradually and successively drawn back and reformed upon the proper alignment, so that the brigade resumed its march in perfect order. This operation took about five and twenty minutes.

Our Cavalry Division did not leave camp with the rest of the Army Corps. This arrangement was made in order not to confuse the movement of the infantry, and, in marching to their position on the extreme right of the line, the cavalry were, with the same motive, ordered not to follow the line of march which had been taken by the infantry. Brigader-General Wilkinson, who commanded the Indian Cavalry Brigade, had had charge of the outposts at Kassassin ever since the arrival of his brigade at that station. He was therefore well acquainted with the ground between Kassassin and Tel el-Kebir, and had on that account been assigned the duty of leading the march on the night of the 12th. He had previously fixed a flagstaff a mile from camp on which the march was at first directed in a due northerly direction.

The Division moved off in the following order:—

The 13th Bengal Lancers in front, followed in succession by the 2nd Bengal Cavalry and the 6th Bengal Cavalry.

Then came N | A and G | B Batteries R.H.A., under Colonel Nairne.

The heavy brigade, with the Mounted Infantry, formed the rear of the column under Sir B. Russell.

On arriving near the previously fixed flagstaff, which was not found till after the cavalry had been halted, and could not be seen at 15 yards distance, the Division formed up.

At 2·15 A.M. the march was resumed in a north-westerly direction. The whole force moved off in column of troops.

At 3·10 A.M. the cavalry halted and fronted towards the west, waiting for the sound of the action having begun as their signal for moving forward, the object for keeping them back till then being to prevent any chance of disturbing the enemy and giving notice of the coming attack.

Sir Garnet, with the Head-quarter Staff, had followed the march of the Highland Brigade, and shortly after the incident above recorded had occurred, sent orders for the brigade to move forward to the attack as soon as it was in hand. He had seen the confusion without knowing the cause.

It was now about 4·35 A.M. A little before this, as it was evident that we must be nearing the parapet, he had sent another order to Colonel Ashburnham, who commanded the supporting brigade, to let his men step out and close up on the brigade in front. A quarter of an hour later, about 4·50, a shaft of light showed itself in the east, as Sir Garnet was still waiting for the sound of the first shots.

It was still nearly an hour before sunrise. It was impossible to see watches. This streak of light, therefore, apparently the harbinger of coming dawn, caused no small anxiety. If it meant that day would be immediately upon us, the attack was clearly too late.

It is now as certain as anything can be that the shaft of light so seen was the comet, which on that day was for the first time reported in Europe, which must therefore have been very conspicuous in the open desert. This strange streak of light, noticed in all parts of the field of Tel el-Kebir, without any one at the time being able to account for it, showed itself always afterwards in the east, shooting upwards during the hour before the dawn, and fading as the sun neared the horizon. It was not till after our arrival in Cairo that the existence of the comet was ascertained, and this strange light before daybreak on the 13th September thus accounted for.

At this moment, when the attack was about to begin, though neither the Highland Brigade nor General Graham's brigade could from the nature of the movement know the exact position of the other, and though the Cavalry Division knew the position of none of the rest of the force, the whole front of the army to the north of the canal was in fact in the form of an irregular échelon, with the left thrown forward thus :—*

Highland Brigade.

Artillery.

2nd Brigade.
(1st Division.)

Cavalry.

It followed that, when a few minutes later, as the Highlanders neared the works, and when, after two or three isolated shots had been discharged, a blaze of fire burst from the whole line of parapet, though the Highland Brigade was within the distance for a single charge, the 2nd, the leading Brigade of General Willis' Division, was some 800 or 900 yards from the parapet, and, the enemy having been roused, it became necessary for the 2nd Brigade to pass over a much longer belt of fire outside the parapet than fell to the lot of the Highland Brigade. On this account also General Willis judged it necessary to make the assault in the ordinary form of a day attack, that is, in "attack formation." This still further delayed the advance of his Division upon the parapet as compared with the Highland Brigade. Hence the history of the seizure of the works for the first ten minutes to a quarter of an hour of the fight is the history of the advance of the Highland Brigade.

It was about five minutes to 5 when it became evident that the brigade was nearing the parapet. The enemy's picquets had just been dimly perceived at about 150 yards off, when a few dropping shots were fired by the sentries close upon the works. The order for bayonets to be fixed without halting, and in perfect silence, was

---

* I believe, from a comparison of much evidence, that this is approximately correct for the hour named. It is possible that the 2nd Brigade and Artillery were more nearly in line than I have shown them. The other relative positions are certainly correct. See, however, note to p. 82 as to General Willis' view of the situation.

given by the Brigadier. The Egyptian bugles sounded the alarm. A shell from a gun came whizzing over the heads of the brigade. The men advanced for 200 yards, and then, from out the darkness, the whole course of the entrenchment was lighted up for a mile or more in length by the flashes of the enemy's rifles, at a range of 150 yards.

The preconcerted signal for storming was at once given. The long night's silence was at length broken, first by the bugler sounding the advance, and then by a ringing cheer from the brigade as the other bugles repeated the signal,* and the High-landers rushed in two long waves upon the rampart in front. In the movement the half-battalion double columns had gradually closed in upon one another, so that the brigade was virtually formed in two nearly continuous lines. Sir E. Hamley had given orders during the night that the men should take ample room. This had tended to close up the intervals. Sir E. Hamley, who was between these two lines, realizing a necessity which was sure immediately to arise, checked the advance of the rear companies of the Gordon and Cameron Highlanders, and formed them into a support.

It was some time before the troops, struggling up the parapet, could make good their foothold on the loose sand of the steep scarps. The enemy's continuous fire told severely upon the attacking line. Not a shot was fired by the Highlanders till the summit was reached.

The first man of the Gordon Highlanders to mount the parapet was Lieutenant Brooks, who fell dead, pierced with four wounds. The first man of the Cameron Highlanders was Private Donald Cameron, who, on reaching the summit, fell forward into the enemy's trench shot through the head.

Gradually the line which had become broken in the struggle to clamber up formed into groups, in which the men helped one another up the parapet. The summit was won at different points, and the groups gathering on the top sprang down upon the terreplein behind.

The desire of correspondents to give an adequate impression of the gallantry and dash of the Highland Brigade has resulted in doing them a great injustice, by representing that the resistance they met with was virtually *nil*, and was overcome immediately. That was by no means the case. The fire was so severe for a con-siderable time, and the defenders held so resolutely to their ground, that, even of the two centre regiments, the Gordon and Cameron Highlanders, though some groups were able very soon to establish a footing within the works, others on the left were driven back from the parapets, so much so that Sir A. Alison himself, who had crossed to lead the advance, was by sheer weight of numbers forced back over the parapet again. Crossing again, he had his horse shot

---

* It is a quaint point that, in consequence of the necessary silence of the night up to this time, the bags of the pipes were not filled, and therefore the pipers could not now strike up, so that, vigorous as were their efforts, it was not till after the brigade was well into the enemy's lines that the proper sound of Highland music was heard.

just as he had dismounted in order to lead the men, and in joining the advancing troops was very nearly cut off by a party of Egyptians falling back from one of the works. Even of those who held their own on the further side of the parapet, large numbers, exposed to the enemy's fire on three sides, began to give way. They turned about again, however, on receiving from Sir E. Hamley the word of command "Right about turn."* Sir E. Hamley had prepared for this very event by retaining in hand, and in close formation, parts of the second line of both regiments. He now, bringing forward this new support, rallied upon them the broken fragments which had not been able to make good their attack, and led the whole mass to the support of those who formed the advancing force on the further side of the front trench, and from this time forward Sir Edward himself led the advance.

How completely dispersed such an attack becomes from the moment when it fairly breaks in upon the enemy may be judged by this, that a Staff officer reports that there was a moment when he saw Sir A. Alison himself, absolutely alone, his pistol in the one hand which previous campaigns have left him, advancing towards a group of the enemy, probably the party which nearly cut him off.

He soon joined a mixed group of all the men able to rally to him. So the fight slowly advanced. Mixed groups of both Camerons and Gordons, in many cases of Camerons, Gordons, and Black Watch, under any officer who could lead them on, attacking first one party of Egyptians and then another till the front rampart between the two higher batteries at H and K was won.

Meantime, on the left of the Highland Brigade, the Highland Light Infantry had struggled in vain to cross the formidable ditch which marked this part of the line. Not only was the work itself here of a more considerable profile than in the other part of the line, but it was occupied by Nubian regiments, who appear to have fought with great courage. Some portion of them, at all events, well handled, seem to have reserved their fire, during the time when darkness made it ineffective, and to have waited till the assailants were involved in the confusion of the scramble up the ditch and exposed to the artillery fire, which, aimed at known distances, now poured from every gun in the entrenchments. Then, after a volley delivered at close quarters upon the Highland Light Infantry, the Nubians were led to charge them in a solid body, driving our men back from the work by the force of formed against unformed troops.

On the right the Black Watch had also struck upon the strong work at K, and were not able to make good their footing as soon as the centre regiments, which were now pushing on into the inclosure, exposed, however, to a biting infantry and artillery fire.

Thus the attack of the Highland Brigade had assumed the form of a wedge, the two flanks held back by the serious nature of

---

* See note to p. 91.

the works they had attacked, the centre pushing on towards the inner lines of entrenchment. The intense severity of the fire from the southern inner line of entrenchment H, b making it for some time impossible to advance over the open ground in the middle space between the two lines of entrenchment, the first part of the inner works which it was possible to attempt was the northern inner face a, Q, c. Here the enemy held out stubbornly, fighting well.

To preserve the relation between different parts of the action, it will be necessary for the time to leave the Highlanders still engaged in this obstinate fight along the line of works a, c, and endeavouring to make good their advance upon the inner line b, c.

The time of the advance of the Highlanders after the outer line of works had been carried may be estimated at about 5·20 A.M.

Meantime, on the right, the 2nd Brigade, belonging to General Willis' division, and under General Graham's command, starting between ten minutes and a quarter of an hour later than the Highlanders, made its attack upon the trenches, and, about the time that the Highlanders were beginning to push on to the interior retrenchments, carried, almost in a rush, the line of works opposed to them, General Graham, with his accustomed gallantry, personally leading the men over the ditch. The enemy, unbroken, fell back stubbornly resisting, and to no great distance from the parapet. The Royal Irish advanced on the right flank, taking up successive positions, admirably selected, and at every successive advance their lines moved forward with a rush as one man. The profile of the work in front of the Royal Irish was, as will be seen from the section, very slight, but that by no means tended to make the fire delivered from it less direct or effective. The York and Lancaster Regiment moved forward with a single rush upon the work at M and the parapet to the right of it. The Royal Irish Fusiliers (of whom it deserves to be recorded that their march upon the enemy's lines was in direct continuation of their march from Ismailia, as they had only arrived on the 12th September in the afternoon at Kassassin and bivouacked there), attacked with a heavy fire the south side of the work at M, and entered it from that side, a little after the York and Lancaster carried it in front.

The Royal Marines advanced without firing a shot up to within 100 yards of the parapet. The marines seized and held the parapet, but the enemy stubbornly kept their ground in a formed body, 50 feet distant.

Time and increasing light had, however, now permitted of new allies being brought in to the support of the attacking infantry of both advanced brigades.

On the extreme right the cavalry had advanced at about 4·40 A.M., at first at a slow walk, soon to be changed into a trot, and at the moment when the first shots were fired, at 5 minutes to 5, were about 2,000 yards distant from the parapet. , As soon as the shots were heard the pace was increased to a swinging trot, and in a very short time the leading part of the division came under the fire of the work on the Egyptian left at O. The Horse

Artillery galloped forward, engaged and silenced this fort, as well as a field battery which showed itself in the open ground in rear of the parapet. The cavalry continued their advance, with the Indian Brigade leading, in line of squadron columns and at about the time that the two centre regiments of the Highland Brigade had driven back the Egyptians from the front parapet, and were beginning to advance into the interior of the work, and that General Graham's brigade was engaged with the enemy, who, driven back from the parapet, was still formed and resisting at various distances within the parapet, the cavalry passed the line of the entrenchments, and began to swing round on to the left rear of the enemy.

Almost at the same time, or very shortly afterwards, Major Lugard passing the rear of the work at K, and observing that the gorge was open, while the guns in it were firing upon the rear of General Graham's brigade, gathered about ten Highlanders and entering the work at the rear shot down the detachments at their guns. As soon as the Black Watch had passed the work at K, a battery of artillery (Major Brancker's) crossed the parapet on the south side of it, while other guns came into action directly in front of the parapet. It will be now, therefore, convenient to follow the movements of the artillery up to this point.

At 10 minutes to 5 A.M., the artillery had been halted, and it was then found that the Highlanders were partially overlapping the front of the guns.

Brigadier-General Goodenough, as soon as the enemy's artillery began to open fire, finding that his position was too much on the sky-line, and that it would be useless to advance further till the light a little improved, dismounted the drivers, and kept his force for a few minutes stationary. He then ordered them to mount again and advanced. The enemy's bullets and shell passed over the heads of the artillery as they moved forward.

About 5·20 A.M. General Goodenough himself passed the gap to the south of the work at K which had just been carried by the Black Watch.

The last part of the artillery advance had been made in an échelon of brigade divisions from the centre, so that, Colonel Elton's division being in front and Lieutenant-Colonel Brancker's battery immediately opposite the gap, this battery was at once pushed on across the gap.* After a little spade work, one gun having broken down in the ditch in crossing, Lieutenant-Colonel Brancker's battery came into action, three guns against the enemy occupying the parapet H, b, from which the Highlanders were suffering so severely, and two guns enfilading the Egyptians to the north.

About the same time, or shortly before this, Colonel Schreiber's batteries on the right came into action, outside the ditch, against a portion of the enemy still holding out to the north of K, at a part of the line still unassailed by any infantry.

---

* This spot is marked on the Plan by a black line.

The enemy's resistance had hitherto been so stubborn that General Willis had thought it necessary to request Sir Garnet to send artillery to the support of the attack, and he had actually dispatched Colonel Gillespie with this request when the first guns, as above described, arrived to his assistance.*

Some short time before the guns came into action Colonel Twynam, the Assistant Adjutant-General of Sir E. Hamley's division, had ridden off to bring up the King's Royal Rifles to the support of the Black Watch, and about this time, just as Lieutenant-Colonel Brancker's battery and Lieutenant-Colonel Schreiber's division came into action, the Rifles and the Black Watch, pouring over the parapet, threatened the Egyptians who still held out to the north of *K* and south of *L*.†

The relative positions of the different parts of the army at this time, between 5·20 and 5·30 A.M., are marked by the fact that when Brigadier-General Goodenough himself crossed the parapet at the beginning of that period, the Highlanders, having just carried the front trench, were moving forward upon the interior line at (*a*), and that towards the end of it, the resistance of the so-called "Abyssinian" Regiment to the north having given way, General Goodenough stopped the fire of Lieutenant-Colonel Schreiber's guns which were directed towards the north-west, *because the Horse Artillery with the Cavalry Division were indicated in the distance by a cloud of dust beyond the enemy's entrenchment*, and might be struck by the shell. Presumably, therefore, the Horse Artillery, and therefore the Brigade of Indian Cavalry, were at this time somewhat to the south of the point marked γ, to which Colonel Buller had ridden on the 9th September.

In the next few minutes, that is, soon after 5·30 A.M., all resistance ceased from the work *K* northwards. General Graham's brigade within that time pushed forward from the parapet upon the formed masses of the enemy beyond. The Egyptians, plied simultaneously by the Horse Artillery on their left, Lieutenant-Colonel Brancker's two guns on their right, Lieutenant-Colonel Schreiber's division on their right front, and threatened by the cavalry in their left rear, gave way at once before the renewed attack of the 2nd Brigade, and soon became a mass of fugitives, only so far affecting the fight further in that they somewhat retarded the advance of the Cavalry Division, which now, sweeping through them, and sparing those who threw down their arms, moved down towards the bridge of Tel el-Kebir.

On the right, then, the next half-hour, or nearly so, from 5·30 to 6 A.M., was occupied thus :—

General Graham's brigade re-formed, and subsequently advanced

---

* Nevertheless, so curiously contradictory are the impressions of men under conditions of such excitement, that General Graham does not admit that the enemy held out long enough for either guns or the appearance of the cavalry to have had any effect on him. I believe the evidence for the narrative as it stands to be unanswerable.

† Part of the Rifles only joined in this attack, the remainder were with the Duke of Cornwall's Light Infantry joining with the Highland Light Infantry in the attack on the part of the lines at and to the south of *H*.

in close order over the high ground towards the bridge. The Guards Brigade, which, exposed to a fire not the less heavy because the Guards had been held in reserve, had advanced steadily upon the parapet, now wheeled towards its left, following General Graham's brigade. Finally, the cavalry, driving the fugitives before them, were sweeping downwards upon the enemy's lines in front of the bridge.

Meantime, on the extreme left of the attack, the Highland Light Infantry, reinforced by part of Colonel Ashburnham's brigade, again attacked the work at H, and at a time which may be put at about 5·40 A.M., carried it. They then swept down southwards towards the canal, carrying the remainder of the works on this side. The two centre regiments, with parts of the Black Watch from the captured work at K, were still pushing forward up to and along the line of entrenchments from a to c, and down the middle of the line between the two parapets of inner entrenchment. Sir Edward Hamley during this time had been both leading the men and giving general directions for the guns to be rendered useless to the enemy as the successive batteries were seized. Observing the numbers of Egyptians, who were now flying from the works, southwards towards the canal, which had been turned, he thought* it possible that they might discover the smallness of the numbers of the Highlanders and attack them from a very dangerous quarter. He therefore formed a part of the Highlanders to their left, but finding that the masses of Egyptians continued their flight he decided that the essential matter was to push them. He sent back Staff officers to form the scattered bodies in rear and bring them on. He then rode to the advanced troops.

It is important to the understanding of the mutual relation of the different parts of the fight that the period occupied in this movement should be carefully noted. At the beginning of it, at 5·20 A.M., the Highland Brigade was exposed to what a Staff officer describes as "a nasty bitter fire," proceeding from the whole line of works from H to b, from the artillery in the works at b and c, and from the infantry in the other trenches. They broke, as has been seen, into detached parties of from 60 up to 300 of mixed regiments, under various officers, and, replying to this fire, advanced by rushes, part over the ground between the two lines of parapets, part along the ditch from a to c. The Egyptians held out stiffly at each turn of the parapet, embrasure, and traverse, so that, though the line of attack had taken the main course of these works in reverse, it required time to dislodge the enemy, and, as far as the hour can be fixed, it must have been about 6 o'clock, or a little before that, when the extreme advanced

---

* It will be obvious, from my using such expressions as "he thought," &c., that I am here and in other parts of the narrative indebted to the personal evidence of Sir E. Hamley. It is the more necessary to make this remark because, from the fact that Sir Edward was not personally as well known to the brigade as Sir Archibald, though all who saw them bear testimony to the personal gallantry of both, it is often difficult to get corroborative evidence of parts of the story.

party of the Highlanders reached the corner of the re-entering angle of the work beyond c.

It must have been about 5·25 A.M. when the three guns of Lieutenant-Colonel Brancker's battery, which had first followed Colonel Goodenough over the parapet south of K, came into action against the line of parapet from H to b, in order to relieve the Highlanders from the dangerous fire which was poured upon them from this parapet as they passed on to the attack upon Q and b, c. The shrapnel fire from these guns at 1,000 yards proved very effective in silencing the guns and infantry in the parapet from H to b, and part of the battery was then turned against the work at Q, which was soon after taken by the Highlanders at the point of the bayonet.

The fire from this part of the line of parapet near Q had, till it was thus taken, been in part directed against General Graham's Brigade, which was at this time (5·35-5·40) showing in formed bodies in the distance beyond the front parapet.

After this the five guns of Lieutenant-Colonel Brancker's battery, in two half-batteries, one of three and one of two guns, moved along the outer face of the parapet a, c, coming into action at various points against such bodies of the enemy as showed any disposition to stand, sometimes in the parapet itself, sometimes on the open ground. Support was shortly afterwards given to these five guns by the whole of Lieutenant-Colonel Straubenzee's, the left Brigade-division of artillery, which had in the meantime passed the front parapet.

It will be convenient now to look at the attack as a whole as it presented itself to the Egyptians. According to Arabi Pasha's own statement, subsequently given in Ceylon, the force which held the lines of Tel el-Kebir, 20,000 strong, with 75 guns, was thus distributed :—*

1 battalion of infantry and 4 guns south of the canal at the point x, which lies between Tel el-Kebir and Kassassin, about 2,300 yards eastwards of the works of Tel el-Kebir.

2 battalions of infantry, 2,000 Bedouins, 300 cavalry, and 2 guns further south, at Abu Nishaba,† on the hill on the edge of the desert and "wady," 4½ miles from Kassassin.

3 battalions of infantry and 6 guns at the dam immediately in rear of the southernmost point of the entrenchments.

1 battalion of infantry and 4 guns at the advanced work in front of the entrenchments.

10 battalions of infantry and 54 guns occupying the line of the entrenchments.

3 battalions of infantry, 5 guns, and the remainder of the cavalry, 1,700, in reserve.

The ten battalions occupying the entrenchment were distributed as follows :—

---

* According to the best information we were able to obtain, he had actually 25,000, and, including Bedouins, 30,000 ; but I give above his own figures.

† ? Sandhills at β. Name does not appear in Survey

6 battalions along the front face south of *K*.

3 battalions on their left, *i.e.*, to the north; 1 battalion still further to the left to the extreme north.

All the regimental officers were with their men; the superior officers slept close behind them.

The Commandant of Tel el-Kebir, Ali Rubi Pasha, slept in Arabi's camp.

The first notice of the coming attack received by the troops was the firing and falling back of the outposts. This notice was, however, virtually *nil* from the nearness of the outposts to the parapet. The troops in the trenches were, he says, absolutely surprised, and he knew nothing of the attack till he heard the firing. Arabi was himself then in bed. By the time he was dressed the soldiers were in full retreat.

Now, it is a remarkable fact that Arabi Pasha, who can have no motive for misstatement on such a subject, maintains firmly what is in itself beyond all question a mistake, that the attack on the Egyptian left was delivered before the Highland attack on their centre. It is interesting and not difficult to account for this statement, and it will serve to show the bearing of the different parts of the attack upon the general result.

The high ground immediately above Arabi's own camp is, as will be seen from the Map, represented by the line of entrenchment from *d* to *e*. This ground forms the point of view from which he, the officers with him, and the Commandant of Tel el-Kebir would necessarily in the first instance view the fight. Now, from 5·30 A.M. up to 6 A.M. what would it have been that Arabi and his Staff, having still in hand nearly the whole of their cavalry, three battalions of infantry, and five guns as an intact reserve, would have seen?

On their right, where the Highlanders had attacked, the inner line from *b* to *c* was still holding out and fighting firmly. Probably the whole of the fight at this point was concealed from Arabi's position by the smoke of the action, but if he could have seen anything of the Highlanders it would have been only small bodies of men, pushing on along the entrenchments and still kept partly in check by infantry and artillery fire from his own men. On the other hand, on the sloping ground in front of him, he must have seen, as he says that he did see, the cavalry and horse artillery sweeping onwards, driving before them a broken mass of fugitives, and in the distance, on the side of the parapet nearest to him, at all events before 5·45, the formed mass of the 2nd, and soon afterwards of the Guards Brigade in full force. Hence it is not difficult to understand his statement that, as he puts it, the cause of the defeat was the flight of the left, and that the part attacked by the Highlanders was only involved in the general confusion when they were joined by the fugitives from the left. What his statement does apparently show is that the cause of the retreat of the intact reserve, and the general attempt to escape to the station which had undoubtedly commenced prior to the arrival of the victorious Highlanders, were due to the advance of the cavalry and horse artillery, and to the threatening appearance of the 1st Division in the distance, and not merely to the advance of the small parties of Highlanders, who towards 6 o'clock began, after their fierce and gallant fight, to push on beyond the point at *c*.

Lieutenant-Colonel Brancker's battery, after coming into action at various points against any of the enemy who showed a disposition to resist, finding finally that all opposition to their advance had given way, pushed on along the ridge towards the point *e*, on the right of the advancing Highlanders who were still engaged in the trenches. Just as the sun rose, throwing shadows over the plain for the first time that morning, that is, soon after 5·52 A.M., they came into action against trains that were already endeavouring to withdraw from the Tel el-Kebir station such portion of the fugitives as were in sufficient order to make good their escape. Arabi himself was already in full flight, and endeavoured to withdraw some portion of his intact reserve. General Willis, who had ridden on with his Staff ahead of his Division, joined, before 6 A.M., the party round the battery, with which at this time was also Brigadier-General Goodenough, commanding the artillery.

The first two trains escaped without being hit, but in the third some ammunition was exploded and the train stopped. Just at this moment, however, the Indian Brigade of Cavalry reached a part of the railway line, and it became necessary to cease further firing against the trains.

Nearly simultaneously, that is, a little after 6 A.M., the advanced body of the Highland Brigade, about 200 men of all three regiments, arrived at the point from which the camp, with the mass of reserves and fugitives struggling to make their escape, appeared below. Sir E. Hamley was in personal command. Sir A. Alison was directing his men. The Colonels of both Gordons and Camerons were present. Sir Garnet, in order to insure the co-operation of the two brigades, had directed that, when this point was reached, and what would probably be the main attack had to be delivered, a halt should be made till General Graham's brigade was able to co-operate by a flank attack. As, however, it was now evident that the Egyptians were only endeavouring to escape, and co-operation in this attack could not be hoped for in time, Sir E. Hamley decided to pursue at once. He therefore ordered Sir Archibald to advance upon the camp, and led the men himself directly through the camp, which they captured, with tents, baggage, and stores, and upon the bridge and railway station, where they seized about 100 carriages.* On the towing-path of the canal beyond the railway station Sir Edward finally halted, checking the fire of the men on the camels and flying people.

As soon as the Highlanders made their attack, just before 5 A.M., the advanced work opened its artillery fire, at first generally upon the plain to the north, but very soon, as the Head-quarters with their escort formed the most conspicuous body within range,

---

* Curiously enough, General Willis from his position near the battery did not see this advance, and is convinced that it did not take place at this time.

directed its fire upon them. Sir Garnet sent back the telegraph troop and led-horses out of range, and remained watching the progress of the attack, the shells fortunately doing very little mischief. In a short time the Egyptian cavalry, which had remained between the advanced work and the parapet, rode slowly out, and were just visible on the sky-line. As there was some danger of their threatening the Highland Brigade in the course of their attack, Sir Garnet ordered the cavalry escort* to advance against them. The Egyptian cavalry did not wait for their attack, but disappeared behind the works.

At 5·35, just after the Highlanders had begun their advance into the interior of the works, the Head-quarters received the order to mount, and rode forward upon the trenches. The advanced work continued to follow the movement, sending shell after shell at the party. Near the trenches Sir Garnet desired Sir John Adye to have some batteries brought up to silence this work, and those of Lieutenant-Colonel Schreiber's division were moved by him, soon after their previous employment was over, to silence this the last part of the entrenchments which held out. Taking up a position on the reverse side of the advanced work, they came into action against it, and in a very short time caused a magazine to explode, which made further resistance impossible. The outwork was evacuated, the defenders making the best of their way towards the canal.

The General, in the meantime, rode forward, and, after speaking to some of the wounded, reached the bridge at Tel el-Kebir just as the victorious Highlanders advanced upon it. There he was soon afterwards joined by the various leaders of divisions from all parts of the field, and at once gave directions for the further advance.

Before detailing these, however, it will be necessary to follow the steps of the Indian and Naval Brigades on the south side of the canal.

The Indian Contingent, under General Macpherson, was formed on the canal bank at 2 A.M. on the morning of the 13th September.

It consisted of the following troops:—

Seaforth Highlanders, under Lieutenant-Colonel Stockwell, C.B., 30 officers, 650 men.

7 | 1 Mountain Battery Royal Artillery, under Major Free, 5 officers, 105 men.

Section of Sappers, under Major Hamilton, 7 officers, 248 men.

20th Native Infantry, under Colonel Rogers, C.B., 5 officers, 268 men.

29th Native Infantry, under Lieutenant-Colonel Galloway, 6 officers, 182 men.

7th Native Infantry, under Colonel Worsley, 6 officers, 271 men.

6th Bengal Cavalry, 1 squadron, 3 officers, 102 men.

Total, 62 officers, 1,826 men.

The Naval Brigade, under Captain Fitzroy, R.N., which moved

along the line of railway, consisted of 210 blue-jackets, with 6 Gatlings. It was attached to General Macpherson's force. The Naval Brigade marched on the northern, while the main body of General Macpherson's infantry advanced along the southern bank, connection between them being maintained by some pontoons, under charge of the Royal Engineers. These moving on the canal kept pace with the Indian and Naval Brigades.

From the restricted nature of the ground the advance was necessarily made in fours. The cavalry followed in rear. The force had marched about 3 miles when the three warning shots which preceded the attack of the Highland Brigade were heard. The brigade continued to move along the towing path, the bank serving them as a protecting traverse.

About a quarter of an hour after the shots had been heard the enemy observed the column, and began to shell it, one of the first shells falling among General Macpherson's Staff.

The Seaforth Highlanders were then pushed forward over the open ground against the guns, which were protected by some pits, and covered by trenches with about 400 infantry in them. The 20th Native Infantry at the same time passed round the battery, taking it in flank. The 7th Native Infantry supported the Seaforth Highlanders. The 29th Native Infantry supported the 20th.

The mountain battery came into action on the top of the bank against the guns in the pits, firing at the flashes of the guns. The Seaforth Highlanders advanced by rushes, firing volleys at intervals; the Gatlings on the north bank gave most effective support, firing with great judgment upon the enemy wherever exposed to them. As soon as the advance had been made close enough to the work, Brigadier-General Tanner gave orders to Colonel Stockwell to fix bayonets and charge. At about 6 A.M. the enemy were driven from their entrenchments on the south bank, and four guns were captured by the Seaforth Highlanders.

The 20th Bengal Infantry had, in the meantime, advanced across the irrigated fields against a native village, which was held in force by the enemy. Colonel Rogers, under Brigadier-General Tanner's orders, carried the village by a bayonet charge.

The whole line advanced, driving the broken enemy before them, and capturing his guns. The squadron of the 6th Bengal Cavalry was pushed forward in pursuit, to cut off the fugitives who were now pouring into the village of Tel el-Kebir from the northern side over the bridge.

Soon after 7 A.M. General Macpherson reported to Sir Garnet on the bridge the complete success of the advance of his brigade.

The total return of ordnance captured in the action will be found in Appendix VI (p. 194). It amounted to fifty-eight guns in all. Of these, General Macpherson's force on the south side captured eight Krupp field guns and four 7-pr. rifled bronze guns, taken in the pits.

The enemy's rout was now complete. The record of the pursuit requires a short chapter to itself.

CHAPTER XIII.

THE PURSUIT AFTER TEL EL-KEBIR. — THE RIDE TO CAIRO.— SURRENDER OF THE REBEL FORCES AND END OF THE WAR. —SIR A. ALISON AT TANTA.

Before leaving the bridge at Tel el-Kebir Sir Garnet issued the following orders. The cavalry were directed to continue their pursuit, and advance upon Cairo with all possible rapidity, to save it, if possible, from the destruction intended by Arabi Pasha. The Indian Contingent was to push on to Zagazig, and so break the connection between the various portions of the Egyptian army dispersed throughout the Delta.

General Wilkinson, with the Indian Cavalry Brigade and Mounted Infantry, marched by the north side of the canal to Aabasa Lock, and there crossed, moving thence along the western side of the canal upon Belbeis. General Drury Lowe himself, with the Horse Artillery and 1st Brigade on the eastern side of the canal, was delayed throughout the earlier part of the day by the difficulty of getting the guns over the narrow bridges across some of the smaller canals. As a consequence General Wilkinson's force reached Belbeis some hours before the heavy brigade. He seized the place about noon on the 13th. Very little resistance of any kind had been met with, only a few stragglers at one or two points venturing to oppose the march. Captain Watson, R.E., who had accompanied General Wilkinson, on seizing the telegraph office, found messages passing from Arabi Pasha to the officer in command at Es-Salihiyeh ordering the Egyptians there stationed to be sent at once to Mansura by train. The object was undoubtedly to arrange for concentrating these troops with those from Damietta either by sending these to Damietta itself, or by bringing all the forces available round by Tanta and Benha upon Cairo. Arabi himself had only arrived at Inshas, the next station towards Cairo on the railway. Arabi's telegrams contained requests for information as to the movements of the English.

Thus the rapid pursuit of the cavalry had already disconcerted the attempt of the Egyptian Commander to gather fresh forces for action. Another important advantage was immediately gained by the opening of the lock sluices so as to send a fresh supply of water down to Tel el-Kebir. The Indian Cavalry Brigade halted at Belbeis for the day. Between 4 and 5 P.M. General Drury Lowe and Sir Baker Russell, with the 4th Dragoon Guards, arrived. The remainder of the heavy brigade and all the guns were still delayed by the heavy sand and the difficulties of the passage of the branch canals.

At 4·30 A.M. on the 14th September the advance was resumed. The column which thus started under the command of General

Drury Lowe consisted of the 2nd Bengal Cavalry, part of the 13th Bengal Cavalry, the 6th Bengal Cavalry, the 4th Dragoon Guards, and the Mounted Infantry. The cavalry moved now on firm desert, good marching ground, on the east of the canal. On the other side of the canal the inhabitants crowded down to the banks, and received with acclamations of pleasure a Proclamation previously prepared in Arabic, which was distributed to them. In it Sir Garnet informed them that the war was over, and that peace had recommenced in Egypt. The cries of " Aman ! Aman ! " (" Peace ! Peace ! ") resounded from the banks, and were repeated from village to village. As the cavalry advanced further they found that the news of the Proclamation had preceded them, and the inhabitants of all the villages came out to meet them with white flags, crying " Aman ! Aman ! "

At Es-Siriakus, in order to keep still in the desert, it was necessary to turn almost due east and bend round the stretch of marshy ground shown on the map. The advantages offered by the desert ground, both as to the facilities of march and in case of necessity for cavalry action, made it well worth while to make this détour. Hitherto a detachment had moved along the western side of the canal, both in order to retain complete command of both banks and in order more easily to establish communication with the people. From Es-Siriakus onwards, however, in order not to separate the force too widely, it became necessary to draw in this detachment, and the whole of the advanced body of the cavalry moved together.

The nearer the approach to Cairo the more demonstrative became the expressions of pleasure of the inhabitants. To the cries of " Aman ! " from the men was now added the appearance of the women on the house-tops raising the wedding song of joy, " Ez Zagharieh." Still, as nothing was known of the state of things in Cairo, General Lowe thought it prudent to halt his force whilst still some miles distant from the Abbassiyeh barracks, which on the eastern side form a kind of outpost to the capital. Thence he sent forward Lieutenant-Colonel Herbert Stewart, with a detachment of about fifty men, composed partly of the 4th Dragoon Guards, and partly of the Indian cavalry, with Captain Watson as Arabic interpreter, and two Egyptian officers, Dhulier Bey and Hussein Effendi, who had accompanied him throughout the march.

The little party as it approached the barracks saw before them large numbers of Egyptian troops. Soon, from among these, a squadron of cavalry advanced towards them, each trooper having a white flag attached to his carbine. It was 4·15 P.M. (14th September). Evidently the Egyptians intended to capitulate.

Everything depended upon not allowing the Egyptians to become aware of the smallness of the body of troops actually present. It was with this object that the cavalry were now and throughout the night kept in the desert, so that the fact of the arrival of forces was known to the Egyptian leaders and troops, but numbers could not be estimated by the Egyptians.

Colonel Herbert Stewart sent for the officer commanding at Abbassiyeh, and received his promise to surrender the barracks and assist in every way. He was ordered to send for the Governor of Cairo, the Chief of the Police, and the officer in charge of the Citadel. The English cavalry still remained about 2 miles outside. The Chief of the Police, on his arrival, reported that Arabi was in his house in Cairo. Colonel Stewart told the Prefect that Arabi must be given up, and the Citadel surrendered that night. The Prefect, begging that no English troops should enter that evening, lest it should create a disturbance, undertook to secure Arabi's surrender, while the Commandant of the Citadel promised to surrender it.

The negotiations having been concluded, General Lowe arranged, ostensibly as a concession to the wishes of the Prefect, that the cavalry should, with the exception of the force intended to occupy the Citadel, bivouac in the desert. The horses were watered at the barracks, where General Drury Lowe himself slept, a dozen men of the 4th Dragoons being placed there as a guard for the reception of Arabi as a prisoner.

At 8 P.M. Captain Watson, R.E., was dispatched to the Citadel in command of a party, consisting of two squadrons of the 4th Dragoon Guards (5 officers, 84 men), and a party of Mounted Infantry (4 officers, 54 men), under command of Captain Lawrence. Several Egyptian officers accompanied the party. Avoiding the city, the little party marched by the tombs of the Khalifs, round the east of Cairo, and entered the town close to the Citadel by the gate Bab el-Wezir.

The night was already exceedingly dark; the clouds of dust raised by the horses in passing over the rubbish-heaps which cover that part of the hill overlooking Cairo added to the obscurity, and the road was therefore not followed without difficulty; but at length, at about a quarter to 10, the 150 men, all told, defiled through the Bab el-Wezir into the narrow streets which lead to the Citadel. The inhabitants, many of whom were standing at the doors of their houses, regarded the troopers with a look of dull curiosity, without demonstration of any kind, and with no apparent surprise.

At the main gate the men were halted and closed up. Captain Watson rode on, and found that up to that time nothing had been done as to the actual evacuation of the Citadel, which was still held by the whole garrison, at least 5,000 strong. Captain Watson rode into the Citadel and arranged with the Governor, Ali Bey Yousif, that he should parade the garrison, and march them out. The Egyptians passed out by the Bab-el-Ayab gate, which opens into Cairo near the mosque of Sultan Hassan. An English officer and a few men were sent to this gate to see the Egyptians defile out, the whole arrangement being treated, as far as possible, as a simple relief of the Egyptian garrison by the English troops. The keys of the Citadel were handed over at once to Captain Watson. Regiment by regiment the Egyptians defiled past into Cairo, towards the Kasr en-Nil barrack, which had been assigned to them for the night, and there the following day they were quietly disarmed. For two hours and a-half, till long past midnight, the defiling of the Egyptians, under the flickering glare of lanterns, into the dark streets went on. As the last troops were leaving, the guards were quietly relieved by the little party of English soldiers. Captain Lawrence, of the Mounted Infantry, was left in charge of the Citadel for the night.

In the middle of the night a frightful noise arose in the Citadel. The prisoners, of whom there were some hundreds in the prisons, having heard that the soldiers were gone, had begun to break their chains and attempt to escape. They were not without some difficulty secured for the night, till their cases could be investigated.

In the course of the evening of 14th September 10,000 men, a mixed force of cavalry, artillery, and infantry, piled their arms in an assigned place in each barrack, and the men were allowed to return to their homes. By soon after daylight on the morning of the 15th the men were streaming out of the various barracks in all directions.

At about 10·45 P.M. on the evening of the 14th Arabi Pasha and Toulba Pasha came in and gave up their swords at Abbassiyeh.

To return to the Indian Contingent. On the 13th it had pushed on to Zagazig. Major-General Macpherson had been strengthened by the attachment to his Contingent of H | I Battery R.A. Starting from Tel el-Kebir at 7·40 A.M., the 6th Bengal Cavalry formed the advanced guard, the Seaforth Highlanders led the Infantry Brigade. At Aabasa, which was reached at 10 A.M., it was found that the sluices of the canal had been opened, and that the water was escaping from the canal. Villagers were collected, under the orders of Colonel Brown, R.E., and the sluice was closed. Colonel Moore, A.Q.M.G., had also collected some boats at Aabasa, and the column thus passed the canal, the Staff and cavalry fording it. The column marched again at 12·10 P.M. by the bank of the Wady Canal to the railway. At the point where the railway line was reached it was found better to move along the embankment. A most curious scene followed. The fugitives from Tel el-Kebir had been overtaken by the rapid march, and were streaming along the banks of the canal. Numbers of them still carried arms, but had evidently not the least notion of fighting. To have forced all of them to lay down their arms would have entailed a long delay, and it was all-important to reach Zagazig as early as possible. Major-General Macpherson therefore judged it better to push on with the head of the column as rapidly as possible, ignoring the armed fugitives. The result was that the two armed and hostile bodies, the one in orderly march, the other in disorderly flight, streamed on side by side, the one on the railway embankment, the other along the canal bank, both heading towards Zagazig. Many of the fugitives, as the Contingent passed them, were gradually disarmed by Colonel Moore, but the leading files continued nearly into Zagazig side by side with the armed Egyptians.

At 3·20 P.M. General Macpherson pushed on at a trot with a squadron of the 6th Cavalry, and reached Zagazig at 4·10 P.M. A running cavalry fight followed with the trains, in which fugitives were endeavouring to escape. The driver of the first train was shot by an officer of the Engineers (Lieutenant Burn-Murdoch). An engine leaving Zagazig in the confusion ran into a train coming from Benha, effectually blocking the line.

Ten engines and over 100 carriages were captured, so that it was possible at once to open up railway communication with Tel el-Kebir.

The telegraph station, as usual, proved one of the most valuable acquisitions. Messages containing all particulars of the enemy's efforts to gather force were seized. A telegram was at once sent to Cairo by General Macpherson, announcing the complete defeat of Arabi, and the fact that the British troops had occupied Zagazig. At the moment General Macpherson was in Zagazig with only twenty sabres. The telegrams seized at the office disclosed the fact that three trains of soldiers were at once to arrive from Es-Salihiyeh. In order to gain time a telegram was dispatched to the second station towards Es-Salihiyeh (Abu Kebir) in the name of the station-master at Zagazig, in which the station-master at Abu Kebir was warned of an imaginary obstruction on the line towards Zagazig, in consequence of which he was desired to detain the troops at Abu Kebir till the line was reported clear. Meantime, a train was sent back down the line to bring in the Seaforth Highlanders, and another train, with a gang of platelayers, was sent 3 miles out towards Abu-Kebir to remove a couple of rails.

By train or on foot the infantry reached Zagazig in the course of the night, having covered 30 miles and fought an action in sixteen hours and a-half.

At 9 P.M. (13th) General Macpherson received the following reply to his telegram :—

" From the Commission named by the Egyptian Nation at Cairo to the Commander-in-Chief of Her Britannic Majesty's Forces at Zagazig.

" The whole Egyptian Nation present their gratitude at the manner your Government have employed in supporting His Highness Tewfik Pasha, our Khedive ; therefore the Nation in general acknowledge your kindness, and beg, in the name of the Nation, to stop any further action on your part until you receive orders from His Highness the Khedive. The army having laid their submission to His Gracious Highness the Khedive, we are leaving immediately by train to lay before him the submission of the army, and beg the favour of any answer to us at Kafr ed-Dauar.

" Raouf Pasha.
" Ali Roubi Pasha.
" Boutrous Pasha."

Major-General Wilkinson, at 4 A.M. on the 14th September, left the force under General Drury Lowe to open communication with

Zagazig; but not being able to effect that purpose, he followed Major-General Lowe with two squadrons (one of the 6th Bengal Cavalry and one of the 13th Bengal Lancers), and not being aware that orders had been given for no troops to enter Cairo on the night of the 14th, passed on towards the " Rond Pont de Faghalla," and by 7 A.M. next morning (15th September) was in possession of the central railway station and telegraph office.

On the 14th September orders were issued for Lieutenant-General Willis to remain in command at Tel el-Kebir with the 2nd Brigade, the Duke of Cornwall's Light Infantry, the part of the 19th Hussars not employed on the line of communications or on escort, and two batteries of artillery.

Three battalions of the Highland Brigade which had marched on the afternoon of the 13th had, by morning of the 14th, reached Zagazig. The remaining Highland Battalion, the Black Watch, which had on the 13th been pushed on by train to Zagazig, reached Belbeis on the 14th. The Marine Artillery and Royal Marines followed the Highland Brigade. The remainder of the artillery moved by road at first on Zagazig, whither also marched the 3rd Battalion King's Royal Rifle Corps.

The general effect of these and the successive movements which followed, as the troops were gradually pushed up on Cairo, was to occupy in strength, and with the utmost possible rapidity, all the points by which any concentration of the dispersed fragments of the Egyptian army could be attempted.

On the afternoon of the 14th September, that is, as soon as the train service could be arranged, Sir Garnet Wolseley, having received by telegraph the reports from Zagazig, started by train for Kalyub the station immediately outside Cairo, with His Royal Highness the Duke of Connaught, and a company of the Scots Guards as escort. Another train containing the remainder of the Scots Guards followed as closely as the nature of the line would permit. The General's intention was to reach Cairo that night if possible. Obstructions on the line of railway delayed Sir Garnet's train for some hours of the night at Zagazig, but as soon as the train could be removed out of Zagazig the Head-quarters and the Guards escort were sent forward by it. Other trains with the remainder of the Guards Brigade followed as soon as they could be sent on.

At Benha, by early morning on the 15th, Colonel Herbert Stewart's account of the surrender of Cairo was received. At Benha, also, Jacoub Pasha came to make submission, and, a strong report in favour of his action of late in Cairo having been made by a deputation of loyal inhabitants, he and Omer Bey were dispatched to secure the surrender to Sir E. Wood of the forces at Kafr ed-Dauar.

By 9·45 A.M. (15th September) the train reached Cairo. Crowds of natives were at the station and in the streets. All received the troops with placid submission. The ordinary peaceful work of the town went on under the charge of the native police. It remained only to secure the surrender in detail of the various detachments of Egyptian troops, and to change the line of communications to Alexandria.

On the 16th news arrived that Rosetta and Abukir were ready to submit.

The war was over, but one striking scene remained to be enacted. It fell to the lot of Sir Archibald Alison.

The town of Tanta had throughout the insurrection, and during the trouble which preceded it, been the centre of fanaticism and of anti-Christian fury. It was necessary to occupy it if possible before any of the dispersed rebel forces reached it. On the 17th, Sir Archibald Alison and 500 of the Gordon Highlanders were dispatched in two trains to Tanta. Another train followed with two guns and the remainder of the battalion. When the first train, with 250 of the Highlanders, approached the station, everything at first seemed to indicate that all was going on in a peaceful way. The Governor, an adherent of Arabi's, with the principal inhabitants, met Sir Archibald at the railway station and assured him that the town was perfectly quiet. Sir Archibald, therefore, with his Staff and an escort of twelve men, went forward with the Governor in order to provide for the quiet entry of his men.

He passed through a narrow winding street which ended in a large open square. It was filled on all sides with armed Egyptian soldiers, hemmed in by a vast crowd of excited townspeople. The fact was that the Es-Salihiyeh force had already slipped round by the line of railway which passes by way of Abu Kebir, Mansura, and Tanta, and that Sir Archibald had struck upon the last portion of that force, consisting of no less than 4 batteries of artillery, 3 squadrons of cavalry, and 2,000 infantry. As soon as the interpreter began to speak to them it appeared that the greater part at least of the officers and men present knew nothing of the defeat of Arabi's forces, and knew only that they had been ordered round from Es-Salihiyeh for purposes of the campaign, which they supposed to be still going on. The moment was critical. The men were all in marching order, the horses saddled, the guns horsed. The General at once sent back Lieutenant Pilkington, his Aide-de-camp, to order up three companies of the Highlanders. Meantime, he sent for the leaders of the soldiers, and through his interpreter made a speech to those of the troopers and gunners who were within hearing. It was some time before the officers appeared. The sullen-looking soldiers and excited Arabs crowded on the twelve Highlanders, who endeavoured to keep a space clear round the General, his Staff, and the Governor of the town, whom they had carefully retained near them. As soon as the officers arrived, Sir Archibald told them that no harm would be done the soldiers if they at once laid down their arms, gave up their guns, and went quietly to their homes.

Whilst the General was still speaking the three companies of Highlanders moved into the square, making their way through the crowd "as if," says Major Hutton, who was present, "they had been in the habit of entering Egyptian towns under such circumstances throughout their lives. With very remarkable steadiness and precision each company in turn came up and took position, forming three sides of a square, with the General in the centre." Each company ordered arms and remained throughout as steady and unconcerned as if in an English barrack-square. The whole fixed bayonets and stood at ease. "It was like a scene on a stage, only to us it had a most satisfactory and reassuring effect, while it impressed the Arab crowd beyond measure."

Very quietly a company was so moved as to interpose between the gunners and their guns. Up to this time the artillery had been much the most hostile part of the Arab force. The crisis was now over. The whole of the troops in succession laid down their arms. Fortunately the remainder of the Es-Salihiyeh force had passed through Tanta towards Rosetta, which had already surrendered. Damietta still held out, and, though Abd el-Al, the Governor, promised surrender, he was apparently only endeavouring to gain time, so that if he had been reinforced by the troops from Es-Salihiyeh he might have given some trouble.

The surrender of Tanta made all further resistance hopeless, but it was necessary to dispatch Sir Evelyn Wood with two battalions and the Maltese Artillery to threaten Abd el-Al on the land side, whilst a portion of the fleet threatened to blockade Damietta on the sea front.

By the 24th September these measures had proved effective, and the last armed force and fortress in Egypt had been surrendered into our hands.

On the 25th September the Khedive made a triumphant entry into Cairo. The English troops lined the streets from the railway to the Palace, and salutes were fired from the Citadel. The local government was immediately placed under charge of the Egyptian authorities.

On the 28th September a serious disaster occurred. It had been a matter of principle that, as far as possible, all the ordinary routine of the country should be left under charge of the Egyptian authorities. For this reason, amongst other things, the railway management had been left in their hands, English officers having been placed at the chief railway stations only to provide for order in the dispatch of troops and military stores. At 3.30 P.M., as the King's Royal Rifles were disembarking at Cairo from Benha, an explosion occurred in a carriage adjoining the platform upon which the troops stood, injuring three or four men. The explosion was followed by others, the wood-work of the carriages was soon in flames, and as it became necessary to remove the troops from the station on account of the continued explosions of shells and gunpowder, the fire began rapidly to spread, and the explosions continually increased in violence.

Arrangements were at once made to place a cordon of troops round the burning station, and to pull down such portions of the building as, when cleared away, would break the course of the fire. But the water-engines were of a poor kind. The day had been one of exceptional and extreme heat under the influence of the Khamseen wind. The fatigues entailed upon the troops, who had to be employed night and day upon the reliefs at the station, were very severe, and the loss of stores of all kinds was most serious.

The explosion was entirely accidental; it was occasioned by shunting some wagons in which there was Egyptian ammunition and a considerable number of percussion shells, one of which must have exploded from the shock of the movement.

A considerable amount of fever, some dysentery, and some ophthalmia soon made their appearance among the troops. The barracks in Cairo had been found to be in a condition so filthy that their occupation was impossible, and the only convenient localities where it was possible to encamp the troops were the Island of Bulak—a dusty plain, presenting many discomforts for encampment—and the desert near Abbassiyeh.

On the 30th September a grand parade before the Khedive of all the troops took place. The army had for the purpose gradually been concentrated on Cairo. It was no mere question of show, and no mere holiday spectacle. It is hardly possible to imagine a sight more calculated to impress an Eastern population than the display of the various arms of the little force which had in so short a time disposed of the fate of Egypt. Not the least effective part of it was the march past of the Indian troops, representative of the many and various Eastern races who contribute to the might of Her Majesty's Empire. The cavalry and infantry from the Far East had, as they passed through the streets of the ancient city, a warlike and stately mien that could not fail to work upon the imagination of a people accustomed to worship power, and power only.

One other spectacle required the presence of English forces throughout the town.

A Sacred Carpet is annually dispatched to Mecca. The ceremony is a very important one in the eyes of the Mahometan world. It is attended by the Khedive in person, and conducted with a variety of ceremonies intended to add to the imposing effect of the demonstration. The whole town, and good numbers of people from the country, are present. To allow such a gathering to take place under conditions tending to produce religious fanaticism, and not to make it evident by the presence of English troops that violent disorder would be immediately repressed, would, under all the circumstances, have been the height of imprudence.

To place the English troops avowedly in any position of opposition to or suspicion of such a gathering would have been a dangerous incentive to disturbance.

The obvious and simple policy was to allow the English troops to attend as a matter of respect to the Khedive and to the faith of his people.

The 5th October was the day fixed for the ceremony. The sight presented by the streams of fanatical Mussulmans passing through the streets of Cairo, attended by the Giaour soldiers and the Indian Mahometan troops, alike wearing Her Majesty's uniform, was a striking and notable one. It only falls to the lot of this history to record the fact as a question of military policy, which it is, unfortunately, the more necessary to explain, because it was a transaction of a kind peculiarly liable to be misunderstood in England, and, in fact, led to considerable misconception.

This may be said to have been the final scene in Cairo prior to the actual dispersal of the army. On the 4th, the previous day, the General had issued a congratulatory order complimenting the troops alike upon their conduct in the campaign, and upon their behaviour as conquerors in Cairo.

Before closing this history, it will be convenient to put together a short summary of the principal dates, which will show the rapidity with which the whole campaign was completed.

On the 27th July, 1882, Her Majesty's Government having decided to send an expedition to Egypt, obtained a Vote of Credit of 2,300,000l.

On the 30th July the troops began to leave England, and troops were dispatched from England from then daily till the 11th August.

On the 15th August, at night, Sir Garnet in person reached Alexandria, a portion only of the expedition having arrived.

On the 20th August the Suez Canal, including Ismailia, was seized.

On the 13th September the Egyptian Army was defeated and dispersed at Tel el-Kebir.

On the 14th September Cairo Citadel and Arabi Pasha surrendered.

It had been decided that the force to be left in Egypt should be reduced to 10,000 men. After the Carpet ceremony the dispersal of the remainder in various directions proceeded rapidly.

On the 21st October Sir Garnet himself sailed from Alexandria, and on the 28th arrived in London.

The three Divisions had already been broken up. The Generals in command were on their way home.

The Indian Contingent had started for India.

Sir Archibald Alison remained in command in Cairo, and a new phase of the Egyptian question had opened.

The old one was closed.

LIST OF APPENDICES.

APPENDIX I.

STATEMENT of Troops conveyed to Egypt from the United Kingdom, and the Transports, &c., in which they proceeded.

Regiment or Corps.	Embarkation Port	Embarkation Date	Transport Name	Transport No.	Full Accommodation of Ship — Officers	Warrant Officers	Men	Horses	Embarked — Officers	Warrant Officers	Men	Horses	Date of Sailing	Arrived Alexandria
Head-quarter Staff and Regimental Staff, B.A.	Liverpool ...	Aug. 5	Capella ...	41	35	2	90	90	36	1	81	65	Aug. 5	Aug. 17
CAVALRY.														
General (in "Calabria") and 3 squadrons Household Cavalry	London (Albert Docks)	,, 1	Holland ...	4	20	1	300	240	14	...	252	239	,, 1	,, 14
	Ditto ...	,, 2	Calabria ...	3	16	...	250	220	18	...	214	219	,, 2	,, 15
	London (South-West India Docks)	,, 5	Egyptian Monarch .	22	15	...	300	266	15	...	290	264	,, 5	,, 17
7th Dragoon Guards ...	Southampton ...	,, 7	Italy	29	36	1	300	274	29	1	293	266	,, 7	,, 18
4th Dragoon Guards ...	Ditto ...	,, 9	Greece ...	16	25	1	250	242	18	1	226	242	,, 9	,, 21
	Ditto ...	,, 9	City of New York...	10	22	1	360	286	17	1	391	286	,, 9	,, 21
19th Hussars, 2 squadrons, 1st Division	Ditto ...	,, 10	Assyrian Monarch...	36	18	1	300	268	18	1	281	263	,, 10	,, 22
Ditto, ditto, 2nd Division ...	Ditto ...	,, 10	Montreal ...	18	13	1	300	270	13	1	305	268	,, 10	,, 22
Cavalry	...	...	... ...	...	165	6	2,360	2,066	142	3	2,252	2,047		
ARTILLERY.														
Royal Artillery, A	1 ...	Portsmouth ...	Aug. 3	Palmyra ...	14	10	...	200	153	10	...	197	153	,, 3	Aug. 14
Royal Horse Artillery, N	A ...	Southampton ...	,, 4	Tower Hill ...	7	16	...	180	176	14	...	178	173	,, 4	,, 16
Royal Artillery, D	1 ...	Portsmouth ...	,, 8	British Prince ...	46	23	...	350	153	13	...	310	150	,, 8	,, 19
Ditto, N	2 ...	Southampton ...	,, 9	Grecian ...	11	7	...	200	153	6	...	196	150	,, 8	,, 20
Royal Horse Artillery, G	B ...	London (Albert Docks)	,, 8	Ludgate Hill ...	26	16	...	180	176	9	...	177	175	,, 8	,, 21
Field Artillery, 1	2 ...	Ditto ...	,, 8	City of Lincoln ...	24	9	...	240	163	8	...	202	150	,, 9	,, 22
Ditto, C	3 ...	Southampton ...	,, 9	Olympus ...	23	10	...	170	127	6	...	170	125	,, 8	,, 22
Ditto, J	3 ...	Portsmouth ...	,, 10	Ascalon ...	35	7	...	170	127	6	...	170	125	,, 9	,, 22
Ammunition Reserve ...	Ditto ...	,, 11	Texas ...	25	13	2	220	220*	7	...	202	205	,, 10	,, 25
Artillery	...	...	... ...	...	111	2	1,910	1,448	79	...	1,802	1,406		

* Seventy being ponies or small mules.

Corps, &c.	Port of Embarkation	Date	Ship										Date (sailed)	Date (arrived)
INFANTRY.														
General and Staff, 1st Division; General and Staff, 1st Brigade; and Scots Guards	London (Albert Docks)	July 30	Orient	20	51	1	850	110	50	1	824	103	July 30	Aug. 10
2nd Battalion Coldstream Guards	Kingstown	Aug. 1	Iberia	21	50	…	780	55	45	…	767	55	Aug. 1	12
Ditto, Grenadier Guards	Queenstown	July 31	Batavia	15	30	1	770	55	29	…	761	55	July 31	12
General 2nd Division, 4th Brigade Staff, and 1st Battalion West Kent	Portsmouth	Aug. 3	Catalonia	33	51	1	920	107	43	1	824	100	Aug. 4	15
2nd Brigade Staff and 2nd Battalion York and Lancaster	Kingstown	Staff, Liverpool, Aug. 4; Kingstown, Aug. 8	Nevada	9	44	1	870	66	31	1	677	58	5	17
1st Battalion Royal Irish Fusiliers	Southampton	Aug. 8	Arab	40	3	1	770	6	32	1	729	4	8	19
General and Staff, 3rd Brigade, and 2nd Battalion Highland Light Infantry	Portsmouth	Aug. 8	France	28	3	1	800	66	30	2	774	59	8	20
1st Battalion Royal Highlanders	London (Albert Docks)	Aug. 8	Nepaul	42	30	1	780	55	31	1	772	55	8	20
Ditto Shropshire	Kingstown	Aug. 10	Lusitania	37	39	1	870	55	29	1	859	54	10	21
2nd Battalion Royal Irish Regiment, and 100 men of 2nd Bearer Company	Portsmouth	Aug. 11	City of Paris	19	39	1	864	6	36	1	812	3	11	21
Infantry	…	…	…	…	397	9	8,274	581	361	9	7,799*	546	…	…
ROYAL ENGINEERS AND VARIOUS.														
10th Company Commissariat and Transport, and detachment Army Hospital Corps and Ordnance Store	Portsmouth	July 27	Dacca (not a transport)	…	5	7	187	…	5	7	187	…	July 27	Aug. 10
2nd and 7th Companies Commissariat and Transport for Cyprus	Woolwich	Aug. 1	Courland	39	13	10	100	…	12	9	91	6	Aug. 2	15 ("Cyprus") Aug. 17
Bearer company, 1 field hospital, and 15th Company Commissariat and Transport	London (South-West India Docks)	Aug. 5	Pelican	8	7	…	210	210	7	…	180	204	5	18 (Port Said) Aug. 17
18th Company Royal Engineers, and 12th Company Commissariat and Transport	Ditto	Aug. 4	Viking	6	8	2	250	132	8	2	213	117	4	Aug. 17
Half bearer company and 2 field hospitals, 1st Division horses of Royal Irish Regiment ("City of Paris")	Portsmouth	Aug. 5	Marathon	43	13	2	200	147	13	1	211	54	6	Aug. 17
24th Company Royal Engineers and detachment 17th Company Commissariat and Transport, and horses of Royal Irish Fusiliers ("Arab")	Southampton	Aug. 8	Duke of Argyll	44	14	4	320	196	9	4	323	187	8	21

* Includes 100 men of 2nd Bearer Company.

Regiment or Corps.	Embarkation.		Transport.		Full Accommodation of Ship.				Embarked.				Date of Sailing.	Arrived Alexandria.
	Port.	Date.	Name.	No.	Officers.	Warrant Officers.	Men.	Horses.	Officers.	Warrant Officers.	Men.	Horses.		
26th Company Royal Engineers, 2nd Division	Southampton ...	Aug. 9	Californian ...	47	17	...	200	50	6	...	183	37	Aug. 9	Aug. 23
8th Company Royal Engineers and Railway Staff	London (Woolwich) ...	", 8	Canadian ...	17	7	6	108	7	6	6	108	7	", 9	", 23 (Port Said)
Pontoon Troop, Telegraph Troop, and Field Park	London (South-West India Docks)	", 9	Oxenholme ...	31	15	...	420	152	16	...	404	152	", 9	Aug. 26
Five field hospitals and staff of hospital ship	London (Albert Docks)	", 9	Carthage ...	32	30	5	220	...	30	2	211	...	", 10	", 21
Detachment 8th Company Commissariat and Transport and Signalling Company	Ditto ...	", 10	Caspian ...	12	22	3	162	92	5	3	133	92	", 11	", 22
17th Company Commissariat and Transport (Head-quarters) and detachment 12th and 15th Companies, and 42 men of 2nd Bearer Company	Portsmouth ...	", 11	Bolivar ...	34	17	6	300	98	6	3	300	98	", 11	", 25
Head-quarters 11th Company Commissariat and Transport	London (Albert Docks)	", 11	Prussian ...	13	8	...	156	106	9	1	162	103	", 12	", 25
Garrison Artillery (1st London and 1st Scottish)	Woolwich ...	", 14	Teviot* ...	38	20	1	250	...	11	1	285	3	", 15 (2 A.M.)	Sept. 5 (Port Said)
Head-quarters 8th and 12th Companies, and detachment 11th Company, Commissariat and Transport	London (Albert Docks) and Portsmouth	", 14	Lydian Monarch ...	57	18	1	300	268	10	5	310	268	Aug. 16	Aug. 27
Police, Mounted and Foot, and various	London (South-West India Docks)	Aug. 16 and 17	Adjutant† ...	60	8	2	350	104	8	4	279	95	", 17	", 30
Ordnance Store Department ...	Woolwich ...	Aug. 19	Irthington ...	45	1	2	100	...	2	2	40	...	", 19	Sept. 4
Royal Engineers, Commissariat and Transport, Army Hospital, and various	...	...	...	...	223	51	3,833	1,562	163	50	3,638‡	1,423		
Grand Total ...	...	...	...	...	931	70	10,467	5,747	781	63	15,572	5,487		

* Detained at Malta six days discharging and shipping stores.

† Includes 3 officers, 3 warrant officers, 143 men, and 6 horses for Malta.

‡ Exclusive of 100 men of 2nd Bearer Company included under infantry.

Note.—This statement represents the number of the Army Corps proceeding from the United Kingdom, and does not include drafts or depôts proceeding to the Mediterranean, in connection with the Army Corps.

BATTALIONS that embarked from Malta, Gibraltar, Cyprus, Aden, and Bombay for Egypt in 1882.

		Officers.	Warrant Officers.	N.C.O.'s and Men.
1st South Staffordshire ..	From Malta .. .. .. Arrived 17th July.	25	1	894*
3rd King's Royal Rifles ..	From Malta .. .. .. Arrived 18th July.	25	1	936*
2nd Duke of Cornwall's ..	From Gibraltar to Malta, and then on to Egypt. Arrived 24th July.	29	1	815*
1st Berkshire	From Malta .. .. .. Arrived 27th July.	28	1	871*
1st Gordon Highlanders ..	From Malta .. .. .. Arrived 7th August.	25	1	826*
1st Cameron Highlanders ..	From Gibraltar .. .. .. Arrived 18th August.	26	1	813*
2nd Manchester	From Malta .. .. .. Arrived 17th August.	22	1	731
2nd Derbyshire	From Gibraltar .. .. .. Arrived 21st August.	27	1	739
1st Sussex	From Cyprus, head-quarters, and 4 companies. Arrived 12th September.	12	2	353
	From Malta, 4 companies. Arrived July.	7	..	328
1st Seaforth Highlanders ..	From Aden .. .. .. Arrived 8th August.	24	2	601
1st Manchester Regiment ..	From Bombay .. .. .. Arrived 6th September.	24	2	648

* These numbers are taken from the Adjutant-General's printed Statement, 6th September, 1882.

THE EXPEDITION TO EGYPT.

Staff.

General Commanding-in-Chief ..	Lieutenant - General Sir Garnet Wolseley, G.C.B., G.C.M.G (with rank of General)
Military Secretary	Major L. V. Swaine, Rifle Brigade.
Private Secretary	Major J. FitzGeorge, 20th Hussars.
Aides-de-Camp	Captain Wardrop, 3rd Dragoon Guards. Lieutenant Childers, R.E. Lieutenant Creagh, R.A. Lieutenant Adye, R.A.
Naval Aide-de-Camp	Commander Rawson, R.N.
Chief of the Staff (second in command)	Lieutenant-General Sir John Adye, K.C.B. (with rank of General while employed).
Aides-de-Camp	Major the Hon. N. G. Lyttelton, Rifle Brigade. Lieutenant the Hon. F. W. Stopford, Grenadier Guards.
Deputy Adjutant-General ..	Colonel the Hon. J. C. Dormer, C.B.
Assistant Adjutant and Quartermaster-Generals	Lieutenant-Colonel F. W. Grenfell, K. O. R. Rifle Corps (60th). Lieutenant-Colonel W. F. Butler, C.B.
Deputy Assistant Adjutant and Quartermaster-Generals ..	Major J. F. Maurice, R.A. Major C. Grove, East Yorkshire Regiment (15th).
Officer Commanding Royal Artillery (Brigadier-General)	Colonel W. H. Goodenough, R.A.
Brigade Major	Major Yeatman Biggs, R.A.
Aide-de-Camp	Captain G. B. Martin, R.A.
Officer Commanding Royal Engineers (Brigadier-General)	Colonel C. B. Nugent, C.B., R.E.
Brigade Major	Major Fraser, R.E.
Aide-de-Camp	Captain T. Waller, R.E.
Commandant at Head-quarters (A.A. and A.Q M.G.)	Colonel the Hon. P. Methuen, Scots Guards.
Command of Base and Lines of Communication—	
Brigadier-General ..	Major-General Wm. Earle, C.S.I.
Aide-de-Camp	Lieutenant H. Earle, South Yorkshire Regiment.
Colonel on Staff	Colonel Sir W. O. Lanyon, K.C.M.G., C.B., 2nd West India Regiment.
Assistant Adjutant-General ..	Colonel R. Harrison, C.B., R.E.

Deputy Assistant Adjutant-General	Major H. G. MacGregor, half-pay.
Deputy Assistant Adjutant and Quartermaster-Generals ..	Major C. W. Murray, Gloucestershire Regiment. Brevet Major J. Alleyne, R.A. Major E. H. Sartorius, V.C., East Lancashire Regiment.
Provost - Marshal (A.A. and A.Q.M.G.)	Colonel H. G. Moore, V.C., Argyleshire and Sutherland Highlanders (83rd).
Senior Commissariat Officer ..	Commissary-General Sir E. Morris, C.B.
Senior Ordnance Store Officer ..	Assistant Commissary-General S. O. Rogers.
Principal Medical Officer ..	Deputy Surgeon-General (local Surgeon-General) Sir J. A. Hanbury, C.B.
Sanitary Officer, Brigade Surgeon (local Deputy Surgeon-General)	J. A. Marston.
Principal Veterinary Surgeon ..	Inspecting Veterinary Surgeon Meyrick.
Intelligence Department . ..	Colonel Buller.* Lieutenant-Colonel Tulloch. Major J. C. Ardagh, R.E. Captain W. J. Gill, R.E. Captain C. M. Watson, R.E. Captain C. R. Conder, R.E. Major A. FitzR. Hart, East Surrey Regiment (31st).
Specially employed	His Serene Highness the Duke of Teck. Lieutenant-Colonel H. H. Jones, R.E. Lieutenant-Colonel M. G. Gerard, Bengal Staff Corps.
Mounted Infantry	Captain H. H. Parr, C.M.G., Somerset Light Infantry (13th).
Attached to the Admiral Commanding-in-Chief	Lieutenant-Colonel Lord Wm. Seymour, Coldstream Guards.

CAVALRY DIVISION.

(As organized on arrival of Indian Brigade, by an Order dated the 27th August, 1882.)

Commanding	Major-General D. C. Drury Lowe, C.B.
Aides-de-Camp	Captain C. E. Swaine, 11th Hussars. Captain Lord St. Vincent, 16th Lancers.

---

* Arrived on the 5th September.

Divisional Staff.

Assistant Adjutant and Quarter-master-General	Lieutenant-Colonel H. Stewart, 3rd Dragoon Guards.
Deputy Assistant Adjutant and Quartermaster-General	Lieutenant-Colonel M. Gerard, Bengal Staff.
Assistant Provost-Marshal ..	
Senior Officer Commissariat and Transport	Assistant Commissary-General Dunn.
Senior Officer Ordnance Store Department	
Principal Veterinary Surgeon ..	
Chaplain	

1st Brigade.

Commanding	Brigadier - General Sir Baker C. Russell, K.C.M.G., C.B.
Orderly Officer	Lieutenant Hon. T. Ashburnham, 7th Hussars.
Brigade Major (Acting).. ..	Lieutenant-Colonel A. McCalmont, 7th Hussars.
Senior Officer, Commissariat and Transport Department	Deputy Assistant Commissary-General M. Graham.
Troops—1,590 men, 1,350 horses	3 squadrons Household Cavalry. 4th Dragoon Guards. 7th ,, ,, 17th Company Commissariat and Transport Corps. One ½ Bearer Company.

2nd Brigade.

Commanding	Brigadier-General H. C. Wilkinson, H.P., late 16th Lancers.
Orderly Officer	Lieutenant Rivett Carnac, 19th Bengal Lancers.
Brigade Major	Major S. D. Barrow, Bengal Staff Corps.
Senior Officer Commissariat and Transport	
Troops—1,497 men, 1,590 horses	13th Bengal Lancers. 2nd Bengal Cavalry. 6th ,, ,,

Divisional Troops.

N	A R.H.A.	Lieutenant - Colonel Borradaile, R.H.A.
Mounted Infantry	Captain Pigott, King's Royal Rifles.
Veterinary Department	
Commissariat and Transport (17th Company)	
Field Hospital	
Postal Department	

FIRST DIVISION.

Staff.

Lieutenant-General	Lieutenant-General G. H. S. Willis, C B.
Aides-de-Camp	{ Captain W. C. James, 2nd Dragoons. Lieutenant A. E. Codrington, Coldstream Guards.
Assistant Adjutant and Quartermaster-General	Colonel R. R. Gillespie.
Deputy Assistant Adjutant and Quartermaster-Generals	{ Major Hildyard, Highland Light Infantry (71st). Captain W. C. F. Molyneux, Cheshire Regiment (22nd).
Officer Commanding Royal Artillery	Lieutenant-Colonel Schreiber, R.A.
Adjutant	Captain F. N. Innes, R.A.
Officer Commanding Royal Engineers	Colonel J. M. C. Drake, R.E.
Adjutant	Captain Barker, R.E.
Senior Ordnance Store Officer ..	Deputy Assistant Commissary-General C. Campbell.
Senior Commissariat Officer ..	Deputy Assistant Commissary-General Saunders.
Principal Medical Officer ..	Deputy Surgeon-General Ekin.
Chaplain	Rev. R. Corbett.

1st Brigade.

Major-General	Major-General H.R.H. the Duke of Connaught and Strathearn, K.G., K.T., K.P., G.C.S.I., G.C.M.G.
Brigade Major	Captain Herbert, Grenadier Guards.
Aide-de-Camp	Major R. B. Lane, Rifle Brigade.

2nd Bn. Grenadier Guards .	Col. P. Smith.	Lt. & Adj. A. J. Acland-Hood.
2nd Bn. Coldstream Guards	Col. G. J. Wigram.	Lt. & Adj. Hon. A. H. Henniker-Major.
1st Bn. Scots Guards ..	Col. G. W. Knox.	Lt. & Adj. Hon. N. de C. Dalrymple.

2nd Brigade.

Major-General	Major-General G. Graham, V.C., C.B., R.E.
Brigade-Major	Captain R. C. Hare, Cheshire Regiment (22nd).
Aide-de-Camp	Brevet Major R. C. Hart, V.C., R.E.

2nd Bn. Royal Irish (18th) .	Col. C. F. Gregorie.	Lt. & Adj. G. H. Symonds.
1st Bn. West Kent (50th) ..	Lt.-Col. A. E. Fyler.	Capt. & Adj. M Wynyard.
2nd Bn. York and Lancaster (84th)	Lt.-Col. F. E. E. Wilson.	Capt. & Adj. W. J. Kirkpatrick.
1st Bn. Royal Irish Fusiliers (87th)	Col. J. N. Beasley.	Lt. and Adj. J. W. H. C. Cusack.

Divisional Troops.

19th Hussars (2 squadrons)	Lt.-Col. K. J. W. Coghill.	Lt. & Adj. J. C. K. Fox.
2nd Bn. Duke of Cornwall's L. I. (46th)	Lt.-Col. W. S. Richardson.	Lt. & Adj. G. A. Ashby.
A Battery, 1st Brig., R.A. .	Major P. T. H. Taylor.	
D Battery, 1st Brig., R.A. .	Major T. J. Jones.	
24th Company Royal Engineers	Captain C. de B. Carey.	
11th Company Commissariat and Transport		
½ Bearer Company		
2 Field Hospitals		
Postal Department.. ..		

SECOND DIVISION.

Staff.

Lieutenant-General	Lieutenant - General Sir Edward Hamley, K.C.M.G., C.B., R.A.
Aides-de-Camp ..	Captain the Hon. H. G. Gough, 14th Hussars. / Lieutenant J. Hanbury Williams, Oxford Light Infantry.
Assistant Adjutant and Quartermaster-General	Colonel P. A. A. Twynam.
Deputy Assistant Adjutant and Quartermaster-Generals	Major K. D. Murray, Royal Irish Fusiliers (89th). / Major E. J. Lugard, Royal Lancaster Regiment (4th).
Officer Commanding Royal Artillery	Lieutenant-Colonel F. C. Alton, R.A.
Adjutant	Lieutenant H. V. Cowan, R.A.
Officer Commanding Royal Engineers	Lieutenant-Colonel J. M. H. Maitland, R.E.
Adjutant	Captain A. O. Green, R.E.
Senior Ordnance Store Officer ..	Deputy Assistant Commissary-General Stevens.
Senior Commissariat Officer ..	
Principal Medical Officer ..	Brigade Surgeon Manby, V.C.

1st Brigade.

Major-General	Major-General Sir Archibald Alison, K.C.B.
Aide-de-Camp	Captain E. T. H. Hutton, King's Own Rifle Corps (60th).
Brigade Major	Major R. W. T. Gordon, Argyleshire and Sutherland Highlanders.

1st Bn. Royal Highlanders (42nd)	Col. D. Macpherson, C.B.	Lt. & Adj. E. Lee.
2nd Bn. Highland Light Infantry (74th)	Col. John Jago.	Capt. & Adj. C. W. Carey.
1st Bn. Gordon Highlanders (75th)	Lt.-Col. D. Hammil.	Lt. & Adj. H. H. Burney.
1st Bn. Cameron Highlanders (79th)	Lt.-Col. J. M. Leith.	Capt. & Adj. K. S. Baines.

117

2nd Brigade.

Major-General	Sir Evelyn Wood, V.C., G.C.M.G., K.C.B.
Aide-de-Camp	Captain Slade, R.A.
Brigade Major	Major Hitchcock, Shropshire Light Infantry.

1st Bn. Sussex Regiment (35th)	Col. S. Hackett.	Capt. H. L. Sapte.
1st Bn. Berksnire Regiment (49th)	Col. W. W. Corban.	Lt. F. B. R. Hemphill.
1st Bn. South Staffordshire Regiment (38th)	Lt.-Col. W. de W. R. Thackwell.	Lt. A. G. Chesney.
1st Bn. Shropshire Light Infantry (53rd)	Col. G. N. Fendall.	Capt. A. H. Murray.

Divisional Troops.

19th Hussars (2 squadrons)	Lt.-Col. K. J. W. Coghill.	Lt. C. R. R. McGrigor.
3rd Bn. King's Royal Rifle Corps (60th)	Lt.-Col. C. Ashburnham, C.B.	
I Battery, 2nd Brig., R A. .	Major W. Ward.	
N Battery, 2nd Brig., R.A..	Lt.-Col. W. G. Brancker.	
26th Company Royal Engineers	Major B. Blood.	
Veterinary Department ..		
12th Company Commissariat and Transport		
½ Bearer Company		
2 Field Hospitals		
Postal Department.. ..		

CORPS TROOPS.

Cavalry Brigade.

(As organized on leaving England; see p. 122 for subsequent organization.)

1st Life Guards (1 squad.) 2nd Life Guards (1 squad.) Royal Horse Guards (1 squad.)	Colonel H. P. Ewart.	Lt. G. Carter. Lt. J. D. Marshall. Lt. Hon. L. F. G. Byng.
4th Dragoon Guards ..	Lt.-Col. J. B. Shaw-Hellier.	Lt. R. L. M. Willoughby.
7th Dragoon Guards ..	Lt.-Col. C. Campbell.	Capt. U. G. C. de Burgh.
N Battery, A Brig., R.H.A.	Major G. W. Borradaile.	
15th Company Commissariat and Transport		
½ Bearer Company		
Postal Department.. ..		

Artillery Corps.

G Battery, B Brigade, Royal Horse Artillery ..	Lt.-Col. W. M. B. Walton.
C Battery, 3rd Brigade, Royal Artillery	Major E. R. Cottingham.
T „ „ „	Lt.-Col. A. A. Stewart.
Ammunition Reserve..	
F Battery, 1st Brigade	Major W. S. Helbert.

Siege Train.

4th Battery, London Division, Royal Artillery ..	Major G. A. Noyes.
5th ,, ,, ,, ..	Lt.-Col. W. H. Graham.
5th Battery, Scottish Division, Royal Artillery ..	Major G. B. Macdonnell.
6th ,, ,, ,, ..	Col. B. L. Forster.

INDIAN CONTINGENT.

Commanding	Major-General* Sir H. T. Macpherson, V.C., K.C.B., B.S.C.

Personal Staff.

Aide-de-Camp	Lieutenant F. C. E. Childers, R.A.
Orderly Officers	{ Lieutenant S. B. Beatson, 11th Bengal Lancers. Lieutenant E. L. S. Brett, Scots Guards

General Staff.

Assistant Adjutant-General ..	Major A. B. Morgan, Norfolk Regiment
Deputy Assistant Adjutant-General	Major A. C. Toker, Bengal Staff Corps
Assistant Quartermaster-General	Captain H. Melliss,† Bombay Staff Corps
Deputy Assistant Quarter-master-Generals	{ Captain E. R. Elles, R.A. Lieutenant E. G. Barrow, Bengal Staff Corps.
Assistant Quartermaster-General (for Intelligence)	Colonel H. Moore, C.B., C.I.E., Bombay Staff Corps.
Deputy Assistant Quarter-master-General (for Intelligence)	Lieutenant J. M. Grierson, R.A.

Deputy Judge Advocate ..	Major M. Clementi, Bengal Staff Corps.
Provost-Marshal	Major H. C. Marsh, Bengal Staff Corps.
Superintendent of Army Signalling	Lieutenant J. E. Dickie, R.E.
Principal Medical Officer ..	Deputy Surgeon-General C. Smith, M.D., Madras Medical Department.
Inspecting Veterinary Surgeon..	Veterinary Surgeon, J. Anderson, A.V.D.
Presbyterian Chaplain	Rev. J. Henderson, M.A.

---

* Local rank, 4th August, 1882, while commanding Indian Division.

† Major King-Harman, Bengal Staff Corps, was appointed Assistant Quartermaster-General, but by reason of illness was unable to take up his appointment.

Infantry Brigade.

Commanding	Brigadier-General* O. V. Tanner, C.B., Bombay Staff Corps.
Orderly Officer	Lieutenant S. D. Gordon, Bengal Staff Corps.
Brigade Major	Brevet-Major R. H. Murray, Seaforth Highlanders.
1st Battalion Seaforth Highlanders (Ross-shire Buffs; the Duke of Albany's)	Lieutenant-Colonel C. M. Stockwell, C.B.
7th Bengal Native Infantry ..	Brevet Colonel H. R. B. Worsley.
20th Bengal (Punjaub) Native Infantry	Brevet Colonel R. G. Rogers, C.B.
29th Company (2nd Belooch) Native Infantry	Lieutenant-Colonel G. Galloway.

Artillery.

Commanding Royal Artillery ..	Lieutenant-Colonel T. Van Straubenzee, R.A.
Adjutant Royal Artillery ..	Captain R. H. S. Baker, R.A.
H Battery, 1st Brigade, Royal Artillery	Major C.·Crosthwaite.
7th Battery, 1st Brigade, Northern Division, Royal Artillery (Mountain Battery)	Major J. F. Free.

Engineers.

Commanding Royal Engineer ..	Colonel J. Browne, C.S.I., R.E.
Field Engineer	Major W. G. Nicholson, R.E.
Assistant Field Engineers ..	Lieutenant G. Burn-Murdoch, R.E. Lieutenant W. D. Lindley, R.E. Lieutenant C. Darling, R.E. Lieutenant A. Speed, R.E. Lieutenant P. Baldwin, R.E.
A and I Companies Madras (Queen's Own) Sappers and Miners	Major Hamilton, R.E. (and Field Engineer).

Additional Infantry Battalion.

1st Battalion Manchester Regiment	Lieutenant-Colonel W. L. Auchinlech.

Reserve at Aden.

4th Madras Native Infantry ..	Colonel Hodding.
31st Madras Native (Light) Infantry	Lieutenant-Colonel R. Griffith, afterwards Colonel Stephens.

Military Accounts Department.

Controller of Military Accounts..	Major M. A. Rowlandson, Madras Staff Corps.
Field Paymaster	Lieutenant W. R. Le G. Anderson, Bombay Staff Corps.

---

* Local rank in Egypt, 4th August, 1882.

Ordnance Department.

Commissary of Ordnance   ..   Captain H. H. Pengree, R.A.

Commissariat Department.

Principal Commissariat Officer ..   Lieutenant-Colonel W. Luckhardt, Bombay Staff Corps.

Deputy Assistant Commissary-General   Captain L. W. Christopher, Bengal Staff Corps.

Sub-Assistant Commissary-Generals   .. ·   ..   ..   ..
{
Lieutenant - Colonel C. McInroy, Madras Staff Corps.
Major A. T. S. A. Rind, Bengal Staff Corps.
Major A. Clarke-Kennedy, Madras Staff Corps.
Captain B. L. P. Reilly, Bombay Staff Corps.
}

Commissariat Transport Department.

Director of Transport   ..   ..   Lieutenant-Colonel C. Hayter, Madras Staff Corps.

Transport Officers   ..   ..
{
Captain S. D. Turnbull, Bengal Staff Corps.
Lieutenant L. E. B. Booth, West Riding Regiment.
Lieutenant E. K. E. Spence, Bengal Staff Corps.
Lieutenant L. G. Clough-Taylor, Connaught Rangers.
}

Appendix III.

REDISTRIBUTION OF TROOPS (ON TRANSFER OF SIR E. HAMLEY'S FORCE TO ISMAILIA).

First Division.

First Brigade ..
- 2nd Grenadier Guards.
- 2nd Coldstream Guards.
- 1st Scots Guards.
- Naval Brigade.

Second Brigade ..
- 2nd Royal Irish.
- 1st Royal West Kent.
- Royal Marine Light Infantry.
- 2nd York and Lancaster.
- 1st Royal Irish Fusiliers.

Divisional Troops ..
- 19th Hussars (2 squadrons).
- 2nd Duke of Cornwall's Light Infantry.
- A-1 Royal Artillery.
- D-1 Royal Artillery.
- 24th Company, Royal Engineers.
- 12th Company, Commissariat and Transport.
- ½ No. 1 Bearer Company.
- No. 3 Field Hospital.

Second Division.

Third Brigade ..
- 1st Royal Highlanders.
- 1st Gordon   „
- 1st Cameron   „
- 2nd Highland Light Infantry.

Indian Contingent (attached) ..
- 7-1 (Mountain Battery).
- 1st Manchester.
- 1st Seaforth Highlanders.
- 7th Bengal Infantry.
- 20th Punjaub Infantry.
- 29th Beloochees.
- Medical Department, Ambulance, &c.
- Transport.
- Commissariat.
- R.E. Field Park.
- Ordnance Department.

Divisional Troops ..
- 19th Hussars (2 squadrons).
- 3rd King's Royal Rifles.
- I-2 Royal Artillery.
- N-2   „
- 26th Company, Royal Engineers.
- 11th Company, Commissariat and Transport.
- ½ No. 2 Bearer Company.
- Nos. 4 and 5 Field Hospitals.
- No. 2 Field Hospital (attached).

CAVALRY DIVISION.

First Brigade .. {
Houschold Cavalry (3 squadrons).
4th Dragoon Guards.
7th   „
17th Company, Commissariat and Transport (part of).
½ No. 1 Bearer Company.

Second Brigade .. {
2nd Bengal Cavalry.
6th   „
13th Bengal Lancers.

Divisional Troops .. {
N-A Royal Horse Artillery.
Mounted Infantry.
Detachment, R.E.
17th Company, Commissariat and Transport (part of).
No. 6 Field Hospital.

CORPS TROOPS.

Corps Artillery .. {
G-B Royal Horse Artillery.
H-1 Royal Artillery.
C-3   „
J-3   „
F-1   „   (Ammunition column).
Royal Marine Artillery.

Siege Train.. .. {
1st London.
5th Scottish.
6th   „

ORDNANCE STORE DEPARTMENT.

Corps Engineers .. {
"A" (Pontoon) Troop.
"C" (Telegraph) Troop.
Field Park.
8th, 17th, and 18th Companies.
Railway Staff.
Queen's Own Sappers and Miners (A and I Companies).

Commissariat and Transport (8, 15, and Auxiliary Companies).
½ No. 2 Bearer Company.
Nos. 1, 7, and 8 Field Hospitals.

Appendix IV.

ALPHABETICAL LIST OF OFFICERS ENGAGED.

Abdy, A. C. S., Lieutenant, 2nd Life Guards.
> Actions of Magfar and Mahsama: two actions at Kassassin; battle of Tel el-Kebir. Medal with clasp; bronze star.

Abercromby, G. C., Lieutenant, Scots Guards.
> Actions of Magfar, Tel el-Maskhuta, and battle of Tel el-Kebir. Medal with clasp; bronze star.

Acheson, Hon. E. A. B., Lieutenant-Colonel, Coldstream Guards.
> Action of Tel el-Maskhuta, and battle of Tel el-Kebir. Medal with clasp; bronze star.

Acland-Hood, A. F., Lieutenant, Grenadier Guards.
> Action of Tel el-Maskhuta; battle of Tel el-Kebir. Medal with clasp; bronze star; 5th class Medjidie.

Addison, C. J., Bombay Medical Staff.
> Medal; bronze star.

Adey, H., Surgeon, Indian Medical Service.
> Battle of Tel el-Kebir. Medal with clasp; bronze star.

Adye, J., Captain, Royal Artillery.
> A.D.C. to G.O.C. Actions of Magfar, Tel el-Maskhuta, Kassassin, 9th September, battle of Tel el-Kebir. Despatches "London Gazette," 2nd November, 1882. Medal with clasp; bronze star; 5th class Medjidie. Brevet of Major.

Adye, Sir J. M., General.
> Chief of Staff. Capture of Mahsama, and battle of Tel el-Kebir. Despatches "London Gazette," 8th September and 6th October, 1882. Thanked by Houses of Parliament. Grand Cross Medjidie; G.C.B.; medal with clasp; bronze star.

Agassiz, Rev. F. W. J. A.
> Promoted 3rd Class Chaplain. Medal with clasp; bronze star.

Alderson, E. A. H., Lieutenant, the Queen's Own Royal West Kent Regiment.
> Served with the Mounted Infantry at actions at Tel el-Maskhuta and Mahsama; both actions at Kassassin; battle of Tel el-Kebir; and occupation of Cairo. Medal with clasp; bronze star.

Alexander, James, Captain, 1st (King's) Dragoon Guards.
> Reconnaissance of 5th August, 1882. Mentioned in despatches. 4th class Osmanieh; medal and bronze star.

Alexander, R. H., Lieutenant, Royal Marines.
> Reconnaissance of 5th August, 1882. Medal; bronze star.

Alexander, W., Medical Staff.
> Medal; bronze star.

Alison, Sir A., Bart., Major-General.
> In command of troops at Alexandria, and at reconnaissance in force on the Mahmudiyeh Canal, and the 3rd Brigade 2nd Division at battle of Tel el-Kebir. Despatches "London Gazette," 29th July, 6th October, and 2nd November, 1882. Promoted Lieutenant-General for distinguished service. Thanked by Houses of Parliament. 2nd class Osmanieh; medal with clasp; bronze star.

CE-I

Allen, A., Captain, Royal Marines.
> Bombardment of forts of Alexandria. Brevet of Major. Medal with clasp; bronze star.

Allen, W. H., Surgeon, Medical Staff.
> Defence of Alexandria; occupation of Kafr ed-Dauar; surrender of Damietta. Medal; bronze star.

Alleyne, J., Brevet Lieutenant-Colonel, Royal Artillery.
> As D.A.A. and Q.M.G. of base, &c. Action at Tel el-Maskhuta and battle of Tel el-Kebir. Despatches "London Gazette," 2nd November, 1882. Brevet of Lieutenant-Colonel. 4th class Osmanieh. Medal with clasp; bronze star.

Allsopp, R., Captain, Royal Artillery.
> Battle of Tel el-Kebir. 4th class Medjidie; medal with clasp; bronze star.

Anderson, John, Veterinary Surgeon, 1st Class.
> Battle of Tel el-Kebir. Medal with clasp; bronze star.

Anderson, M., Veterinary Surgeon.
> Action of Kassassin; battle of Tel el-Kebir. Medal with clasp; bronze star.

Anderson, R., Surgeon, Medical Staff.
> Medal; bronze star.

Anderson, W. R. Le G., Lieutenant, Bombay Staff Corps.
> Medal; bronze star.

Anderson, W. S., Captain, King's Royal Rifle Corps.
> Reconnaissance at Ramleh; affair at Tel el-Maskhuta; action at Kassassin; battle of Tel el-Kebir. Medal with clasp; bronze star.

Andrews-Speed, H. S., Lieutenant, Royal Engineers.
> Battle of Tel el-Kebir. Medal with clasp; bronze star.

Anstruther, R. W., Lieutenant, Royal Engineers.
> Battle of Tel el-Kebir. Medal with clasp; bronze star.

Anthonisz, A. H., Surgeon, Medical Staff.
> Medal; bronze star.

Aplin, H. M., Deputy Assistant Commissary-General of Ordnance.
> Medal; bronze star.

Apthorp, D. R., Captain, 19th Hussars.
> Medal; bronze star.

Archer, F. W., Captain, King's Royal Rifle Corps.
> Reconnaissance at Ramleh; affair at Tel el-Maskhuta; action at Kassassin; and battle of Tel el-Kebir. Medal with clasp; bronze star.

Ardagh, J. C., Brevet Lieutenant-Colonel, Royal Engineers.
> Operations at Alexandria; battle of Tel el-Kebir. Despatches "London Gazette," 2nd November, 1882. Brevet of Lieutenant-Colonel. 4th class Osmanieh; medal with clasp; bronze star. See General Orders, 4th September, 1882.

Armstrong, F. H., Assistant Commissary-General.
> Medal; bronze star.

Armstrong, H. D., Captain, the Queen's Own Royal West Kent Regiment
> Medal; bronze star.

Armstrong, J. A., Major, Royal Engineers.
> Brevet of Lieutenant-Colonel.

Armstrong, O. R., Lieutenant, Seaforth Highlanders.
> Engagement of Shaluf; seizure of Suez Canal east of Ismailia; battle of Tel el-Kebir; occupation of Zagazig and of Cairo. Medal with clasp; bronze star.

Armstrong, T. H., Lieutenant, Northumberland Fusiliers.
At Alexandria and Ismailia. Medal; bronze star.
Arnold, F. A. M., Lieutenant, Queen's Own Royal West Kent Regiment.
Medal; bronze star.
Arrowsmith, C. H. M., Lieutenant, Queen's Own Royal West Kent Regiment.
Medal; bronze star.
Arthur, Rev. D.
Battle of Tel el-Kebir; mentioned in despatches. Medal with clasp; bronze star.
Arthur, Sir G. C. A., Bart., Lieutenant, 2nd Life Guards.
Action at Kassassin; battle of Tel el-Kebir. Medal with clasp; bronze star.
Ash, R. V., Surgeon-Major, Medical Staff.
Battle of Tel el-Kebir. Medal with clasp : bronze star.
Ashburnham, C., Colonel (Half-pay).
Reconnaissance of 5th August; affair at Tel el-Maskhuta; action at Kassassin; and commanded a brigade at battle of Tel el-Kebir. Despatches "London Gazette," 6th October and 2nd November, 1882. Medal with clasp. A D.C. to the Queen. 3rd class Medjidie; bronze star; K.C.B.
Ashburnham, Hon. T., Lieutenant, 7th (Queen's Own) Hussars.
Capture of Mahsama; actions at Kassassin and battle of Tel el-Kebir. 5th class Medjidie; medal with clasp; bronze star. See General Orders, 7th September, 1882.
Ashby, G. A., Lieutenant, Duke of Cornwall's Light Infantry.
Actions at Magfar and Tel el-Maskhuta; both actions at Kassassin; battle of Tel el-Kebir. Despatches "London Gazette," 19th September, 1882. 5th class Medjidie; medal with clasp; bronze star.
Aspinwall, J. H., Lieutenant, 7th Dragoon Guards.
Actions of Magfar, Mahsama, and Kassassin; battle of Tel el-Kebir; and forced march to Cairo. Medal with clasp; bronze star.
Atherton, W. H., Captain, 5th Dragoon Guards.
Battle of Tel el-Kebir. Medal with clasp; bronze star.
Atkinson, F. G., Lieutenant, Bengal Staff Corps.
Battle of Tel el-Kebir. Medal with clasp; bronze star.
Auchinleck, W. L.
Commanded 1st Battalion Manchester Regiment. Medal; bronze star.
Austen, A. R., Lieutenant, King's Shropshire Light Infantry.
Defence of Alexandria; occupation of Kafr ed-Dauar; surrender of Damietta. Medal; bronze star.
Aylmer, E. K. G., Lieutenant, 19th Hussars.
Battle of Tel el-Kebir. Medal with clasp; bronze star.
Aylmer, J. A., Captain, 4th (Royal Irish) Dragoon Guards.
Actions at Magfar and Tel el-Maskhuta; capture of Mahsama; first action at Kassassin; battle of Tel el-Kebir; subsequent pursuit to Belbeis; surrender and occupation of Cairo. Medal with clasp; bronze star.

Baird, D., Lieutenant, York and Lancaster Regiment.
Battle of Tel el-Kebir. Medal with clasp; bronze star.
Baker, A. A., Deputy Assistant Commissary-General.
Battle of Tel el-Kebir. Medal with clasp; bronze star.

Baker, F. B., Surgeon-Major.
> Battle of Tel el-Kebir. 3rd class Medjidie; medal with clasp; bronze star.

Boker, G. C. B., Lieutenant, King's Royal Rifle Corps.
> Action at Kassassin, and battle of Tel el-Kebir. Medal with clasp; bronze star.

Baker, J. V. V., Captain, Royal Artillery.
> Battle of Tel el-Kebir. Medal with clasp; bronze star.

Baker, R. H. S., Captain, Royal Horse Artillery.
> Battle of Tel el-Kebir. Despatches "London Gazette," 17th November, 1882. 4th class Medjidie; medal with clasp; bronze star.

Baldwin, F., Captain, Royal Marine Light Infantry.
> 4th class Medjidie.

Baldwin, P. B., Lieutenant, Royal Engineers.
> Battle of Tel el-Kebir. Medal with clasp; bronze star.

Balfour, C. B., Lieutenant, Scots Guards.
> Actions of Magfar, Tel el-Maskhuta, and battle of Tel el-Kebir. Medal with clasp; bronze star.

Balfour, J. H., Lieutenant, Bengal Staff Corps.
> Action of Kassassin; battle of Tel el-Kebir. Medal with clasp; bronze star.

Balfour, R. F., Major and Lieutenant-Colonel, Grenadier Guards.
> Died of wounds received in action at Tel el-Kebir.

Banks, J. H., Captain, 7th Dragoon Guards.
> Actions of Mahsama and Kassassin. Medal; bronze star; 4th class Medjidie.

Barclay, D. E. D., Lieutenant, 19th Hussars.
> Battle of Tel el-Kebir. Wounded. Medal with clasp; bronze star.

Barker, G., Captain, Royal Engineers.
> Action at Tel el-Maskhuta and at Kassassin, 9th September; and battle of Tel el-Kebir. Despatches "London Gazette," 2nd November, 1882; brevet of Major. 4th class Medjidie. Medal with clasp; bronze star.

Barlow, M. J., Captain, Royal Artillery.
> Battle of Tel el-Kebir. Medal with clasp; bronze star.

Barnard, H. C., Lieutenant, Royal Irish Fusiliers.
> Battle of Tel el-Kebir. Medal with clasp; bronze star.

Barnard, W. O., Lieutenant-Colonel, Manchester Regiment.
> Commanded 2nd Battalion Manchester Regiment; and commanded troops in charge of Ras et-Tin, after the bombardment of Alexandria. Medal; bronze star; 3rd class Medjidie.

Barnett, O., Brigade Surgeon.
> Despatches "London Gazette," 2nd November, 1882. Medal; bronze star; 3rd class Medjidie.

Barnwell, T., Surgeon-Major.
> Medal; bronze star.

Barrell, W. J., Quartermaster, Commissariat and Transport Staff.
> Granted honorary rank of Captain. Medal; bronze star.

Barrett, A. L., Lieutenant, Bengal Staff Corps.
> Battle of Tel el-Kebir. Medal with clasp; bronze star.

Barrett, L., Lieutenant, Royal Artillery.
> Medal; bronze star.

Barron-Stanton, W., Captain, Gordon Highlanders.
> Battle of Tel el-Kebir. Medal with clasp; bronze star.

Barrow, C. T., Captain, Scottish Rifles.
 Commanding Auxiliary Transport. Medal; bronze star. See
 General Orders, 11th September, 1882.
Barrow, E. G., Lieutenant, Bengal Staff Corps.
 As Deputy Assistant Quartermaster-General to the Indian Contin-
 gent. Battle of Tel el-Kebir. Medal with clasp; 5th class of
 Medjidie ; bronze star.
Barrow, F. E., Surgeon.
 Medal; bronze star.
Barrow, S. D., Major, Bengal Staff Corps.
 As Brigade Major 2nd Cavalry Brigade, Indian Contingent. Battle
 of Tel el-Kebir. Despatches "London Gazette," 2nd November,
 1882. Brevet of Lieutenant-Colonel. 4th class Osmanieh.
Barry, W. S. J., Lieutenant, Royal Irish Fusiliers.
 Medal ; bronze star.
Bartleman, John, Lieutenant-Colonel, Bengal Staff Corps.
 Battle of Tel el-Kebir. Medal with clasp ; bronze star.
Barttelot, E. M., Lieutenant, 2nd Battalion Royal Fusiliers.
 Served with the Mounted Infantry, battle of Tel el-Kebir. Medal
 with clasp ; bronze star.
Barton, F. A., Lieutenant, 7th Dragoon Guards.
 Actions of Mahsama and Kassassin. Medal; bronze star.
Barton, G., Major, Royal Fusiliers.
 As D.A.A. and Q.M.G. Commanded Foot Police ; action at Kas-
 sassin ; and battle of Tel el-Kebir. Despatches "London Gazette,"
 2nd November, 1882. Brevet of Lieutenant-Colonel. 4th class
 Osmanieh ; medal with clasp ; bronze star. See General Orders,
 13th September, 1882 ; ditto, 16th September, 1882.
Bateman, H. W., Paymaster (Captain).
 Medal; bronze star.
Bateman Hanbury, Hon. W. S., Lieutenant, 2nd Life Guards.
 Actions of Magfar, Mahsama, and Kassassin ; battle of Tel el-Kebir.
 Medal with clasp ; bronze star.
Bathurst, A. C. H., Lieutenant, Royal Sussex Regiment.
 Defence of Alexandria ; surrender of Kafr ed-Dauar ; occupation
 of Damanhur ; and surrender of Damietta. Medal and bronze
 star.
Battersby, F., Quartermaster, Commissariat and Transport Staff.
 Battle of Tel el-Kebir. Granted honorary rank of Captain. Medal
 with clasp ;. bronze star.
Battersby, J., Surgeon (Captain).
 Battle of Tel el-Kebir. Medal with clasp ; bronze star.
Bayly, R. K., Major, Royal Highlanders.
 Battle of Tel el-Kebir. Medal with clasp ; bronze star ; 4th class
 Osmanieh.
Bayley, W. H., Major, Royal West Kent Regiment.
 Medal ; bronze star.
Baynes, D. L., Captain, Gordon Highlanders.
 Defence of Alexandria.
Baynes, K. S., Captain, Queen's Own Cameron Highlanders.
 Battle of Tel el-Kebir. Medal with clasp ; bronze star.
Beal, H., Major, South Staffordshire.
 Medal and bronze star.
Bean, A. W., Lieutenant, Berkshire Regiment.
 Surrender of Kafr ed-Dauar. Medal ; bronze star.

Beath, J. H., Surgeon-Major (Lieutenant-Colonel).
 Despatches "London Gazette," 17th November, 1882.   Medal;
  bronze star ; 3rd class Medjidie ; C.B.
Beatson, S. B., Lieutenant, Bengal Staff Corps.
 Medal; bronze star.
Beattie, J. F., Surgeon-Major.
 Battle of Tel el-Kebir.   Medal with clasp ; bronze star.
Beatty, J. W., Surgeon.
 Battle of Tel el-Kebir.   Medal with clasp ; bronze star.
Beaumont, D., Staff Paymaster, Grenadier Guards.
 Medal ; bronze star.
Beaumont, F. M., Lieutenant, King's Royal Rifle Corps.
 Reconnaissance at Ramleh ; affair at Tel el-Maskhuta ; action at
  Kassassin ; and battle of Tel el-Kebir.   Medal with clasp ; bronze
  star.
Becher, C. L., Captain, 7th Dragoon Guards.
 Actions of Magfar, Mahsama, and Kassassin ; battle of Tel el-
  Kebir, and forced march to Cairo.   Medal with clasp ; bronze
  star.
Becher, E. F., Captain, Royal Artillery.
 Medal; bronze star.
Beckett, C. E., Captain, 3rd Hussars.
 Commanded Mounted Police.   Action at Kassassin, 9th September,
  and battle of Tel el-Kebir.   Despatches "London Gazette," 2nd
  November, 1882.   Medal with clasp ; bronze star.   Brevet of
  Major.   4th class Medjidie.
Beech, J. R., Lieutenant, Veterinary Surgeon.
 Action at Kassassin, and battle of Tel el-Kebir.   Medal with clasp ;
  bronze star.
Bell, W., Paymaster (Hon. Captain), Army Pay Department.
 Medal ; bronze star.
Bellord, Rev. J. (Captain).
 Battle of Tel el-Kebir.   Slightly wounded.   Promoted 3rd Class
  Chaplain.   Medal with clasp ; bronze star.
Bennett, E. E., Veterinary Surgeon (Lieutenant).
 Actions of Tel el-Maskhuta and Kassassin ; battle of Tel el-Kebir.
  Medal with clasp ; bronze star.
Bennett, F. W., Lieutenant, Royal Engineers.
 Medal and bronze star.
Bent, W. H. M., Lieutenant, South Staffordshire Regiment.
 Reconnaissance of 5th August.   Medal and bronze star.
Beresford, H. de la P., Captain, Royal Marine Artillery.
 Medal ; bronze star.
Bernard, J., Lieutenant, Royal Marine Light Infantry.
 Actions at Mallaha Junction, Tel el-Maskhuta, Mahsama, both
  actions at Kassassin, and battle of Tel el-Kebir.   Medal with
  clasp ; bronze star.
Bertram, W., Lieutenant, Manchester Regiment.
 Medal ; bronze star.
Bevan, E. B. L., Captain, West Kent Regiment.
 Medal.
Bevan, R. B.
 Battle of Tel el-Kebir.   Medal with clasp ; bronze star.
Beville, H. E. W., Lieutenant, Bombay Staff Corps.
 Battle of Tel el-Kebir.   Medal with clasp ; bronze star.

Bibby, A., Major, 7th Dragoon Guards.
  Actions of Magfar and Mahsama. Severely wounded; horse shot.
  Mentioned in despatches. Brevet of Lieutenant-Colonel; medal;
  bronze star.
Bigg, G. K. S., Surgeon.
  Medal; bronze star.
Billings, M., now Quartermaster, 1st Staffordshire Regiment.
  Medal; bronze star.
Binning, G. Lord, Lieutenant, Royal Horse Guards Blue.
  Battle of Tel el-Kebir. Medal with clasp; bronze star.
Birch, H. G., Lieutenant, Royal Artillery.
  Medal; bronze star.
Bishop, C. L. N., Lieutenant, Royal Marines.
  Medal; bronze star.
Blackburn, A. G., Lieutenant, Cameron Highlanders.
  Battle of Tel el-Kebir. Severely wounded. Medal with clasp
  bronze star; 5th class Medjidie.
Blackburn, J. E., Lieutenant, Royal Engineers.
  Battle of Tel el-Kebir. Medal with clasp; bronze star.
Blagrove, H. J., Lieutenant, 13th Hussars.
  Attached to 19th Hussars, and served as Orderly Officer to Briga-
  dier-General, 1st Cavalry Brigade. Action at Kassassin on 9th
  September; and battle of Tel el-Kebir. March to, and occupation
  of, Cairo. Medal with clasp; bronze star.
Blakeney, W. E. A., Lieutenant, Shropshire Light Infantry.
  Defence of Alexandria; occupation of Kafr ed-Dauar; surrender of
  Damietta. Medal; bronze star.
Blaxland, A. H., Captain, Royal Marines.
  Reconnaissance of 5th August, 1882; action of Kassassin; battle of
  Tel el-Kebir. Medal with clasp; bronze star.
Blood, B., Major, Royal Engineers.
  Battle of Tel el-Kebir. Despatches "London Gazette," 2nd
  November, 1882. Brevet of Lieutenant-Colonel. 4th class
  Osmanieh. Medal with clasp; bronze star.
Blood, W. P., Lieutenant, Royal Irish Fusiliers.
  Battle of Tel el-Kebir. Medal with clasp; bronze star.
Bond, F. G., Lieutenant, Royal Engineers.
  Actions at Kassassin 8th and 9th September; and battle of Tel el-
  Kebir. March to, and occupation of, Cairo. Medal with clasp;
  bronze star.
Bond, R. J., Major, Royal Engineers.
  Battle of Tel el-Kebir. Despatches "London Gazette," 2nd
  November, 1882. Brevet of Lieutenant-Colonel. 3rd class
  Medjidie; medal with clasp; bronze star.
Booth, L. E. B., Lieutenant, 1st Battalion Duke of Wellington's
  Regiment.
  Battle of Tel el-Kebir. Medal with clasp; bronze star.
Booth, T. G., Paymaster (H. Captain).
  Medal; bronze star.
Borradaile, G. W., Major, Royal Horse Artillery.
  Battle of Tel el-Kebir. Despatches "London Gazette," 2nd
  November, 1882. Medal with clasp; bronze star. 3rd class
  Medjidie; C.B.
Boscawen, Hon. E. E. T., Captain, Coldstream Guards.
  Action of Tel el-Maskhuta and battle of Tel el-Kebir. 4th class
  Osmanieh; medal with clasp; bronze star.

Boulger, A., Quartermaster, York and Lancaster Regiment.
Battle of Tel el-Kebir. Medal with clasp; bronze star. Granted
honorary rank of Major.

Bourchier, H. S., Major, Royal Marines.
Operations at El-Meks; occupation of Port Saïd and surrender of
Fort Gemil. 4th class Osmanieh. Medal; bronze star.

Bourns, D. C. G., Surgeon-Major (Major).
Battle of Tel el-Kebir. Medal with clasp; bronze star.

Bowen, C. E. H., Lieutenant, Scots Guards.
Action at Tel el-Maskhuta and battle of Tel el-Kebir. Medal with
clasp; bronze star.

Bower, R. L., Lieutenant, King's Royal Rifle Corps.
Reconnaissance at Ramleh; affair at Tel el-Maskhuta; action at
Kassassin; battle of Tel el-Kebir. Medal with clasp; bronze star.

Bowles, A. M., Major, Derbyshire Regiment.
Medal; bronze star.

Bowman, H., now Lieutenant, Coast Brigade, Royal Artillery.
Battle of Tel el-Kekir.✦ Despatches "London Gazette," 2nd
November, 1882. Medal with clasp; bronze star.

Bowman, H. J., Lieutenant, Derbyshire Regiment.
Medal; bronze star.

Boyd, T., Surgeon (Captain).
Battle of Tel el-Kebir. Medal with clasp; bronze star.

Boyes, J. E., Major, Gordon Highlanders.
Battle of Tel el-Kebir. Despatches "London Gazette," 2nd
November, 1882. Brevet of Lieutenant-Colonel. 4th class
Osmanieh. Medal with clasp; bronze star.

Boyle, G. V., Lieutenant, Coldstream Guards.
Action of Tel el-Maskhuta and battle of Tel el-Kebir. Medal with
clasp; bronze star.

Boyle, M. C., Captain, King's Royal Rifle Corps.
Mentioned in despatches.

Bradford-Atkinson, T. H. H., Lieutenant, Grenadier Guards.
Action of Tel el-Maskhuta; battle of Tel el-Kebir. Medal with
clasp; bronze star.

Braithwaite, Captain, 13th Hussars.
Battle of Tel el-Kebir. Medal with clasp; bronze star. See
General Orders, 13th September, 1882.

Brancker, W. G., Major, Royal Artillery.
Despatches "London Gazette," 2nd November, 1882. 3rd class
Medjidie; C.B.

Bridge, C. H., Deputy Assistant Commissary General (Captain).
Medal; bronze star.

Bridge, W. C., Lieutenant, South Staffordshire Regiment.
Medal and bronze star.

Bridges, E. S., Major, Grenadier Guards.
Despatches "London Gazette," 2nd November, 1882. 4th class
Osmanieh; medal; bronze star.

Briggs, W., Major (Honorary). (Staff Paymaster.)
Medal; bronze star.

Brindle, Rev. R. (Captain).
Medal; bronze star.

Broackes, C., Quartermaster.
Provost-Marshal at Base. Medal; bronze star.

Broadwood, F., Lieutenant, South Staffordshire Regiment.
Medal and bronze star.

Brock-Hollinshead, L., Lieutenant, Royal West Kent Regiment.
Medal; bronze star.
Brocklehurst, J. F., Captain, Royal Horse Guards Blue.
Battle of Tel el-Kebir. Medal with clasp; bronze star.
Bromhead, E. R., Major, York and Lancaster Regiment.
'Battle of Tel el-Kebir. Medal with clasp; bronze star. 4th class Osmanieh.
Brooke-Hunt, R. H., Captain, Seaforth Highlanders.
Seizure of Suez Canal east of Ismailia; battle of Tel el-Kebir; occupation of Zagazig and of Cairo. Medal with clasp; bronze star.
Brooks, A., Conductor of Supplies.
Battle of Tel el-Kebir. Medal with clasp; bronze star. Promoted to Quartermaster, Commissariat and Transport Staff.
Brooks, H. G., Lieutenant, Gordon Highlanders.
Killed in action at Tel el-Kebir.
Broome, G. S., Lieutenant, Shropshire Light Infantry.
Defence of Alexandria, occupation of Kafr ed-Dauar, and surrender of Damietta. Medal; bronze star.
Broome, W. A., Captain, Bombay Staff Corps.
Battle of Tel el-Kebir, forced march on, and seizure of, Zagazig, and occupation of Cairo. Medal with clasp; bronze star.
Browell, E. T., Captain, Royal Artillery.
Medal; bronze star.
Browne, G. J. D., now Lieutenant, 1st Leinster Regiment.
Battle of Tel el-Kebir. Wounded. Medal with clasp; bronze star.
Browne, James, Colonel, Royal Engineers.
Commanded Royal Engineers, Indian Contingent. Battle of Tel el-Kebir. Despatches "London Gazette," 17th November, 1882. 3rd class Osmanieh; C.B. Medal with clasp; bronze star.
Browne, J. W., Riding Master.
Medal; bronze star.
Browne, W. B., Captain, Duke of Cornwall's Light Infantry.
Actions of Magfar, Tel el-Maskhuta, both actions at Kassassin, and battle of Tel el-Kebir. Mentioned in despatches. Medal with clasp; bronze star. Brevet of Major.
Bryant, G. F., Major, Bombay Staff Corps.
4th class Osmanieh.
Buchanan-Riddel, H. E., Lieutenant, King's Royal Rifle Corps.
Reconnaissance at Ramleh; affair at Tel el-Maskhuta; action at Kassassin; and battle of Tel el-Kebir. Medal with clasp; bronze star.
Buller, Sir R. H., Colonel.
As D.A. and Q.M.G., Intelligence Department. Battle of Tel el-Kebir. Despatches "London Gazette," 2nd November, 1882. 3rd class Osmanieh; K.C.M.G. Medal with clasp; bronze star. See General Orders, 2nd September, 1882; ditto, 11th September, 1882.
Burke, J. L., now Quartermaster, Military Police.
Medal; bronze star.
Burke, M. A., Captain, 7th Dragoon Guards.
Actions of Magfar, Mahsama, and Kassassin; battle of Tel el-Kebir, and forced march to Cairo. Medal with clasp; bronze star.
Burke, R. W., Lieutenant, Veterinary Department.
Medal; bronze star.

Burke, T. E., Lieutenant, Royal Lancaster Regiment.
   Battle of Tel el-Kebir. Medal with clasp ; bronze star.
Burney, E., Lieutenant, Berkshire Regiment.
   Surrender of Kafr ed-Dauar. Medal ; bronze star.
Burney, H. H., Lieutenant, Gordon Highlanders.
   Battle of Tel el-Kebir. Medal with clasp ; bronze star ; 5th class
   Medjidie.
Burney, P. de S., Lieutenant, Royal Artillery.
   Surrender of Kafr ed-Dauar. Medal ; bronze star.
Burn-Murdoch, J., Lieutenant, Royal Engineers.
   Battle of Tel el-Kebir. Despatches "London Gazette," 17th No-
   vember, 1882. 5th class Medjidie ; medal with clasp ; bronze star.
Burr, C. E. G., Captain, Royal Irish Regiment.
   Battle of Tel el-Kebir. Medal with clasp ; bronze star.
Burrell, E., Captain, Shropshire Light Infantry.
   Battle of Tel el-Kebir. Medal with clasp ; bronze star.
Burrowes, A. L. S., Captain, Royal Marine Artillery.
   Reconnaissance of 5th August, 1882 ; actions of Kassassin ; battle
   of Tel el-Kebir. Medal with clasp ; bronze star.
Burrowes, A. St. L., Captain, Royal Marines.
   Actions of Tel el-Maskhuta and Kassassin ; battle of Tel el-Kebir.
   Medal with clasp ; bronze star.
Burt, W., Veterinary Surgeon (Captain).
   Mentioned in despatches. Medal ; bronze star.
Burtenshaw, J., now Quartermaster, Royal Marine Light Infantry.
   Actions of Mallaha, Tel el-Maskhuta, Kassassin, and battle of Tel el-
   Kebir. Medal with clasp ; bronze star.
Burton, E. B., Lieutenant, West Riding Regiment.
   Battle of Tel el-Kebir. Medal with clasp ; bronze star
Burton, E. M., Lieutenant, Royal Engineers.
   Employed on special service under the Admiralty in connection with
   the murder of Professor Palmer and his party. Medal and bronze
   star ; 5th class Medjidie.
Buscarlet, J. R. B., Major, Royal Sussex.
   Medal and bronze star.
Butler, W. F., Lieutenant-Colonel (Half-pay).
   As A.A.G., Head-quarters. Actions of Magfar, Tel el-Maskhuta ;
   Kassassin, 9th September ; battle of Tel el-Kebir Despatches
   "London Gazette," 2nd November, 1882. A.D.C. to the Queen.
   3rd class Medjidie ; medal with clasp ; bronze star.
Byrch, E. B., Captain, Royal Marines.
   Reconnaissance of 5th August, 1882. Medal ; bronze star.

Cafe, C. H. W., Captain, Royal Sussex Regiment.
   Defence of Alexandria ; surrender of Kafr ed-Dauar ; occupation of
   Damanhur ; and surrender of Damietta. Medal and bronze star.
Cuillard, V. H. P., Lieutenant, Royal Engineers.
   Actions at Tel el-Maskhuta, Mahsama, and Kassassin. Medal and
   bronze star ; 5th class Medjidie.
Caledon, J. A., Earl of, Captain, 4th Battalion Royal Inniskilling Fusiliers.
   Engagements of Magfar and Mahsama, both actions at Kassassin,
   battle of Tel el-Kebir, and occupation of Cairo. Medal with
   clasp ; bronze star.
Calley, T. C. P., Lieutenant, 1st Life Guards.
   Actions of Magfar, Mahsama, Kassassin ; battle of Tel el-Kebir ;
   march to and occupation of Cairo. Medal with clasp ; bronze star.

Calvert, H. H., Lieutenant, 7th Dragoon Guards.
Actions of Mahsama and Kassassin ; battle of Tel el-Kebir ; and forced march to Cairo. Medal with clasp ; bronze star.
Cameron, C. B., Lieutenant, York and Lancaster Regiment.
Battle of Tel el-Kebir. Medal with clasp ; bronze star.
Campbell, A. L., Lieutenant, Seaforth Highlanders.
Battle of Tel el-Kebir. Medal with clasp ; bronze star.
Campbell, B. B. D., Major, Scots Guards.
Actions of Magfar and Tel el-Maskhuta ; battle of Tel el-Kebir. Medal and clasp ; bronze star.
Campbell, C., Lieutenant-Colonel, 7th Dragoon Guards.
Actions of Magfar, Mahsama, and Kassassin ; battle of Tel el-Kebir ; and forced march to Cairo. Despatches "London Gazette," 2nd November, 1882. 3rd class Medjidie ; C.B. Medal with clasp ; bronze star.
Campbell, C. G. L., Deputy Assistant Commissary-General of Ordnance (Captain).
Battle of Tel el-Kebir. Despatches "London Gazette," 2nd November, 1882. Promoted Assistant Commissary-General of Ordnance. Medal with clasp ; bronze star ; 4th class Medjidie
Campbell, Chas. Wm., Captain Bengal Staff Corps.
Medal ; bronze star.
Campbell, E. P., Lieutenant, Black Watch.
Battle of Tel el-Kebir. Medal with clasp ; bronze star.
Campbell, F. S., Captain, Royal Sussex Regiment.
Medal and bronze star.
Campbell, J. A., Lieutenant, Seaforth Highlanders.
Seizure of Suez Canal east of Ismailia ; battle of Tel el-Kebir ; occupation of Zagazig and of Cairo. Medal with clasp ; bronze star.
Campbell, J. C. L., Lieutenant, Royal Engineers.
Action at Kassassin, 9th September ; and battle of Tel el-Kebir. Medal with clasp ; bronze star.
Campbell, W., Surgeon, M. B., Scots Guards.
Actions of Magfar and Tel el-Maskhuta ; battle of Tel el-Kebir. Medal with clasp ; bronze star.
Campbell, William, Captain, Royal Marine Artillery.
Bombardment of forts of Alexandria. Medal with clasp ; bronze star. Brevet of Major.
Candy, J., Surgeon-Major.
Medal ; bronze star.
Cane, C. R. J., Lieutenant, Royal Artillery.
Battle of Tel el-Kebir. Medal with clasp.
Capper, W. B., Lieutenant, Shropshire Light Infantry.
See General Orders, 11th September, 1882. Medal ; bronze star.
Carden, H. P., Lieutenant, Duke of Cornwall's Light Infantry.
Actions at Magfar and Tel el-Maskhuta, both actions at Kassassin (wounded 28th August, 1882), and battle of Tel el-Kebir. Medal with clasp ; bronze star.
Carden, H. W., Lieutenant, Duke of Cornwall's Light Infantry.
Battle of Tel el-Kebir. Medal with clasp ; bronze star.
Carey, C. de B., Captain, Royal Engineers.
Actions at Kassassin, 9th September. Despatches "London Gazette," 2nd November, 1882. Brevet of Major. Medal ; bronze star.
Carey, C. W., Captain, Highland Light Infantry.
Battle of Tel el-Kebir. 4th class Medjidie. Medal with clasp ; bronze star.

Carey, G. T. J., Lieutenant, Highland Light Infantry.
  Battle of Tel el-Kebir (severely wounded). Medal with clasp :
  bronze star.
Carey, J. T., Surgeon.
  Medal ; bronze star.
Carlaw, H., now Quartermaster, Gordon Highlanders.
  Battle of Tel el-Kebir. Medal with clasp ; bronze star.
Carleton. A. W., Surgeon.
  Medal ; bronze star.
Carmichael, J. C. G., Surgeon-Major, Indian Medical Service.
  Battle of Tel el-Kebir. Medal with clasp ; bronze star.
Carr, A. N., Lieutenant, Bengal Staff Corps.
  Medal ; bronze star.
Carr, E. H., Captain, Royal West Kent Regiment.
  4th class Medjidie. Medal ; bronze star.
Carré, G. T., Major (Half-pay), Royal Artillery.
  Battle of Tel el-Kebir. Medal with clasp ; bronze star.
Carter, S. H., Surgeon.
  Battle of Tel el-Kebir. Medal with clasp ; bronze star.
Case, M. F. M., Veterinary Surgeon, 1st class.
  Battle of Tel el-Kebir. Medal with clasp ; bronze star.
Catherwood, W. A., Surgeon Major.
  Battle of Tel el-Kebir. Medal with clasp ; bronze star.
Cautley, J. C., Captain, Royal West Kent Regiment.
  Action at Kassassin. Medal ; bronze star.
Cavarra, A., Lieutenant, Royal Malta Fencible Artillery.
  Medal ; bronze star.
Cavage, G. R., Lieutenant, Queen's Own Cameron Highlanders.
  Battle of Tel el-Kebir. Medal with clasp ; bronze star.
Chads, H. C., Lieutenant, South Staffordshire Regiment.
  Medal and bronze star. See General Orders, 11th September, 1882.
Chalmers, N. G., Major, Queen's Own Cameron Highlanders.
  Battle of Tel el-Kebir. Medal with clasp ; bronze star.
Chapman, F. S., Captain, Queen's Own Cameron Highlanders.
  Battle of Tel el-Kebir. Medal with clasp ; bronze star.
Chapman, J. F., Lieutenant-Colonel, 7th Dragoon Guards.
  Actions of Mahsama and Kassassin, battle of Tel el-Kebir, and
  forced march to Cairo. Medal with clasp ; bronze star ; 4th
  class Osmanieh.
Charteris, Hon. A. D., Lieutenant, Coldstream Guards.
  Action of Tel el-Maskhuta and battle of Tel el-Kebir. Medal with
  clasp ; bronze star.
Chase, R. G., Lieutenant, Berkshire Regiment.
  Surrender of Kafr ed-Dauar. Medal ; bronze star.
Chauncy, C. H., Staff Paymaster, Coldstream Guards.
  Medal and bronze star.
Chawner, J. H., Lieutenant, Royal Irish Regiment.
  Battle of Tel el-Kebir. Medal with clasp ; bronze star.
Cheetham, C. J., Captain, Royal Marines.
  Bombardment of Alexandria. Medal with clasp ; bronze star
  4th class Medjidie.
Chermside, H. C., Captain, Royal Engineers.
  Medal and bronze star.
Chesney, A. G., Lieutenant, South Staffordshire Regiment.
  Reconnaissance of 5th August. Mentioned in despatches. 5th
  class Medjidie ; medal and bronze star.

Chevers, H., Captain, Manchester Regiment.
Medal ; bronze star.

Chichester, A. G., Lieutenant, Royal Irish Regiment.
Battle of Tel el-Kebir (severely wounded). Medal with clasp ; bronze star ; 5th class Medjidie.

Childe-Pemberton, C. B., Lieutenant, Royal Horse Guards Blue.
Battle of Tel el-Kebir. Medal with clasp ; bronze star.

Childers, E. S. E., Lieutenant, Royal Engineers.
A.D.C. to G.O.C. Actions at Magfar, Tel el-Maskhuta, Kassassin, 9th September; and battle of Tel el-Kebir. Despatches " London Gazette," 2nd November, 1882. 5th class Medjidie ; medal with clasp ; bronze star. Brevet of Major.

Childers, F. C. E., Lieutenant, Royal Artillery.
As A.D.C. to O. C. Indian Contingent. Despatches " London Gazette," 2nd November, 1882. 5th class Medjidie.

Christopher, L. W., Captain, Bengal Staff Corps.
Medal ; bronze star.

Church, A. G. H., Lieutenant-Colonel, Manchester Regiment.
Medal ; bronze star.

Churchward, W. S., Lieutenant, Royal Artillery.
Battle of Tel el-Kebir. Medal with clasp ; bronze star.

Clapp, W. H. B., Brigade Surgeon.
Medal ; bronze star.

Clark, H. H., Lieutenant, Royal Artillery.
Battle of Tel el-Kebir.

Clark, J. E., Brigade Surgeon.
Medal ; bronze star.

Clark-Kennedy, A., Captain, Madras Staff Corps.
Medal ; bronze star.

Clarke, C., Lieutenant, Royal Marine Light Infantry.
Several minor actions at El-Meks. Medal; bronze star.

Clarke, G. S., Captain, Royal Engineers.
Medal and bronze star.

Cleeve, S. D., Lieutenant, Royal Engineers.
Medal and bronze star.

Cleland, W., Lieutenant-Colonel, Royal Dublin Fusiliers.
As Chief of Police in Alexandria. Mentioned in despatches. 3rd class Medjidie. Medal and bronze star.

Cleland-Henderson, J. M., Lieutenant, Manchester Regiment.
Medal ; bronze star.

Clementi, M., Major, Bengal Staff Corps.
Deputy Judge Advocate, Indian Contingent. Battle of Tel el-Kebir. Medal with clasp ; bronze star ; 4th class Osmanieh.

Cochran, A. G., Lieutenant, Royal Marines.
Transport Officer to advance force at Ramleh. Reconnaissance of 5th August; action of Kassassin, 9th September; battle of Tel el-Kebir. Medal with clasp ; bronze star.

Cochrane, W. F. D., Captain, Duke of Cornwall's Light Infantry.
Medal and bronze star. See General Orders, 11th September, 1882.

Cockburn, C. J., Lieutenant, 1st Battalion Royal Warwickshire Regiment.
With Reserve Depôt at Alexandria.

Cocks, H. H. S., Lieutenant, Coldstream Guards.
Battle of Tel el-Kebir. Medal with clasp ; bronze star.

Codrington, A. E., Lieutenant, Coldstream Guards.
> A.D.C. to Lt.-Gen., 1st Division. Actions of Magfar, Tel el-Maskhuta, Kassassin, 9th September, and battle of Tel el-Kebir. Despatches "London Gazette," 2nd November, 1882. Medal with clasp; bronze star; 5th class Medjidie.

Codrington, E. W., Lieutenant, Manchester Regiment.
> Medal; bronze star.

Coffin, R. P., Captain, Royal Marines.
> Occupation of Port Saïd; actions of Magfar, Tel el-Maskhuta, Mahsama, both actions at Kassassin, battle of Tel el-Kebir. Medal with clasp; bronze star. Despatches "London Gazette," 8th September and 2nd November, 1882. Brevet of Major.

Coghill, K. J. W., Lieutenant-Colonel, 19th Hussars.
> Battle of Tel el-Kebir. Despatches "London Gazette," 2nd November, 1882. 3rd class Medjidie; C.B. Medal with clasp; bronze star

Coghlan, J. D., Captain, Gloucester Regiment.
> In transport service. Medal and bronze star.

Coke, Viscount Thos. Wm., Captain, Scots Guards.
> Actions of Magfar, Tel el-Maskhuta, and battle of Tel el-Kebir. Medal with clasp; bronze star.

Cole, E., Quartermaster, Royal Irish Fusiliers.
> Battle of Tel el-Kebir. Medal with clasp; bronze star.

Colebrook, G. T., Deputy Assistant Commissary-General (Captain).
> Medal; bronze star.

Cole-Hamilton, A. R., Lieutenant, Shropshire Light Infantry.
> Defence of Alexandria; occupation of Kafr ed-Dauar; surrender of Damietta. Medal; bronze star.

Colhoun, C. K., Honorary Captain! York and Lancaster Regiment.
> Battle of Tel el-Kebir. Meda with clasp; bronze star.

Collett, W., Quartermaster, Commissariat and Transport Corps.
> Medal; bronze star.

Collins, Rev. R. F. (Captain).
> Battle of Tel el-Kebir. Medal with clasp; bronze star

Colville, T., Major, Highland Light Infantry.
> Killed in action at Tel el-Kebir.

Comyn, J. S., Surgeon Major.
> Promoted Brigade Surgeon. Medal; bronze star.

Conder, C. R., Captain, Royal Engineers.
> Action at Kassassin; and battle of Tel el-Kebir 4th class Medjidie. Medal with clasp; bronze star.

Coney, W. B., Captain, Derbyshire Regiment.
> Medal; bronze star.

Connaught and Strathearn, His Royal Highness A. W. P. A., Duke of Honorary Colonel, Rifle Brigade.
> Commanded Brigade of Guards. Action at Tel el-Maskhuta; and battle of Tel el-Kebir. Despatches "London Gazette" 8th September, 6th October, and 7th November, 1882. Thanked by Houses of Parliament. 2nd class Medjidie; C.B.; medal with clasp; bronze star.

Connolly, B. B., Surgeon.
> Battle of Tel el-Kebir Medal with clasp; bronze star. Promoted Surgeon-Major.

Conolly, P. B., Surgeon.
> Battle of Tel el-Kebir Medal with clasp; bronze star.

Connor, T., Lieutenant of Orderlies, Army Hospital Corps.
Medal and bronze star.

Conran, W. L., Lieutenant, Royal Irish Fusiliers.
Battle of Tel el-Kebir. Medal with clasp; bronze star.

Cook, H. R., Captain, Manchester Regiment.
Medal; bronze star.

Cooke, W. N. M., Lieutenant, York and Lancaster Regiment.
Medal; bronze star.

Cooper, F. E., Lieutenant, Royal Artillery.
Battle of Tel el-Kebir. Medal with clasp; bronze star.

Cooper, R. J., Lieutenant, Grenadier Guards.
Action of Tel el-Maskhuta; battle of Tel el-Kebir. Medal with clasp; bronze star.

Cooper-Key, C. A. McN., Lieutenant, Royal Artillery.
Medal; bronze star.

Corban, L., Surgeon Major.
Action at Kassassin; battle of Tel el-Kebir Mentioned in despatches. Medal with clasp; bronze star Surgeon-Major, with relative rank of Lieutenant-Colonel.

Corban, W. W., Lieutenant-Colonel, Berkshire Regiment.
Surrender of Kafr ed-Dauar. Medal; bronze star; 3rd class Medjidie.

Corbet, W. O., Lieutenant, Coldstream Guards.
Action of Tel el-Maskhuta, and battle of Tel el-Kebir. Medal with clasp; bronze star.

Corbett, Rev. J. (Captain).
Medal; bronze star.

Corbett, Rev. R. A. (Major).
Battle of Tel el-Kebir. Medal with clasp; bronze star.

Cossey, J. F., Quartermaster, Commissariat and Transport Staff.
Battle of Tel el-Kebir. Medal with clasp; bronze star.

Cotterill, H. G., Lieutenant, Royal Marines.
Capture of Port Saïd, Ismaïlia, and Nefisha; both actions at Kassassin. Medal; bronze star.

Cottingham, E. R., Major, Royal Artillery.
Battle of Tel el-Kebir. Despatches " London Gazette," 2nd November, 1882. Medal with clasp; bronze star. Brevet of Lieutenant-Colonel. 3rd class Medjidie.

Cotton, J., Lieutenant, Gordon Highlanders.
Battle of Tel el-Kebir. Medal with clasp; bronze star. Granted hon. rank of Captain.

Coveny, R. C., Captain, Royal Highlanders.
Battle of Tel el-Kebir (wounded). Despatches " London Gazette," 2nd November, 1882. Brevet of Lieutenant-Colonel. Medal with clasp; bronze star

Cowan, H. V., Lieutenant, Royal Artillery.
As Adjutant, Royal Artillery, 2nd Division. Battle of Tel el-Kebir (severely wounded). Despatches " London Gazette," 2nd November, 1882. Brevet of Major. 5th class Medjidie; medal with clasp; bronze star.

Cox, G., Major, Royal Irish Fusiliers.
As D.A.A. and Q.M.G. of base and lines of communication. Medal and bronze star. Brevet of Lieutenant-Colonel.

Cox, K. M. M., Lieutenant, Royal Highlanders.
Medal; bronze star.

Crabbe, A. B., Lieutenant, 3rd Hussars.
Battle of Tel el-Kebir. Medal with clasp; bronze star.

Crabbe, E. M. S., Lieutenant, Commissariat and Transport Staff.
    See General Orders, 11th September, 1882. Medal ; bronze star
Craig, J. F., Lieutenant, Royal Artillery.
    Battle of Tel el-Kebir. Medal with clasp ; bronze star.
Craigie, J., Captain, Royal Marines.
    Brevet of Major.
Cramer, C. P., Major, King's Royal Rifle Corps.
    Affair at Tel el-Maskhuta ; action at Kassassin ; battle of Tel el-Kebir.
    Despatches " London Gazette," 2nd November, 1882. Medal with
    clasp. Brevet of Lieutenant-Colonel. 4th class Osmanieh ;
    bronze star.
Creagh, A. G., Lieutenant, Royal Artillery.
    A.D.C. to G.O.C. Despatches " London Gazette," 2nd November,
    1882. Medal with clasp. Brevet of Major. Bronze star ; 5th
    class Medjidie.
Crealock, J. N., Lieutenant-Colonel, Derbyshire Regiment.
    Commandant at Alexandria and at El-Meks. Medal ; bronze
    star.
Creighton, W. M., Paymaster (Captain).
    Medal ; bronze star.
Crofts, A. M., Surgeon, Indian Medical Service.
    Battle of Tel el-Kebir. Medal with clasp ; bronze star
Cross, A. E. A., Captain, Gordon Highlanders.
    Battle of Tel el-Kebir. Despatches " London Gazette," 2nd November, 1882. Medal with clasp ; bronze star.
Crosthwaite, C., Major, Royal Artillery.
    Despatches " London Gazette," 2nd November, 1882. Medal with
    clasp ; bronze star. Brevet of Lieutenant-Colonel. 3rd class
    Medjidie.
Crow, W. A., Veterinary Department (Lieutenant).
    Action of Kassassin ; battle of Tel el-Kebir. Medal with clasp ;
    bronze star.
Crumplin, W., Quartermaster, Commissariat and Transport Staff.
    Medal ; bronze star.
Crutchley, C., Lieutenant, Scots Guards.
    Actions of Magfar, Tel el-Maskhuta ; battle of Tel el-Kebir. 5th
    class Medjidie. Medal with clasp ; bronze star.
Cumberland, G. B. M., Captain, Royal Highlanders.
    Battle of Tel el-Kebir. Severely wounded. Medal with clasp ;
    bronze star.
Cumming, Gordon, Sir Wm. G., Captain and Lieutenant-Colonel, Scots
    Guards.
    Actions of Magfar, Tel el-Maskhuta, and battle of Tel el-Kebir.
    Medal with clasp ; bronze star.
Cummings, H., Captain, Royal West Kent Regiment.
    Medal ; bronze star.
Cuningham, G. W. H., Captain, Cheshire Regiment.
    Medal ; bronze star.
Cunningham, G. G., Lieutenant, Duke of Cornwall's Light Infantry.
    Actions at Magfar and Tel el-Maskhuta ; action at Kassassin. Twice
    wounded. Despatches " London Gazette," 19th September
    and 2nd November, 1882. 5th class Medjidie. Medal ; bronze
    star.
Cusack, J. W. H. C., Lieutenant, Royal Irish Fusiliers.
    Battle of Tel el-Kebir. Medal with clasp ; bronze star ; 5th class
    Medjidie.

Dalbiac, H. S., Captain, Royal Artillery.
  Battle of Tel el-Kebir (severely wounded). Despatches "London Gazette," 2nd November, 1882. Medal with clasp; bronze star 4th class Medjidie.
Dalrymple, Hon. N. de C., Lieutenant, Scots Guards.
  Actions of Magfar, Tel el-Maskhuta, and battle of Tel el-Kebir. Medal with clasp; bronze star. 5th class Medjidie.
Daly, F. A. B., Surgeon.
  Medal; bronze star.
Daly, H. D., Lieutenant, Royal Irish Regiment.
  Battle of Tel el-Kebir. Medal with clasp; bronze star.
Daly, M., Conductor of Supplies.
  Actions at Kassassin of 28th August and 9th September; battle of Tel el-Kebir. Medal with clasp; bronze star.
Daniell, F. F., Lieutenant-Colonel, Gordon Highlanders.
  Medal; bronze star.
Daniell, O. J., Lieutenant, Royal West Kent Regiment.
  Medal; bronze star.
D'Arcy, E. B., Quartermaster, Ordnance Store Department.
  Medal; bronze star.
Darley, J. W. W., Captain, 4th Dragoon Guards.
  Battle of Tel el-Kebir. Medal with clasp; bronze star.
Darling, C. H., Lieutenant, Royal Engineers.
  Battle of Tel el-Kebir. Medal with clasp; 5th class Medjidie; bronze star.
Darling, J. B., Lieutenant, Royal Marines.
  Reconnaissance of 5th August, 1882; actions of Tel el-Maskhuta, Kassassin, and battle of Tel el-Kebir. Medal with clasp; bronze star.
Daubeny, H. J., Captain, Royal Irish Regiment.
  Battle of Tel el-Kebir. Despatches "London Gazette," 2nd November, 1882. Brevet of Major. 4th class Medjidie; medal with clasp; bronze star.
Dauncey, T. H. E., now Lieutenant 21st Hussars.
  Battle of Tel el-Kebir. Medal with clasp; bronze star.
Davidge, J., Surgeon-Major (Lieutenant-Colonel).
  Medal; bronze star.
Davidson, Arthur, Lieutenant, King's Royal Rifle Corps.
  5th class Medjidie. Medal with clasp; bronze star. See General Orders, 30th August, 1882.
Davidson, C. F. H., Lieutenant, Queen's Own Cameron Highlanders.
  Battle of Tel el-Kebir. Medal with clasp; bronze star.
Davidson, D. F., Lieutenant, Queen's Own Cameron Highlanders.
  Battle of Tel el-Kebir. Medal with clasp; bronze star.
Davie, G. S., Surgeon-Major (Lieutenant-Colonel).
  Battle of Tel el-Kebir. Despatches "London Gazette," 2nd November, 1882. 3rd class Medjidie; medal with clasp; bronze star.
Davies, A. M., Lieutenant-Colonel, Madras Staff Corps.
  Medal; bronze star.
Davies, J. D., Surgeon-Major (Captain).
  Battle of Tel el-Kebir. Medal with clasp; bronze star.
Davison, T., Major, 16th Lancers.
  Battle of Tel el-Kebir. Medal with clasp; bronze star.
Dawes, B. M., Major, Prince of Wales' Leinster Regiment.
  Staff Commandant at Gabbari. Despatches "London Gazette," 2nd November, 1882. Medal; 4th class Osmanieh; bronze star. Brevet of Lieutenant-Colonel.

Dawnay, Hon. E. H., Lieutenant, Coldstream Guards.
Action at Tel el-Maskhuta; and battle of Tel el-Kebir. Medal with clasp; bronze star.

Dawson, D. F. R., Lieutenant, Coldstream Guards
Served with the Mounted Infantry at action of Tel el-Maskhuta; and battle of Tel el-Kebir. 5th class Medjidie; medal with clasp; bronze star.

Dawson, R. H., Lieutenant, Manchester Regiment.
Medal; bronze star.

Day, M. C., Captain, 7th Dragoon Guards.
Despatches "London Gazette," 2nd November, 1882. Brevet of Major.

Day, R. V., Captain, Commissariat and Transport Staff.
Medal; bronze star.

Deane, G. W., Captain, Bengal Staff Corps.
Battle of Tel el-Kebir. Despatches "London Gazette," 2nd November, 1882. Medal with clasp; bronze star.

De Burgh, W. G. C., Captain, 7th Dragoon Guards.
Actions of Magfar, Mahsama, Kassassin; battle of Tel el-Kebir and forced march to Cairo. Medal with clasp; bronze star.

De Crespigny, T. D. W. C., Lieutenant, 15th Hussars.
Battle of Tel el-Kebir. Medal with clasp; bronze star.

Delamain, W. S., Lieutenant, Berkshire Regiment.
Surrender of Kafr ed-Dauar. Medal; bronze star.

Denne, G. R. A., Major, 4th Dragoon Guards.
Magfar, Tel el-Maskhuta. Commanded 4th Dragoon Guards at battle of Tel el-Kebir. Despatches "London Gazette," 2nd November, 1882. Brevet of Lieutenant-Colonel. 3rd class Medjidie. Medal with clasp; bronze star.

Denne, H. W. D., Lieutenant, Gordon Highlanders.
Battle of Tel el-Kebir. Medal with clasp; bronze star.

Des Barres, A. H., Captain, Royal Marines.
4th class Medjidie.

De Vesci, J. R. W., *Viscount*, Major, Coldstream Guards.
Action of Tel el-Maskhuta; and battle of Tel el-Kebir. Medal with clasp; bronze star.

Dickie, J. E., Lieutenant, Royal Engineers.
Battle of Tel el-Kebir. 5th class Medjidie. Medal with clasp; bronze star.

Dickinson, E., Captain, Royal Engineers.
Medal and bronze star.

Ditmas, E., Lieutenant, 7th Dragoon Guards.
Battle of Tel el-Kebir, and forced march to Cairo. Medal with clasp; bronze star.

Dixon, C. E., Captain, Royal Irish Regiment.
Battle of Tel el-Kebir. Medal with clasp; bronze star.

Donald, A., Major, Royal Marines.
Reconnaissance of 5th August. Actions of Magfar, Tel el-Maskhuta, both actions at Kassassin, and battle of Tel el-Kebir. Mentioned in despatches. Medal with clasp; bronze star.

Donne, B. D. A., Lieutenant, Royal Sussex Regiment.
Medal and bronze star.

Donovan, H. L., Surgeon (Captain).
Medal; bronze star.

Dopping-Hepenstal, L. I., Lieutenant, Royal Engineers.
Medal and bronze star.

Doran, R. H. P., Lieutenant-Colonel, Royal West Kent Regiment.
Medal; bronze star.

Doran, W. R. B., Lieutenant, Royal Irish Regiment
Battle of Tel el-Kebir. Medal with clasp; bronze star.

Dorman, J. C., Surgeon (Captain).
Medal; bronze star.

Dormer, Hon. J. C., Colonel (Half-pay).
Acting Chief of Staff and D.A.G. Reconnaissance of 5th August near Ramleh; and battle of Tel el-Kebir. Despatches "London Gazette," 6th October and 2nd November, 1882. Promoted Major-General for distinguished service. 2nd class Medjidie; medal with clasp; bronze star. See General Orders, 23rd August, 1882.

Dorward, J. F., Captain, Royal Engineers.
Action at Kassassin. Medal and bronze star.

Dougherty, E. M., Paymaster (Honorary Captain), York and Lancaster Regiment.
Medal; bronze star.

Douglas, G. P., Lieutenant, 2nd Dragoon Guards.
Battle of Tel el-Kebir. Medal with clasp; bronze star.

Dowdall, A. P. G., Paymaster (Honorary Captain), Royal Sussex Regiment.
Medal and bronze star.

Dowell, A. J. W., Lieutenant, Berkshire Regiment.
Surrender of Kafr ed-Dauar. Medal; bronze star.

Drake, J. M. C., Lieutenant-Colonel, Royal Engineers.
Commanding Royal Engineer, 1st Division. Action at Tel el-Maskhuta and at Kassassin, 9th September; and battle of el Tel-Kebir. Despatches "London Gazette," 17th November, 1882. 3rd class Osmanieh; C.B.; medal with clasp; bronze star.

Draper, J., Assistant Commissary General (Lieutenant-Colonel).
Mentioned in despatches. Medal; bronze star.

Drummond-Wolff, H. H., Lieutenant, Royal Fusiliers.
Battle of Tel el-Kebir (severely wounded). Despatches "London Gazette," 17th November, 1882. Medal with clasp; bronze star.

Drury Lowe, Sir D. C., Major-General, Cavalry Division.
Commanded Cavalry Brigade, and afterwards Cavalry Division, throughout the campaign. Actions at Magfar and Tel el-Maskhuta; capture of Mahsama; action at Kassassin; battle of Tel el-Kebir; and subsequent pursuit to Belbeis; and surrender and occupation of Cairo. Despatches "London Gazette," 8th September, 19th September, 6th October, and 2nd November, 1882. Thanked by Houses of Parliament. 2nd class Osmanieh; K.C.B.; medal with clasp; bronze star.

Du Boulay, D. de la M., Captain, 7th Dragoon Guards.
Actions of Magfar, Mahsama, and Kassassin; battle of Tel el-el-Kebir, subsequent pursuit, and occupation of Cairo. Medal with clasp; bronze star.

Duff, A. G., Lieutenant, Black Watch (Royal Highlanders).
Battle of Tel el-Kebir. Medal with clasp; bronze star.

Dundas, R., Lieutenant, Scots Guards.
Actions of Magfar, Tel el-Maskhuta, and battle of Tel el-Kebir. Medal with clasp; bronze star.

Dunne, W. A, Major, Commissariat and Transport Staff.
Battle of Tel el-Kebir. Medal with clasp; bronze star.

Earle, H., Lieutenant, South Yorkshire Regiment.
    A.D.C. to O.C. base and lines of communication. Battle of Tel el-Kebir 5th class Medjidie; medal with clasp; bronze star.

Earle, W., Major-General.
    Commanded base and lines of communication. Despatches "London Gazette," 6th October and 2nd November, 1882. Thanked by both Houses of Parliament. C.B.; 2nd class Medjidie; medal with clasp; bronze star.

Eaton, J. B., Surgeon, Indian Medical Service.
    Medal; bronze star.

Eden, C. J., Captain, Black Watch (Royal Highlanders).
    Battle of Tel el-Kebir. Medal with clasp; bronze star.

Eden, F. M., Captain, Royal Marines.
    Occupation of Port Saïd; battle of Tel el-Kebir. Despatches "London Gazette," 8th September, 1882. Medal with clasp; bronze star.

Eden, J. M. R., Lieutenant, Duke of Cornwall's Light Infantry.
    Actions of Magfar, Tel el-Maskhuta, both actions at Kassassin, and battle of Tel el-Kebir. Medal with clasp; bronze star.

Edge, J. D. (M.D.), Major, Cheshire Regiment.
    Battle of Tel el-Kebir; forced march to, and occupation of, Zagazig. 4th class Osmanieh; medal with clasp; bronze star.

Edwards, H. H., Captain, Royal Welsh Fusiliers.
    Action at Kassassin (wounded). Despatches "London Gazette," 19th September, 1882.

Edwards, W. M. M., Lieutenant, Highland Light Infantry.
    Battle of Tel el-Kebir (severely wounded). Bronze star; medal with clasp; V.C.

Edye, L., Captain, Royal Marines.
    Actions of Mallaha Junction, Magfar, Tel el-Maskhuta, Mahsama, Kassassin; battle of Tel el-Kebir. Medal with clasp; bronze star.

Egerton, G. G. A., Lieutenant, Seaforth Highlanders.
    Seizure of Suez Canal east of Ismailia; battle of Tel el-Kebir; occupation of Zagazig and of Cairo. Medal with clasp; bronze star.

Ekin, J., Deputy Surgeon-General (Colonel).
    As P.M.O., 1st Division, throughout the campaign; and present at the battle of Tel el-Kebir. Despatches "London Gazette," 2nd November, 1882. C.B.; 3rd class Osmanieh. Medal with clasp; bronze star.

Elderton, Allan, Lieutenant, Bengal Staff Corps.
    Battle of Tel el-Kebir. Medal with clasp; bronze star.

Elles, E. R., Captain, Royal Artillery.
    D.A.Q.M.G. Indian Contingent. Battle of Tel el-Kebir. Despatches "London Gazette," 2nd November, 1882. Brevet of Major. 4th class Medjidie. Medal with clasp; bronze star.

Elliot, G. R., Lieutenant, Seaforth Highlanders.
    Seizure of Suez Canal east of Ismailia; battle of Tel el-Kebir; occupation of Zagazig and of Cairo. Medal with clasp; bronze star.

Elliot, H. F., Lieutenant, Royal Highlanders.
    Battle of Tel el-Kebir. Medal with clasp; bronze star.

Elliot, M., Lieutenant-Colonel, Royal Artillery.
    Commanding Siege Train. Despatches "London Gazette," 2nd November, 1882. 3rd class Medjidie. Medal; bronze star.

Elrington, M., Lieutenant, Royal Engineers.
    Medal and bronze star.

Elton, F. Coulthurst, Lieutenant-Colonel, Royal Artillery.
Commanding Royal Artillery, 2nd Division. Battle of Tel el-Kebir.
Despatches " London Gazette," 2nd November, 1882. 3rd class
Medjidie; C.B. Medal with clasp; bronze star.
Emeris, J., Captain, South Staffordshire Regiment.
Medal and bronze star.
England, J. M. F., Captain, Royal Irish Fusiliers.
Battle of Tel el-Kebir Brevet of Major. 4th class Medjidie.
Medal with clasp; bronze star.
Enright, E., Lieutenant, Orderlies.
Medal and bronze star.
Enthoven, P. H., Lieutenant, Royal Artillery.
Battle of Tel el-Kebir. Medal with clasp; bronze star.
Erskine, H. W., Lieutenant, Gordon Highlanders.
Actions of Magfar, Tel el-Maskhuta, and battle of Tel el-Kebir
Medal with clasp; bronze star.
Evans, C. W. H., Lieutenant, Royal West Kent Regiment.
Medal; bronze star.
Evans, F. S., Lieutenant, Derbyshire Regiment.
Medal; bronze star.
Evans, J. W., Surgeon, Indian Medical Service.
Battle of Tel el-Kebir. Medal with clasp; bronze star.
Evans-Gordon, C., Captain, Berkshire Regiment.
Surrender of Kafr ed-Dauar. Medal; bronze star.
Ewart, C. F. S., Lieutenant, Seaforth Highlanders.
Battle of Tel el-Kebir. Medal with clasp; bronze star.
Ewart, H. P., Lieutenant-Colonel, 2nd Life Guards.
Commanded Household Cavalry. Actions at Magfar, Mahsama,
Kassassin, battle of Tel el-Kebir. Despatches " London Gazette,"
19th September and 2nd November, 1882. 3rd class Medjidie;
C.B. Medal with clasp; bronze star.
Ewart, J. S., Lieutenant, Cameron Highlanders.
Battle of Tel el-Kebir. Medal with clasp; bronze star.
Eyre, P. H., Lieutenant-Colonel, South Staffordshire Regiment.
Reconnaissance of 5th August. Mentioned in despatches. Medal
and bronze star; 4th class Osmanieh.
Eyton, J. H. W., Captain, Shropshire Light Infantry.
Defence of Alexandria; occupation of Kafr ed-Dauar; surrender of
Damietta. Medal; bronze star.

Facer, W., Quartermaster, Manchester Regiment.
Medal; bronze star.
Falls, J. A. W., Lieutenant, Duke of Cornwall's Light Infantry.
Action at Kassassin; battle of Tel-el-Kebir. Despatches " London
Gazette," 19th September and 2nd November, 1882. Medal with
clasp; bronze star.
Falvey, J. J., Surgeon.
Medal; bronze star.
Fanshawe, H. D., Lieutenant, 19th Hussars.
Battle of Tel el-Kebir. Medal with clasp; bronze star.
Farmar-Bringhurst, E. D., Surgeon, Medical Department.
Medal; bronze star.
Farquharson, M. H., Major, Royal Marines.
Medal; bronze star. 4th class Osmanieh.

Farwell, W., Captain, Duke of Cornwall's Light Infantry.
Battle of Tel el-Kebir. Medal with clasp ; bronze star.
Faught, J. G., Brigade Surgeon.
Mentioned in despatches. Medal ; bronze star.
Fegen, M. F., Lieutenant, Royal Artillery.
Battle of Tel el-Kebir. Medal with clasp ; bronze star.
Feilding, R. H. B. A. A., *Viscount*, Lieutenant, Royal Artillery.
Battle of Tel el-Kebir. Medal with clasp ; bronze star.
Fendall, G. N., Lieutenant-Colonel, King's Shropshire Regiment.
Defence of Alexandria ; occupation of Kafr ed-Dauar ; and sur
render of Damietta. Medal ; bronze star.
Fenning, H., Lieutenant, King's Shropshire Regiment.
Defence of Alexandria ; occupation of Kafr ed-Dauar ; surrender of
Damietta. Medal ; bronze star.
Ferguson, H., Brigade Surgeon.
Medal ; bronze star.
Ferguson, R. P., Surgeon-Major.
Medal ; bronze star.
Fergusson, C. H., Captain, Seaforth Highlanders.
Engagement of Shaluf ; seizure of Suez Canal east of Ismailia.
Despatches "London Gazette," 8th September, 1882. Medal
and bronze star.
Field, C., Lieutenant, Royal Marines.
Actions of Mallaha; Tel el-Maskhuta, both actions at Kassassin ;
battle of Tel el-Kebir. Medal with clasp ; bronze star.
Firth, S., now Quartermaster, Royal Artillery.
Battle of Tel el-Kebir. Despatches "London Gazette," 2nd November, 1882. Medal with clasp ; bronze star.
FitzGeorge, G. W. A., Major, 20th Hussars.
Battle of Tel el-Kebir. Brought home despatches. Despatches
"London Gazette," 6th October, 1882. Brevet of Lieutenant-
Colonel. 4th class Osmanieh ; medal with clasp ; bronze star.
Fitzgerald, Lord F.; Lieutenant, King's Royal Rifle Corps.
Action of Kassassin of 9th September ; battle of Tel el-Kebir.
Medal with clasp ; bronze star.
FitzStubbs, E., Major, Commissariat and Transport Staff.
Medal ; bronze star.
Fletcher, H. A., Major, Indian Forces (Bengal).
Medal ; bronze star.
Fludyer, H., Captain, Scots Guards.
Actions of Magfar, Tel el-Maskhuta, and battle of Tel el-Kebir.
Medal with clasp ; bronze star.
Follett, R. W. W., Captain, Coldstream Guards.
Action of Tel el-Maskhuta ; and battle of Tel el-Kebir. Medal with
clasp; bronze star.
Foord, E., Lieutenant, Bengal Artillery.
Medal ; bronze star.
Foote, F. O. B., Captain, Royal Artillery.
Mentioned in despatches. Medal ; 4th class Medjidie ; bronze
star.
Forbes, C. D'O., Staff Paymaster (Major).
Medal ; bronze star.
Forbes, J., Quartermaster, Royal Highlanders.
Battle of Tel el-Kebir. Mentioned in despatches. Granted honorary rank of Captain. Good service pension. Medal with clasp ;
bronze star.

Ford, R. W., Surgeon.
Medal ; bronze star.
Ford, T., Quartermaster, Berkshire Regiment.
Surrender of Kafr ed-Dauar. Medal ; bronze star.
Forrester, J. S., Surgeon.
Actions at Kassassin ; battle of Tel el-Kebir. Medal with clasp
bronze star.
Forster, J. F., Major, Royal Irish Rifles.
Reconnaissance at Ramleh ; action at Magfar ; and action at Kassassin (severely wounded). Medal and bronze star.
Fortescue, Hon. A. G., Lieutenant, Coldstream Guards.
Action of Tel el-Maskhuta ; and battle of Tel el-Kebir. Medal with
clasp ; bronze star.
Foss, J. E. V., Surgeon.
Medal ; bronze star.
Foster, H. J., Lieutenant, Royal Engineers.
Actions at Kassassin of 8th and 9th September ; and battle of
Tel el-Kebir. Medal with clasp ; bronze star.
Foster, W., Major, King's Royal Rifle Corps.
Action at Kassassin ; and battle of Tel el-Kebir.
Fox, A. N., Surgeon-Major.
Medal ; bronze star.
Fox, G. M., Captain, Royal Highlanders.
Battle of Tel el-Kebir (wounded). Medal with clasp ; bronze
star.
Fox, J. C. K., Lieutenant, 19th Hussars.
Battle of Tel el-Kebir. Medal with clasp ; bronze star.
Fox, T. C. A., Paymaster, Princess of Wales' Berkshire Regiment.
Surrender of Kafr ed-Dauar. Medal ; bronze star.
Frampton, C., Captain, Royal Marines.
Reconnaissance of 5th August ; actions of Tel el-Maskhuta ; both
actions at Kassassin ; and battle of Tel el-Kebir. Medal with
clasp ; bronze star.
Fraser, E. L., Major, King's Royal Rifle Corps.
Reconnaissance at Ramleh ; affair at Tel el-Maskhuta ; action at
Kassassin ; and battle of Tel el-Kebir. 4th class Osmanieh ;
medal with clasp ; bronze star.
Fraser, Hon. H. T., Major, Scots Guards.
Actions of Magfar, Tel el-Maskhuta, and battle of Tel el-Kebir.
4th class Osmanieh ; medal with clasp ; bronze star.
Fraser, T., Major, Royal Engineers.
As Brigade Major Royal Engineers. Capture of Ismailia ; actions
at Magfar, Mahsama, Tel el-Maskhuta, Kassassin, 9th September ; and battle of Tel el-Kebir. Despatches "London Gazette,"
8th September and 2nd November, 1882. Brevet of Lieutenant-Colonel. 4th class Osmanieh ; medal with clasp ; bronze
star.
Free, J. F., Major, Royal Artillery.
Despatches "London Gazette," 2nd November, 1882. Medal with
clasp ; bronze star. Brevet of Lieutenant-Colonel. 3rd class
Medjidie.
Freer, H. C., Lieutenant, South Staffordshire Regiment.
Medal and bronze star.
French, A., Major, Suffolk Regiment.
Mentioned in despatches. Brevet of Lieutenant-Colonel. Medal ;
bronze star.

French, H., Major, Bombay Staff Corps.
Actions of Magfar, Mahsama, Kassassin (28th August), and battle of Tel el-Kebir. Medal with clasp; bronze star.

Frend, G., Lieutenant, Northumberland Fusiliers.
Medal; bronze star.

Fryer, E., Deputy Assistant Commissary-General (Captain).
Battle of Tel el-Kebir. 4th class Medjidie. Medal with clasp; bronze star.

Fuller, S., Brigade Surgeon.
Battle of Tel el-Kebir. Medal with clasp; bronze star.

Fyler, A. E., Lieutenant-Colonel, West Kent Regiment.
3rd class Medjidie; medal; bronze star.

Gaitskell, W. J., Lieutenant, Royal Marines.
Medal; bronze star.

Galindo, R. E., now Lieutenant, 1st Dragoon Guards.
Medal; bronze star.

Galloway, J., Lieutenant-Colonel, Bombay Staff Corps.
Battle of Tel el-Kebir, march on Zagazig, and occupation of Cairo. Despatches "London Gazette," 2nd November, 1882. Medal with clasp; bronze star. 3rd class Medjidie; C.B.

Gallwey, T. J., Surgeon.
Action at Kassassin and battle of Tel el-Kebir. Medal with clasp; bronze star.

Galton, H. G. H., Lieutenant, Royal Artillery.
Medal; bronze star.

Gardner, H., Captain, Royal Irish Fusiliers.
Battle of Tel el-Kebir. Medal with clasp; bronze star.

Gardner, R. H., Surgeon.
Action at Magfar, both actions at Kassassin, and battle of Tel el-Kebir. Medal with clasp; bronze star.

Garland, E. A. C., Lieutenant, 1st Battalion Highland Light Infantry.
Battle of Tel el-Kebir. Medal with clasp; bronze star.

Garnett, R., Major, Seaforth Highlanders.
Engagement of Shaluf; seizure of Suez Canal east of Ismailia; battle of Tel el-Kebir; occupation of Zagazig and of Cairo. Despatches "London Gazette," 8th September, 1882. Medal with clasp; bronze star.

Gascoigne, W. J., Major and Lieutenant-Colonel, Scots Guards.
Actions at Magfar, Tel el-Maskhuta, and battle of Tel el-Kebir. Medal with clasp; bronze star.

Gavegan, F. C., Major, Berkshire Regiment.
Surrender of Kafr ed-Dauar. Medal; bronze star.

Gerard, M. G., Brevet Lieutenant-Colonel, Bengal Staff Corps.
Defence of Alexandria. D.A.A. and Q.M.G. Cavalry Division. Reconnaissance of 5th August. Action of Kassassin, battle of Tel el-Kebir, and occupation of Cairo. Despatches "London Gazette," 2nd November, 1882. C.B.; 3rd class Medjidie. Medal with clasp; bronze star.

Gifford, R., Lieutenant, Derbyshire Regiment.
Acting A.D.C. to Commandant of Alexandria. Medal; bronze star.

Gill, W. J., Captain, Royal Engineers.
See General Orders, 17th August, 1882. Medal; bronze star.

Gillespie, R. R., Colonel (Half-pay).
A.A.G. 1st Division. Actions of Magfar, Tel el-Maskhuta, Kassassin (9th September), battle of Tel el-Kebir. Despatches "London Gazette," 2nd November, 1882. C.B.; 3rd class Osmanieh. Medal with clasp; bronze star.

Gillespie, W. J., Major, Berkshire Regiment.
Surrender of Kafr ed-Dauar. Medal; bronze star

Gimlette, G. H. D., Surgeon, Indian Medical Service.
Battle of Tel el-Kebir, and pursuit to Zagazig. Medal with clasp; bronze star.

Giraud, B. T., Brigade Surgeon.
Battle of Tel el-Kebir. Medal with clasp; bronze star. Promoted Brigade Surgeon.

Gladstone, J. R., Lieutenant, Coldstream Guards.
Action of Tel el-Maskhuta; and battle of Tel el-Kebir. Medal with clasp; bronze star.

Gleig, A., Assistant Paymaster (Lieutenant), Shropshire Regiment.
Defence of Alexandria; occupation of Kafr ed-Dauar; surrender of Damietta. Medal; bronze star.

Godsal, W. C., Lieutenant, Royal Engineers.
Medal and bronze star.

Golding, E. W., Lieutenant-Colonel, Derbyshire Regiment
Temporary command, 2nd battalion Derbyshire Regiment Medal; bronze star.

Goldsmid, Sir F. J., Honorary Colonel, Cinque Ports Artillery Volunteers.
Organized an Intelligence Department at Alexandria at the commencement of the operations. Mentioned in despatches. 2nd class Osmanieh

Goodenough, W. H., Brigadier-General, Royal Artillery.
Commanded Royal Artillery. Battle of Tel el-Kebir. Despatches "London Gazette," 6th October and 10th November, 1882. 2nd class Medjidie; C.B. Medal with clasp; bronze star.

Goodwyn, H. E., Lieutenant, Royal Engineers.
Battle of Tel el-Kebir. Medal with clasp; bronze star

Goold-Adams, R. E., Lieutenant, Highland Light Infantry.
Battle of Tel el-Kebir. Medal with clasp; bronze star]

Gordon, A. W. B., Lieutenant, Royal Artillery.
Battle of Tel el-Kebir. Medal with clasp; bronze star.

Gordon, C. H., Captain, Royal Engineers.
Medal; bronze star.

Gordon, F., Lieutenant, Gordon Highlanders.
Battle of Tel el-Kebir. Medal with clasp; bronze star.

Gordon, J. C. F., Captain, Bengal Staff Corps.
Battle of Tel el-Kebir. Despatches "London Gazette," 2nd November, 1882. Medal with clasp; bronze star.

Gordon, O. B., Major, Queen's Own Cameron Highlanders.
Battle of Tel el-Kebir. Medal with clasp; bronze star

Gordon, R. W. T., Lieutenant-Colonel, Argyll and Sutherland Highlanders.
Brigade Major, 3rd Brigade, 2nd Division. Battle of Tel el-Kebir. Despatches "London Gazette," 2nd November, 1882. Brevet of Lieutenant-Colonel 4th class Osmanieh. Medal with clasp; bronze star.

Gordon, S. D., Lieutenant, Bengal Staff Corps.
Battle of Tel el-Kebir. 5th class Medjidie. Medal with clasp; bronze star.

Gordon-Lennox, Lord A. C., Captain and Lieutenant-Colonel, Grenadier Guards.
Battle of Tel el-Kebir.   Medal with clasp ; bronze star.
Gore, G. A. E., Captain, Royal Marines.
Capture of Ismailia.   Despatches "London Gazette," 8th September, 1882.   4th class Medjidie.   Medal ; bronze star.
Gorman L., Captain, Army Hospital Corps.
Action at Kassassin ; battle of Tel el-Kebir.   Medal with clasp ; bronze star.
Gosset, E. A. G., Lieutenant, Derbyshire Regiment.
Medal ; bronze star.
Gosset, M. W. E., Lieutenant-Colonel, Dorsetshire Regiment.
Medal ; bronze star.   4th class Osmanieh.
Gough, Hon. H. G., Captain, 14th Hussars.
A.D.C. to G.O.C. 2nd Division.   Battle of Tel el-Kebir (horse killed).   Despatches "London Gazette," 2nd November, 1882.   Brevet of Major.   4th class Medjidie ; medal with clasp ; bronze star.
Gough, W. A., Lieutenant, Oxfordshire Light Infantry.
Served with the Military Foot Police.   Brevet of Major.   5th class Medjidie.
Graham, Gerald, Major-General, Royal Engineers.
Commanded 2nd Brigade, 1st Division, throughout the campaign.   Actions at Magfar and Kassassin, 28th August and 9th September ; battle of Tel el-Kebir.   Despatches "London Gazette," 8th September, 19th September, 26th September, 6th October, and 2nd November, 1882.   Thanked by both Houses of Parliament.   K.C.B. ; 2nd class Medjidie ; medal with clasp ; bronze star.
Graham, H., Quartermaster, Army Hospital Corps.
Medal and bronze star.
Graham, M., Captain, Commissariat and Transport Staff
Battle of Tel el-Kebir.   Medal with clasp ; bronze star.
Graham, S. J., Lieutenant-Colonel, Royal Marines.
Occupation of Port Saïd and Ismaïlia ; actions of Tel el-Maskhuta, Kassassin (9th September), and battle of Tel el-Kebir.   Despatches "London Gazette," 2nd September and 2nd November, 1882   Medal with clasp ; bronze star ; 4th class Osmanieh ; C.B.
Graham, T. P., Surgeon-Major, Argyll and Sutherland Highlanders.
Actions of Magfar, Tel el-Maskhuta, and battle of Tel el-Kebir   Medal with clasp ; bronze star.
Graham, W. B., Lieutenant, Manchester Regiment.
Medal ; bronze star.
Graham, W. H., Major, Royal Artillery.
Medal ; bronze star.
Graham-Stirling, T. J., Lieutenant, Black Watch.
Killed in action at Tel el-Kebir.
Grant, E. J., Lieutenant, Royal Irish Regiment.
Battle of Tel el-Kebir.   Medal with clasp ; bronze star
Grant, I. R. J. M., Lieutenant, Queen's Own Cameron Highlanders.
Battle of Tel el-Kebir.   Medal with clasp ; bronze star.
Grant, J. G., Surgeon-Major.
Medal ; bronze star.
Grant, J. J. F., Major, Duke of Cornwall's Light Infantry.
Medal ; bronze star.
Grant, John, Captain, Bombay Staff Corps.
Medal ; bronze star.

Grant, J. W., Lieutenant, Royal Marines.
Actions of Magfar, Kassassin, and battle of Tel el-Kebir. Medal with clasp; bronze star.
Grattan, E., Major, Commissariat and Transport Staff.
Medal; bronze star; 4th class Osmanieh.
Grattan, H., Major, Royal Sussex Regiment.
Defence of Alexandria; surrender of Kafr ed-Dauar; and occupation of Damanhur. Medal and bronze star.
Green, A. O., Captain, Royal Engineers.
Battle of Tel el-Kebir. 4th class Medjidie. Medal with clasp; bronze star.
Green, R. S., Captain, Berkshire Regiment.
Surrender of Kafr ed-Dauar. Medal; bronze star.
Green, W., Lieutenant-Colonel, Black Watch (Royal Highlanders).
Battle of Tel el-Kebir. Despatches "London Gazette," 2nd November, 1882. 4th class Osmanieh. Medal with clasp; bronze star.
Greer, W., Lieutenant, Seaforth Highlanders.
Seizure of Suez Canal east of Ismailia; battle of Tel el-Kebir; occupation of Zagazig and of Cairo. Medal with clasp; bronze star.
Gregorie, C. F., Lieutenant-Colonel, Royal Irish Regiment.
Battle of Tel el-Kebir. Despatches "London Gazette," 2nd November, 1882. 3rd class Medjidie; C.B. Medal with clasp; bronze star.
Gregorie, D. G., Lieutenant, Royal Irish Regiment.
Battle of Tel el-Kebir. Medal with clasp; bronze star.
Grenfell, F. W., Major, King's Royal Rifle Corps.
A.A.G., Head-quarters. Action of Tel el-Maskhuta; battle of Tel el-Kebir. Despatches "London Gazette," 2nd November, 1882. A.D.C. to the Queen. 3rd class Medjidie; medal with clasp; bronze star.
Gribble, H. C., Lieutenant, 3rd Dragoon Guards. Attached to 7th Dragoon Guards.
Killed in action at Kassassin on 28th August, 1882.
Grierson, J. M., Lieutenant, Royal Artillery.
D.A.Q.M.G., Indian Contingent. Action at Kassassin, 9th September, and battle of Tel el-Kebir. Despatches "London Gazette," 2nd November, 1882. 5th class Medjidie. Medal with clasp; bronze star.
Grieve, F., Major, Duke of Cornwall's Light Infantry.
Reconnaissance in force on Kafr ed-Dauar; actions of Magfar, Tel el-Maskhuta, at Kassassin (28th August), and battle of Tel el Kebir. Despatches "London Gazette," 19th September, 1882. Brevet of Lieutenant-Colonel. Medal with clasp; bronze star.
Griffith, C. B., Honorary Captain (Paymaster), Highland Light Infantry.
Medal and bronze star.
Griffith, G. R., Veterinary Surgeon (Lieutenant).
Actions of Magfar, Mahsama, Kassassin, battle of Tel el-Kebir. and forced march to Cairo. Medal with clasp; bronze star.
Griffiths, C., Lieutenant, York and Lancaster Regiment.
Battle of Tel el-Kebir. Medal with clasp; bronze star.
Griffiths, W., Quartermaster, Shropshire Light Infantry.
Defence of Alexandria, occupation of Kafr ed-Dauar, and surrender of Damietta. Medal; bronze star.
Grosvenor, S. F., Lieutenant, York and Lancaster Regiment.
Battle of Tel el-Kebir. Medal with clasp; bronze star.

Grove, C., Major, East Yorkshire Regiment.
D.A.A.G., Head-quarters. Actions of Tel el-Maskhuta, Kassassin (9th September), battle of Tel el-Kebir. Despatches " London Gazette," 2nd November, 1882. Brevet of Lieutenant-Colonel. 4th class Osmanieh; medal with clasp; bronze star.

Grove, H. C., Captain, Royal Sussex Regiment.
Defence of Alexandria; operations at Ramleh; surrender of Kafr ed-Dauar; and occupation of Damanhur. Medal and bronze star.

Groves, E. A. W. S., Captain, Royal West Kent Regiment.
Battle of Tel el-Kebir. Brevet of Major. Medal with clasp; bronze star.

Guinness, C. W. N., Lieutenant-Colonel, Seaforth Highlanders.
Seizure of Suez Canal east of Ismailia; battle of Tel el-Kebir; occupation of Zagazig and of Cairo. Despatches " London Gazette," 2nd November, 1882. Medal with clasp; bronze star; 4th class Osmanieh.

Gunton, T. W., Quartermaster, Grenadier Guards.
Action of Tel el-Maskhuta and battle of Tel el-Kebir. Medal with clasp; bronze star.

Gwatkin, F. S., Lieutenant, Bengal Staff Corps.
Action at Kassassin, 9th September; battle of Tel el-Kebir, and occupation of Cairo. Medal with clasp; bronze star.

Hacket-Thompson, F., Lieutenant, Queen's Own Cameron Highlanders.
Battle of Tel el-Kebir. Medal with clasp; bronze star.

Hackett, Rev. J., Chaplain 4th class (Captain).
Medal; bronze star.

Hackett, Simpson, Lieutenant-Colonel, Royal Sussex Regiment.
Medal and bronze star.

Haggard,
See General Orders, 11th September, 1882.

Hagger, W. R., Veterinary Surgeon (Lieutenant).
Medal; bronze star.

Haines, C. S., Quartermaster, 2nd Life Guards.
Medal; bronze star.

Hall, C. A. K., Lieutenant, Royal Munster Fusiliers.
Medal; bronze star. See General Orders, 11th September, 1882.

Hall, R. S., Major, Coldstream Guards.
Action of Tel el-Maskhuta; and battle of Tel el-Kebir. Medal with clasp; bronze star.

Haly, R. H. O'G., Lieutenant-Colonel, York and Lancaster Regiment.
Actions of Magfar, Kassassin, and battle of Tel el-Kebir. Medal with clasp; bronze star. Brevet of Lieutenant-Colonel.

Hamilton, A. F., Major, Royal Engineers (late Madras).
Battle of Tel el-Kebir. Brevet of Lieutenant-Colonel. Medal with clasp; bronze star.

Hamilton, D. J., Lieutenant, Coldstream Guards.
Action of Tel el-Maskhuta and battle of Tel el-Kebir. Medal with clasp; bronze star.

Hamilton, G. V., Captain, Commissariat and Transport Corps.
Medal; bronze star; 4th class Medjidie.

Hamilton, S. G., Surgeon (Lieutenant), Life Guards.
Actions of Magfar, Mahsama, Kassassin; battle of Tel el-Kebir; march to and occupation of Cairo. Mentioned in despatches. Medal with clasp; bronze star.

Hamilton, T., Quartermaster, Royal Irish Regiment.
Action of Kassassin, and battle of Tel el-Kebir. Mentioned in despatches. Honorary rank of Major. Medal with clasp; bronze star.

Hamley, Sir E. B., Lieutenant-General, Royal Artillery.
Commanded 2nd Division, battle of Tel el-Kebir. Despatches "London Gazette," 6th October and 2nd November, 1882. Thanked by Houses of Parliament. 2nd class Osmanieh; K.C.B.; medal with clasp; bronze star.

Hammill, D., Lieutenant-Colonel, Gordon Highlanders.
Battle of Tel el-Kebir. Despatches "London Gazette," 2nd November, 1882. 3rd class Medjidie; C.B. Medal with clasp; bronze star.

Hanbury, E. E., Lieutenant, Scots Guards.
Action at Tel el-Maskhuta, and battle of Tel el-Kebir. Medal with clasp; bronze star.

Hanbury, Sir J. A., Deputy Surgeon-General.
Principal Medical Officer. Battle of Tel el-Kebir. Despatches "London Gazette," 6th October and 2nd November, 1882. 2nd class Medjidie; K.C.B. Medal with clasp; bronze star.

Hanbury-Williams, J., Lieutenant, Oxfordshire Light Infantry.
As A.D.C. to G.O.C. 2nd Division. Battle of Tel el-Kebir. Horse killed. Despatches "London Gazette," 2nd November, 1882. 5th class Medjidie; medal with clasp; bronze star.

Hancock, W. W., Lieutenant, Derbyshire Regiment.
Medal; bronze star.

Hanford-Flood, J. C., Captain, 19th Hussars.
Battle of Tel el-Kebir. Despatches "London Gazette," 2nd November, 1882. Brevet of Major. 4th class Medjidie. Medal with clasp; bronze star.

Harden, G., Captain, Royal Sussex Regiment.
Medal and bronze star.

Harding, A., Surgeon.
Battle of Tel el-Kebir. Medal with clasp; bronze star.

Hardy, Hon. Gathorne.
See General Orders, 11th September, 1882.

Hare, R. C., Captain, Cheshire Regiment.
Brigade Major, 2nd Brigade, 1st Division. Action at Kassassin. Despatches "London Gazette," 19th September and 2nd November, 1882. Brevet of Major. 4th class Medjidie; medal and bronze star.

Hare, T. L., Lieutenant, Scots Guards.
Actions of Magfar, Tel el-Maskhuta, and battle of Tel el-Kebir. Medal with clasp; bronze star.

Harman, G. B., Major-General.
Commanded garrison at Alexandria. Thanked by the Houses of Parliament. Medal and bronze star.

Harris, Geo., Quartermaster, Ordnance Store Department.
Despatches "London Gazette," 2nd November, 1882. Granted honorary and relative rank of Captain. Medal; bronze star.

Harris, F. A., Lieutenant, Bengal Staff Corps.
Medal; bronze star.

Harris, W. O., Lieutenant, Bengal Staff Corps.
Battle of Tel el-Kebir. Medal with clasp; bronze star.

Harrison, C. E., Surgeon.
Action of Tel el-Maskhuta; battle of Tel el-Kebir. Medal with clasp; bronze star.

Harrison, C. E. C. B., Lieutenant, 2nd Battalion Royal West Kent Regiment.
Medal; bronze star.

Harrison, R., Colonel, Royal Engineers,
Appointed A.A.G. Served as Chief Staff Officer on lines of communication throughout the campaign. Action of Magfar; and battle of Tel el-Kebir. Despatches "London Gazette," 2nd November, 1882. C.M.G.; 3rd class Osmanieh; medal with clasp; bronze star.

Harrison, W., Lieutenant, 11th Hussars.
Battle of Tel el-Kebir. Medal with clasp; bronze star.

Hart, A. F., Major, East Surrey Regiment.
As D.A.A. and Q.M.G., Intelligence Branch. Reconnaissance of 5th August; actions at Magfar, Tel el-Maskhuta, and Kassassin (wounded, horse wounded); and battle of Tel el-Kebir. Mentioned in despatches. Brevet of Lieutenant-Colonel. 4th class Osmanieh; medal with clasp; bronze star.

Hart, H. C., Quartermaster, 2nd Battalion Duke of Cornwall's Light Infantry.
Battle of Tel el-Kebir. Medal with clasp; bronze star.

Hart, R. C., Brevet Major, Royal Engineers.
As A.D.C. to Major-General, 2nd Brigade, 1st Division. Reconnaissance of 5th August; engagements of Magfar and Tel el-Maskhuta; both actions at Kassassin, and battle of Tel el-Kebir. Despatches "London Gazette," 19th September and 2nd November, 1882. Brevet of Lieutenant-Colonel. 4th class Osmanieh; medal with clasp; bronze star.

Hartopp, C. E., Lieutenant, Scots Guards.
Actions of Magfar and Tel el-Maskhuta. Medal and bronze star.

Harvest, W. S. S., Lieutenant, Royal Marines.
Actions of Mallaha, Tel el-Maskhuta, Magfar, Mahsama, Kassassin; battle of Tel el-Kebir; and occupation of Cairo. Medal with clasp; bronze star.

Harvey, C. H., Surgeon-Major.
Medal; bronze star.

Harvey, W. L., Lieutenant, Duke of Cornwall's Light Infantry.
Battle of Tel el-Kebir. Medal with clasp; bronze star.

Haselden, R., Surgeon.
Medal; bronze star.

Hatch, G. P., Lieutenant, Wiltshire Regiment.
Battle of Tel el-Kebir. Medal with clasp; bronze star.

Hatchell, H. M., Captain, Royal Irish Regiment.
Battle of Tel el-Kebir. Medal with clasp; bronze star.

Hawkins, H. T., Lieutenant, Royal Artillery.
Medal; bronze star.

Hawkins, J. W., Captain, Royal Artillery.
Action of Kassassin; and battle of Tel el-Kebir. Medal with clasp; bronze star.

Hay, Hon. A., Lieutenant, Scots Guards.
Actions of Magfar, Tel el-Maskhuta; and battle of Tel el-Kebir. Medal with clasp; bronze star.

Hay, E. O., Captain, Royal Artillery.
Battle of Tel el-Kebir. Despatches "London Gazette," 2nd No-

vember, 1882. Brevet of Major. 4th class Medjidie. Medal with clasp ; bronze star.

Hay, J. A., Captain, Highland Light Infantry.
Battle of Tel el-Kebir. Medal with clasp; bronze star.

Haynes, A. E., Lieutenant, Royal Engineers.
Employed on special service under the Admiralty in connection with the murder of Professor Palmer and his party. Medal and bronze star ; 5th class Medjidie.

Hayter, C., Major, Madras Staff Corps.
Director of Transports, Indian Contingent. Despatches "London Gazette," 17th November, 1882. 3rd class Medjidie ; C.B. Medal with clasp ; bronze star.

Healy, R. C., Major-General, Commissariat and Transport Staff.
Medal ; bronze star.

Heath, F. C., Lieutenant, Royal Engineers.
Engagement at Magfar ; and battle of Tel el-Kebir. Medal with clasp ; bronze star.

Heath, H. N. C., Lieutenant, South Staffordshire Regiment.
As Transport Officer ; and present at reconnaissance of 5th August. Medal and bronze star.

Heathcote, R. W., Captain, Royal Marines.
Reconnaissance of 5th August ; battle of Tel el-Kebir. Mentioned in despatches. Brevet of Major. 4th class Medjidie ; medal with clasp ; bronze star.

Hebbert, W. S., Major, Royal Artillery.
Battle of Tel-el-Kebir. Despatches "London Gazette," 2nd November, 1882. Brevet of Lieutenant-Colonel. 3rd class Medjidie. Medal with clasp ; bronze star.

Hellard, R. C., Lieutenant, Royal Engineers.
Action at Kassassin on 9th September. Medal and bronze star.

Hemphill, F. B. R., Lieutenant, Berkshire Regiment.
Surrender of Kafr ed-Dauar. Medal ; bronze star.

Henderson, G. F. R., Lieutenant, York and Lancaster Regiment.
Battle of Tel el-Kebir. 5th class Medjidie. Medal with clasp ; bronze star. Brevet of Major.

Henderson, J. S., Lieutenant, Gordon Highlanders.
Battle of Tel el-Kebir. Medal with clasp ; bronze star.

Henderson, R. A., Lieutenant, Manchester Regiment.
Medal ; bronze star.

Heneage, A. R., Lieutenant, Highland Light Infantry.
Battle of Tel el-Kebir (wounded). Medal with clasp ; bronze star.

Henley, R., Captain, King's Royal Rifle Corps.
Action at Kassassin ; and battle of Tel-el-Kebir. Medal with clasp ; bronze star.

Henniker-Major, Hon. A. H., Lieutenant, Coldstream Guards.
Medal and bronze star.

Henry, W. F. R., Lieutenant, Royal Irish Fusiliers.
Battle of Tel el-Kebir. Medal with clasp ; bronze star.

Herbert, I. J. C., Lieutenant, Grenadier Guards.
Brigade Major, 1st Brigade, 1st Division. Action of Tel el-Maskhuta ; battle of Tel el-Kebir. Despatches "London Gazette," 2nd November, 1882. Brevet of Major. 4th class Medjidie. Medal with clasp ; bronze star.

Herring-Cooper, C. H., Captain, Royal Artillery.
Medal ; bronze star.

Hetherington, R. P., Surgeon.
Medal ; bronze star.
Heyman, C. E. H., Lieutenant, Royal Artillery.
Battle of Tel el-Kebir. Medal with clasp ; bronze star.
Hickie, H., Conductor of Supplies.
Medal ; bronze star.
Hickman, S. C., Lieutenant, Royal Artillery.
Action at Tel el-Maskhuta. Battle of Tel el-Kebir. Despatches "London Gazette," 8th September, 1882. Brevet of Major. 5th class Medjidie. Medal with clasp ; bronze star.
Hickson, R. C. C., Surgeon-Major.
Action of Kassassin. Mentioned in despatches. Medal; bronze star.
Higginson, C. T. M., Major, Indian Local Forces (Bengal).
Medal ; bronze star.
Hildyard, H. J. T., Major, Highland Light Infantry.
D.A.A. and Q.M.G., 1st Division. Actions of Magfar, Tel el-Maskhuta, Kassassin, 9th September; battle of Tel el-Kebir. Despatches "London Gazette," 2nd November, 1882. Brevet of Lieutenant-Colonel. 4th class Osmanieh. Medal with clasp ; bronze star.
Hill, G. M. D., Major, Indian Local Forces (Bengal).
Medal ; bronze star.
Hippisley, R. L., Lieutenant, Royal Engineers.
Medal and bronze star.
Hirst, W. H., now Quartermaster, Netley.
Medal ; bronze star.
Hitchcock, T. B., Captain, Shropshire Light Infantry.
4th class Medjidie. Medal ; bronze star.
Hodson, G. B., Lieutenant, Bengal Staff Corps.
Reconnaissance of 5th August. Medal and bronze star.
Hoey, J., Surgeon, Indian Medical Service.
Battle of Tel el-Kebir. Medal with clasp ; bronze star.
Holbech, W. H., Captain, King's Royal Rifle Corps.
Brigade Major, 2nd Brigade, 1st Division. Affair at Tel el-Maskhuta ; action at Kassassin ; and battle of Tel el-Kebir. Despatches "London Gazette," 2nd November, 1882. Brevet of Major. 4th class Medjidie ; medal with clasp ; bronze star.
Holden, H. W., Captain, Berkshire Regiment.
Surrender of Kafr ed-Dauar. Medal ; bronze star.
Holland, P., Lieutenant, Duke of Cornwall's Light Infantry.
Actions at Magfar, Tel el-Maskhuta, and Kassassin ; battle of Tel el-Kebir. Medal with clasp ; bronze star.
Hollway, E. J., Lieutenant, Duke of Cornwall's Light Infantry.
Battle of Tel-el-Kebir. Medal with clasp ; bronze star.
Home, D. M., Lieutenant-Colonel, Royal Horse Guards.
4th class Osmanieh. Medal ; bronze star.
Home, J., Lieutenant, Royal Highlanders.
Battle of Tel el-Kebir. Medal with clasp ; bronze star.
Home, Hon. W. S. D., Major, Grenadier Guards.
Action of Tel el-Maskhuta. Battle of Tel el-Kebir. 4th class Osmanieh. Medal with clasp ; bronze star.
Hood, T. C., Paymaster, Seaforth Highlanders.
Medal ; bronze star.
Hope, M., Major, Gordon Highlanders.
Battle of Tel el-Kebir. Medal with clasp ; bronze star.

Hopkins, W., Quartermaster, Commissariat and Transport Corps.
Battle of Tel el-Kebir. Medal with clasp; bronze star.
Hore, C. O., Lieutenant, South Staffordshire Regiment.
Served with the Mounted Infantry at reconnaissance of 5th August;
and in actions at Magfar, Tel el-Maskhuta, and Mahsama;
second action at Kassassin; and battle of Tel el-Kebir. 5th class
Medjidie. Medal; bronze star.
Hornblower, E., Quartermaster, Commissariat and Transport Staff
Medal; bronze star.
Horsbrugh, A. B., Captain, South Staffordshire Regiment.
Reconnaissance of 5th August. Medal and bronze star.
Houghton, E., Captain, Ordnance Store Department.
Medal; bronze star.
Houghton, E. R., Lieutenant, Shropshire Light Infantry.
Medal.
Howard, Francis (M.D.), Surgeon-Major.
Medal; bronze star.
Howard, W., Quartermaster, Cameron Highlanders.
Battle of Tel el-Kebir. Medal with clasp; bronze star.
Howard-Vyse, H. G. L., Lieutenant, King's Royal Rifle Corps.
Killed in action near Alexandria.
Howe, R. C. A., Lieutenant, York and Lancaster Regiment.
Battle of Tel el-Kebir. Medal with clasp; bronze star.
Howell, R., Quartermaster, Army Hospital Corps.
Action at Kassassin. Medal and bronze star.
Hubbard, H. W., Surgeon.
Battle of Tel el-Kebir. Medal with clasp; bronze star.
Hughes, E., Major, Commissariat and Transport Staff.
Senior Commissariat Officer. Battle of Tel el-Kebir. Promoted to
Assistant Commissary-General, with relative rank of Lieu-
tenant-Colonel. Medal with clasp; bronze star; 3rd class
Medjidie.
Hughes-Hallett, J. W., Brevet Major, Seaforth Highlanders.
Engagement of Shaluf; seizure of Suez Canal east of Ismailia;
battle of Tel el-Kebir; occupation of Zagazig and of Cairo.
Despatches "London Gazette," 8th September, 1882. Medal
with clasp; bronze star.
Huleatt, H., Lieutenant, Royal Engineers.
Medal and bronze star.
Hume, J. S. M., Lieutenant, South Staffordshire Regiment.
Reconnaissance of 5th August. Mentioned in despatches. Medal
and bronze star.
Hume-Spry, G. F., Surgeon-Major, 2nd Life Guards.
Actions of Magfar and Mahsama, and battle of Tel el-Kebir. Medal
with clasp; bronze star.
Humphreys, H.
Medal and bronze star.
Hunt, J. M., Captain, Queen's Own Cameron Highlanders.
Battle of Tel el-Kebir. Despatches "London Gazette," 2nd Novem-
ber, 1882. Brevet of Major. 4th class Medjidie. Medal with
clasp; bronze star.
Hunter, F. E. A., Lieutenant, Royal Artillery.
Battle of Tel el-Kebir. Medal with clasp; bronze star.
Hunter, W. H., Lieutenant, Seaforth Highlanders.
Seizure of Suez Canal east of Ismailia; battle of Tel el-Kebir;
occupation of Zagazig and of Cairo. Medal with clasp; bronze star.

Hunter-Blair, R. S., Lieutenant, Gordon Highlanders.
Battle of Tel el-Kebir. Medal with clasp; bronze star.
Hussey, J. H., Captain, 4th Dragoon Guards.
Battle of Tel el-Kebir. Despatches "London Gazette," 2nd November, 1882. Brevet of Major. 4th class Medjidie. Medal with clasp; bronze star.
Hutton, E. T. H., Captain, King's Royal Rifle Corps.
Reconnaissance of 5th August; and battle of Tel el-Kebir (horse killed). Despatches "London Gazette," 2nd November, 1882. Brevet of Major. 4th class Medjidie; medal with clasp; bronze star.
Huyshe, A. G., Lieutenant-Colonel, Berkshire Regiment.
Surrender of Kafr ed-Dauar. Medal; bronze star.
Huyshe, E. V., Captain, Welsh Regiment.
Battle of Tel el-Kebir. Medal with clasp; bronze star.
Hyslop, R. M., Captain, Royal Engineers.
Medal; bronze star.

Ievers, O. G., Lieutenant, Royal Sussex Regiment.
Medal and bronze star.
Iggulden, H. A., Lieutenant, Derbyshire Regiment.
Medal; bronze star.
Ind, F. W., Lieutenant, Royal Artillery.
Battle of Tel el-Kebir. Medal with clasp; bronze star.
Innes, E. S., Captain, Royal Marines.
Bombardment and occupation of Alexandria; operations in the Suez Canal. Mentioned in despatches. Medal with clasp; bronze star. Brevet of Major.
Innes, F. N., Captain, Royal Artillery.
Battle of Tel el-Kebir. Despatches "London Gazette," 2nd November, 1882. Brevet of Major. 4th class Medjidie medal with clasp; bronze star.
Irvine, J. L., Lieutenant, Royal Engineers.
Battle of Tel el-Kebir. Medal with clasp; bronze star.
Irwin, L. B., Captain, Bengal Staff Corps.
Battle of Tel el-Kebir. Medal with clasp; bronze star.

Jackson, H. W., Lieutenant, Gordon Highlanders.
Medal; bronze star.
Jackson, R. W., Brigade Surgeon.
Battle of Tel el-Kebir. Despatches "London Gazette," 2nd November, 1882. 3rd class Medjidie. Medal with clasp; bronze star. Knighted.
Jago, Trelawny J., Lieutenant-Colonel, Highland Light Infantry.
Medal and bronze star.
James, Wm. Christopher, Captain, 2nd Dragoons.
A.D.C. to G.O.C. 1st Division. Actions of Magfar, Tel el-Maskhuta, Kassassin, 9th September. Battle of Tel el-Kebir. Despatches "London Gazette," 2nd November, 1882. Brevet of Major. 4th class Medjidie. Medal with clasp; bronze star.
Jamieson, E. W., Lieutenant, Berkshire Regiment.
Surrender of Kafr ed-Dauar. Medal; bronze star.
Jarrett, T., Quartermaster, South Staffordshire Regiment.
Medal and bronze star.

Jazdowski, B. J., Surgeon-Major.
  Medal ; bronze star.
Jenkins, H. C., Captain, 17th Lancers.
  See General Orders, 9th September, 1882.   Medal ; bronze star.
Jenkins, C. B. H., Captain, 19th Hussars.
  Battle of Tel el-Kebir.   Medal with clasp ; bronze star.
Jenkins, R., Lieutenant, Shropshire Regiment.
  Defence of Alexandria ; occupation of Kafr ed-Dauar ; surrender of
  Damietta.   Medal ; bronze star.
Jennings, R. M., Major, Bengal Staff Corps.
  Battle of Tel el-Kebir.   Despatches "London Gazette," 2nd
  November, 1882.   Brevet of Lieutenant-Colonel.   4th class Osma-
  nieh.   Medal with clasp ; bronze star.
Jessop, G. H., Captain, Commissariat and Transport Staff.
  Medal ; bronze star.
John, T., Lieutenant-Colonel, Duke of Cornwall's Light Infantry.
  Action at Kassassin.   Battle of Tel el-Kebir.   Despatches "London
  Gazette," 19th September, 1882.   4th class Osmanieh.   Medal
  with clasp ; bronze star.
Johnson, F. F., Lieutenant, West Kent Regiment.
  Battle of Tel el-Kebir.   Medal with clasp ; bronze star.   4th class
  Medjidie.
Johnson, William, Quartermaster, Commissariat and Transport Staff.
  Medal ; bronze star.
Johnston, J. K., Major, Commissariat and Transport Staff.
  Medal ; bronze star.
Johnston, R. C., Captain, King's Royal Rifle Corps.
  Medal ; bronze star.
Johnston, W. T., Surgeon.
  In medical charge of 1st Battalion South Staffordshire Regiment.
  Reconnaissances near Ramleh.   Medal ; bronze star.
Johnstone, J. R., Lieutenant, Royal Marine Light Infantry.
  Medal ; bronze star.
Jones, C. M., Captain, Connaught Rangers.   Attached to 2nd battalion
  Royal Irish Regiment.
  Killed in action at Tel el-Kebir.
Jones, F. W. R., Major, Manchester Regiment.
  Medal ; bronze star.
Jones, G. T., Colonel, Bengal Staff Corps.
  Medal ; bronze star.
Jones, H. H., Lieutenant-Colonel, Royal Engineers.
  Was specially employed and present at occupation of Suez by
  Naval Brigade; affair at Shaluf ; action at Tel el-Maskhuta;
  capture of Mahsama ; and battle of Tel el-Kebir.   Despatches
  "London Gazette," 8th September, 1882.   3rd class Medjidie ;
  medal with clasp ; bronze star.
Jones, H. S., Lieutenant-Colonel, Royal Marines.
  Commanded Royal Marines throughout the campaign.   Actions of
  Tel el-Maskhuta, Mahsama ; both actions at Kassassin ; and
  battle of Tel el-Kebir.   Despatches "London Gazette," 19th
  September, 26th September, and 2nd November, 1882.   A.D.C
  to the Queen.   C.B. ; 2nd class Medjidie.   Medal with clasp ;
  bronze star.   See also General Orders, 31st August, 1882 ; ditto,
  3rd September, 1882.
Jones, J. W., Captain, Royal West Kent Regiment.
  Medal ; bronze star.

Jones, T. J., Major, Royal Artillery.
Battle of Tel el-Kebir. Despatches "London Gazette," 2nd November, 1882. Brevet of Lieutenant - Colonel. 3rd class Osmanieh. Medal with clasp; bronze star.
Joseph, W., Captain of Orderlies
Medal and bronze star.

Kappey, F. G., Lieutenant, Royal Marines.
Medal; bronze star.
Kay, A. G., Surgeon.
Medal; bronze star.
Kays, D. S., Lieutenant, Highland Light Infantry.
Killed in action at Tel el-Kebir.
Keays, W., Surgeon.
Medal and bronze star.
Keefer, W. N., Surgeon-Major, Indian Medical Service.
Action of Kassassin. Battle of Tel el-Kebir. 4th class Osmanieh. Medal with clasp; bronze star.
Kelham, H. R., Captain, Highland Light Infantry.
Battle of Tel-el-Kebir. Medal with clasp; bronze star.
Kelly, W. F., Captain, Royal Sussex Regiment.
Medal and bronze star.
Kelsall, E. W., Surgeon.
Action at Kassassin. Battle of Tel el-Kebir. Mentioned in despatches. Medal with clasp; bronze star.
Kelsey, W. F., Major, Seaforth Highlanders.
Engagement at Shaluf. Commanded half-battalion Seaforth Highlanders; present at seizure of Suez Canal east of Ismailia; battle of Tel el-Kebir; occupation of Zagazig and of Cairo. Despatches "London Gazette," 8th September and 2nd November, 1882. Brevet of Lieutenant-Colonel. Medal with clasp; bronze star; 4th class Osmanieh.
Kemble, H. C., Major, Indian Local Forces (Bengal).
Battle of Tel el-Kebir. Despatches "London Gazette," 2nd November, 1882. Brevet of Lieutenant-Colonel. 4th class Osmanieh. Medal with clasp; bronze star.
Kennedy, Lord A., Lieutenant, Royal Highlanders.
Battle of Tel el-Kebir. Medal with clasp; bronze star.
Kennedy, T. F. A., Lieutenant, Royal Highlanders.
Battle of Tel el-Kebir. Medal with clasp; bronze star.
Kennedy, W. H., Lieutenant, King's Royal Rifle Corps.
Reconnaissance at Ramleh; affair of Tel el-Maskhuta; action at Kassassin; and battle of Tel el-Kebir. Medal with clasp; bronze star.
Kenyon-Slaney, W. S., Captain, Grenadier Guards.
Action of Tel el-Maskhuta; battle of Tel el-Kebir. Medal with clasp; bronze star.
Keppel, E. G., Captain, Highland Light Infantry.
Battle of Tel el-Kebir. Medal with clasp; bronze star.
Keraus, W. R., Surgeon-Major.
Medal; bronze star.
Kevill-Davies, S. E. O'B., Lieutenant, Gordon Highlanders.
Battle of Tel el-Kebir. Medal with clasp; bronze star.
Keyser, F. C., Lieutenant-Colonel, Royal Fusiliers.
Commanded Corps of Signallers, battle of Tel el-Kebir. Despatches

"London Gazette," 19th September and 2nd November, 1828. 3rd class Medjidie; C.B.; medal with clasp; bronze star. See General Orders, 30th August, 1882.

Kidston, A. F., Major, Royal Highlanders.
Battle of Tel el-Kebir. 4th class Osmanieh. Medal with clasp; bronze star.

Killick, G. L. B., Lieutenant, King's Royal Rifle Corps.
Action at Kassassin and battle of Tel el-Kebir. Medal with clasp; bronze star.

Kinahan, J., Surgeon-Major.
Medal; bronze star.

Kincaid, C. S., Lieutenant, Royal Irish Fusiliers.
Battle of Tel el-Kebir. Medal with clasp; bronze star.

King, C. D., Lieutenant, Royal Artillery.
Battle of Tel el-Kebir. Medal with clasp; bronze star.

King, P. M., Lieutenant, 21st Hussars.
Actions of Mahsama, Kassassin; battle of Tel el-Kebir, and occupation of Cairo. Medal with clasp; bronze star.

King, R. F., Captain, Ordnance Store Department.
Medal; bronze star.

King, T. F., Captain, Berkshire Regiment.
Medal; bronze star.

Kirchhoffer, R. B., Captain, Royal Marine Light Infantry.
Operations in the Suez Canal; occupation of Ismaïlia; bombardment of Nefisha; with Naval Brigade at battle of Tel el-Kebir. Medal; bronze star.

Kirkpatrick, W. J., Captain, York and Lancaster Regiment.
Actions of Magfar, Tel el-Maskhuta, Kassassin; and battle of Tel el-Kebir. Mentioned in despatches. Brevet of Major. Medal with clasp; bronze star.

Kirkwood, J. K., Captain, Shropshire Regiment.
Defence of Alexandria; occupation of Kafr ed-Dauar; surrender of Damietta. Medal; bronze star.

Kirwan, G. H., Lieutenant, Manchester Regiment.
Medal; bronze star.

Kneller, G. T. St. J. (Captain), Paymaster, Derbyshire Regiment.
Medal; bronze star.

Knight, H., Captain, Royal Artillery.
4th class Medjidie. Medal; bronze star.

Knocker, C. G., Captain, Scots Fusiliers.
Medal; bronze star.

Knowles, F., Major, Bengal Staff Corps.
Battle of Tel el-Kebir. Despatches "London Gazette," 2nd November, 1882. Brevet of Lieutenant-Colonel. 3rd class Medjidie. Medal with clasp; bronze star.

Knox, G. W., Colonel, Scots Guards.
Actions of Magfar, Tel el-Maskhuta; and battle of Tel el-Kebir. Despatches "London Gazette," 2nd November, 1882. Medal with clasp; bronze star; and 3rd class Medjidie; C.B.

Kysh, D. J., Lieutenant, Royal Marines.
Actions of Mallaha, Tel el-Maskhuta, Kassassin, and battle of Tel el-Kebir. Medal with clasp; bronze star.

Laffan, R. C. K., Surgeon.
Battle of Tel el-Kebir. Medal with clasp; bronze star.

Lambton, A., Major and Brevet Colonel, Coldstream Guards.
Action of Tel el-Maskhuta; and battle of Tel el-Kebir. 4th class
Osmanieh; medal with clasp; bronze star.

Lane, A. V., Surgeon.
Medal; bronze star.

Lane, H. F., Captain (Paymaster), 4th Dragoons.
Action at Kassassin. Medal; bronze star.

Lane, W. R., Surgeon-Major, Scots Guards.
Actions of Magfar, Tel el-Maskhuta; and battle of Tel el-Kebir.
Medal with clasp; bronze star.

Lane, R. B., Captain, Rifle Brigade.
A.D.C. to Major-General, Guards Brigade. Actions of Tel
el-Maskhuta and Magfar. Despatches "London Gazette,"
2nd November, 1882. Brevet of Lieutenant-Colonel. 4th class
Osmanieh; medal with clasp; bronze star.

Lang, H. G., Lieutenant, Seaforth Highlanders.
Engagement of Shaluf; seizure of Suez Canal east of Ismailia;
battle of Tel el-Kebir; occupation of Zagazig and of Cairo.
Despatches "London Gazette," 8th September, 1882. Medal
with clasp; bronze star.

Lanyon, Sir W. O., Lieutenant-Colonel, 2nd West India Regiment.
Colonel on Staff and Commandant of the Base of Operations.
Despatches "London Gazette," 2nd November, 1882. 3rd class
Osmanieh; medal and bronze star.

La Terrière, F. B. de S., Lieutenant, 18th Hussars.
Battle of Tel el-Kebir. Medal with clasp; bronze star.

Lauder, R. R., now Quartermaster, 1st Battalion Seaforth Highlanders.
Seizure of Suez Canal east of Ismailia, battle of Tel el-Kebir,
occupation of Zagazig and of Cairo. Medal with clasp; bronze star.

Lawrence, R. C. B., Captain, 5th Dragoon Guards.
Despatches "London Gazette," 2nd November, 1882. Brevet of
Major. 4th class Medjidie. See General Orders, 30th August,
1882.

Lea, S. J., Captain, 3rd Hussars.
Battle of Tel el-Kebir. Medal with clasp; bronze star; 4th class
Medjidie.

Leach, E., Major, West Kent Regiment.
4th class Osmanieh. Medal; bronze star.

Leader, N., Surgeon.
Medal; bronze star.

Le Bailly, A. C., Lieutenant, York and Lancaster Regiment.
Surrender of Kafr ed-Dauar. Medal; bronze star.

Lecky, F. B., Lieutenant, Royal Artillery.
Battle of Tel el-Kebir. Medal with clasp; bronze star.

Lee, H. L., Lieutenant, Berkshire Regiment.
Battle of Tel el-Kebir. Medal with clasp; bronze star.

Lees, A. R., Major, York and Lancaster Regiment.
Battle of Tel el-Kebir. Mentioned in despatches. Brevet of Lieutenant-Colonel. Medal with clasp; bronze star.

Le Grand, F. G., Lieutenant-Colonel, Royal Marines.
Several minor actions at El-Meks. 3rd class Medjidie. Medal;
bronze star.

Leigh, H. G., Lieutenant, 1st Life Guards.
Actions of Magfar, Mahsama, Kassassin, 9th September; battle
of Tel el-Kebir; march to and occupation of Cairo. Medal with
clasp; bronze star.

Leigh, Hon. R., Lieutenant, 15th Hussars.
Battle of Tel el-Kebir.   Medal with clasp; bronze star.
Leigh, R., Lieutenant-Colonel, Highland Light Infantry.
Battle of Tel el-Kebir.   Despatches "London Gazette," 2nd November, 1882.   Brevet of Lieutenant-Colonel.   4th class Osmanieh; medal with clasp; bronze star.
Leigh-Lye, C., Lieutenant, York and Lancaster Regiment.
Battle of Tel el-Kebir.   Medal with clasp; bronze star.
Leith, J. M., Lieutenant, Royal Artillery.
Battle of Tel el-Kebir.   Despatches "London Gazette," 2nd November, 1882.   3rd class Medjidie; C.B.   Medal with clasp; bronze star.
Le Marchant, O. C., Lieutenant, Royal Sussex Regiment.
Medal and bronze star.
Lendrum, J. V., Captain, Seaforth Highlanders.
Engagement of Shaluf; seizure of Suez Canal east of Ismailia; battle of Tel el-Kebir; occupation of Cairo.   Despatches "London Gazette," 8th September, 1882.   Medal with clasp; bronze star.
Leonard, A. G., Lieutenant, East Lancaster Regiment.
Medal; bronze star.   See General Orders, 11th September, 1882.
Le Quesne, J. C., Captain, Royal Marines.
Battle of Tel el-Kebir.   Medal with clasp; bronze star.
Leslie, A. M., Lieutenant, Suffolk Regiment.
As Acting D.A.C.G., Commissariat and Transport Staff.   Medal; bronze star.
Leslie, J., Lieutenant, Grenadier Guards.
Action of Tel el-Maskhuta; battle of Tel el-Kebir.   Medal with clasp; bronze star.
Leslie, W. C. G., Lieutenant, York and Lancaster Regiment.
Battle of Tel el-Kebir.   Medal with clasp; bronze star.
Leverson, J. J., Lieutenant, Royal Engineers.
As Acting Deputy Assistant Commissary-General from 11th August to 1st November; and present in action at Kassassin on 9th September.   Medal and bronze star.
Lewis, A. T., now Quartermaster, Royal Engineers.
Action of Kassassin; and battle of Tel el-Kebir.   Medal with clasp; bronze star.
Lewis, H., Quartermaster, 7th Dragoon Guards.
Action of Mahsama; battle of Tel el-Kebir, and forced march to Cairo.   Mentioned in despatches.   Medal with clasp; bronze star.   Granted honorary rank of Major.
Lima, A. G., Sergeant-Major, 19th Hussars.
Battle of Tel el-Kebir.   Medal with clasp; bronze star.
Lindley, W. D., Lieutenant, Royal Engineers.
Battle of Tel el-Kebir.   Medal with clasp; bronze star.
Lindsay, C. L., Lieutenant, Grenadier Guards.
Action of Tel el-Maskhuta; battle of Tel el-Kebir.   Medal with clasp; bronze star.
Lindsay, W. F. L., Lieutenant, Royal Artillery.
Battle of Tel el-Kebir.   Medal with clasp; bronze star.
Litster, T., Staff Paymaster.
Battle of Tel el-Kebir.   Medal with clasp; bronze star.
Littledale, H. A., Major, Derbyshire Regiment.
Battle of Tel el-Kebir.   Medal with clasp; bronze star.

Livingston, P. J. C., Lieutenant, Royal Highlanders.
  Battle of Tel el-Kebir (wounded).
Livingstone, C. P., Lieutenant, Royal Highlanders.
  Battle of Tel el-Kebir. Medal with clasp; bronze star.
Lloyd, F. T., Major, Royal Artillery.
  Medal; bronze star.
Lloyd, H. J. G., Lieutenant, Duke of Cornwall's Light
  Infantry.
  Reconnaissance in force on Kafr ed-Dauar, actions at Magfar, Tel
  el-Maskhuta, and Kassassin; Battle of Tel el-Kebir. Medal
  with clasp; bronze star.
Lloyd-Barrow, T. S., Surgeon Major.
  Battle of Tel el-Kebir. Medal with clasp; bronze star.
Lockhart, Sir S. M., Captain, 1st Life Guards.
  Actions of Magfar, Mahsama, Kassassin; battle of Tel el-Kebir;
  march to and occupation of Cairo. Medal with clasp; bronze star.
Long, R. L., Paymaster (Captain).
  Medal; bronze star.
Loraine, F. E. B., Major, Royal Artillery.
  Medal; bronze star.
Lousada, F. P., Captain, York and Lancaster Regiment.
  Battle of Tel el-Kebir. 4th class Medjidie. Medal with clasp;
  bronze star
Lovell, P. A. D. A., Lieutenant, Coldstream Guards.
  Action of Tel el-Maskhuta; and battle of Tel el-Kebir. Medal
  with clasp; bronze star.
Lovett, H. R., Lieutenant, King's Royal Rifle Corps.
  Action of Kassassin; and battle of Tel el-Kebir. Medal with clasp;
  bronze star.
Lowe, W. H. M., Lieutenant, 7th Dragoon Guards.
  Actions of Magfar, Mahsama, Kassassin; battle of Tel el-Kebir;
  and forced march to Cairo. Medal with clasp; bronze star.
Lowry, J., Lieutenant, York and Lancaster Regiment.
  Battle of Tel el-Kebir. Medal with clasp; bronze star.
Lucas, T. R., Captain, Lincolnshire Regiment.
  Action at Kassassin; battle of Tel el-Kebir. Mentioned in
  despatches. Medal with clasp; bronze star.
Luckhardt, W., Brevet Lieutenant-Colonel, Bombay Staff Corps.
  Principal Commissariat Officer, Indian Contingent. Battle of Tel
  el-Kebir. Despatches "London Gazette," 17th November, 1882.
  3rd class Medjidie; C.B. Medal with clasp; bronze star.
Lugard, E. J., Major, Lancaster Regiment.
  D.A.A. and Q.M.G., 2nd Division. Despatches "London Gazette,"
  2nd November, 1882. Brevet of Lieutenant-Colonel. 4th class
  Osmanieh; medal with clasp; bronze star.
Luke, E. V., Lieutenant, Royal Marine Light Infantry.
  Actions of Tel el-Maskhuta, Mahsama, Kassassin, and battle of
  Tel el-Kebir. Medal with clasp; bronze star.
Lye, H. S., Captain, Royal Irish Regiment.
  Battle of Tel el-Kebir. Medal with clasp; bronze star.
Lysley, W. Du V., Lieutenant, King's Royal Rifle Corps
  Reconnaissance at Ramleh; affair at Tel el-Maskhuta; action of
  Kassassin; and battle of Tel el-Kebir. Medal with clasp; bronze
  star.
Lyttelton, Hon. N. G., Major, Rifle Brigade.
  A.D.C. to Chief of Staff. Battle of Tel el-Kebir. Despatches

"London Gazette," 2nd November, 1882. Brevet of Lieutenant-Colonel. 4th class Osmanieh; medal with clasp; bronze star.

McBlain, J., Quartermaster, Scots Guards.
4th class Medjidie. Actions of Magfar, Tel el-Maskhuta; and battle of Tel el-Kebir. Medal with clasp; bronze star. Honorary rank of Major.

McCalmont, H., Lieutenant-Colonel, 7th Hussars.
Brigade Major, 1st Cavalry Brigade. Capture of Mahsama; both actions at Kassassin; battle of Tel el-Kebir; and pursuit to Cairo. Despatches "London Gazette," 8th September and 2nd November, 1882. 3rd class Medjidie; medal with clasp; bronze star.

McCausland, E. L., Lieutenant, Royal Marines.
Occupation of Port Saïd and Ismaïlia. Actions of Tel el-Maskhuta and Kassassin; battle of Tel el-Kebir (severely wounded). Medal with clasp; bronze star.

McCausland, W. H., Lieutenant-Colonel, Royal Artillery (Madras).
Battle of Tel el-Kebir. Despatches "London Gazette," 2nd November, 1882. Brevet of Lieutenant-Colonel. 4th class Osmanieh. Medal with clasp; bronze star.

McCheane, W. H., Captain, Royal Marine Light Infantry.
Occupation of Ismailia, actions at Magfar and Tel el-Maskhuta. Medal; bronze star.

McClintock, B., Captain, Shropshire Light Infantry.
Defence of Alexandria; occupation of Kafr ed-Dauar; surrender of Damietta. Medal; bronze star.

McClintock, W. K., Lieutenant, Berkshire Regiment.
Surrender of Kafr ed-Dauar. Medal; bronze star.

McComb, R. B., Captain, Commissariat and Transport Staff.
Medal; bronze star.

McCracken, F. W. N., Lieutenant, Berkshire Regiment.
Surrender of Kafr ed-Dauar. Medal; bronze star.

McDonald, C. M., Lieutenant-Colonel, Highland Light Infantry.
Battle of Tel el-Kebir. Despatches "London Gazette," 2nd November, 1882. Brevet of Major. Medal with clasp; bronze star.

McDowell, C. G.
See General Orders, 27th August, 1882.

McDowell, E. G., Brigade Surgeon.
3rd class Medjidie. Medal; bronze star.

McGrath, E., Brigade Surgeon.
Mentioned in despatches. 3rd class Medjidie. Medal; bronze star.

McGrigor, C. R. R., Lieutenant, King's Royal Rifle Corps.
Reconnaissance of Ramleh; affair at Tel el-Maskhuta; action at Kassassin; and battle of Tel el-Kebir. Medal with clasp; bronze star.

McInroy, C., Lieutenant-Colonel, Madras Staff Corps.
Battle of Tel el-Kebir. Medal with clasp; bronze star.

McKay, W., Lieutenant of Orderlies.
Medal and bronze star.

McLaughlin, G. H., Lieutenant, Royal Artillery.
Medal; bronze star.

McLoughlin, J.
(Q.M., C. and T. Staff). Medal; bronze star.

McNair, J. M., Major (Paymaster), Cameron Highlanders.
> Medal ; bronze star.

McNalty, G. W., Surgeon.
> Battle of Tel el-Kebir.   4th class Osmanieh.   Medal with clasp ; bronze star.

McNamara, W. H., Surgeon.
> Battle of Tel el-Kebir.   Medal with clasp ; bronze star.

McNeil, J. G., Lieutenant, Black Watch.
> Killed in action at Tel el-Kebir.

McNeill, Sir J. C., Colonel (Half-pay).
> Despatches "London Gazette," 2nd November, 1882.   K.C.B. ; 2nd class Medjidie.   Medal and bronze star.

McQuaid, P. J., Surgeon.
> Action at Kassassin ; battle of Tel el-Kebir.   Medal with clasp ; bronze star.

Macbay, W. G. W., Captain, Bombay Staff Corps.
> Battle of Tel el-Kebir.   Despatches "London Gazette," 2nd November, 1882.   Brevet of Major.   Medal with clasp ; bronze star.

Macdonald, C. E. W., Lieutenant, Bengal Staff Corps.
> Actions of Kassassin, and battle of Tel el-Kebir.   Medal with clasp ; bronze star.

Macdonald, C. M., Captain, Highland Light Infantry.
> Battle of Tel el-Kebir.   Despatches "London Gazette," 2nd November, 1882.   Brevet of Major.   Medal with clasp ; bronze star.

Macdonald, G. G., Lieutenant, Grenadier Guards.
> Action of Tel el-Maskhuta, and battle of Tel el-Kebir.   Medal with clasp ; bronze star.

Macdonald, H. C. F., Lieutenant, Seaforth Highlanders.
> Seizure of Suez Canal east of Ismailia ; battle of Tel el-Kebir ; occupation of Zagazig and of Cairo.   Medal with clasp ; bronze star.

Macdonnel, G. B., Major, Royal Artillery.
> Despatches "London Gazette," 2nd November, 1882.   3rd class Medjidie.   Medal and bronze star.

MacDougall, S., Lieutenant, Argyll and Sutherland Highlanders.
> Battle of Tel el-Kebir (severely wounded)   Medal with clasp ; bronze star.

MacFarlane, H. H., Lieutenant, 3rd Dragoon Guards.
> Action of Tel el-Maskhuta.   In command of Remount Depôt, Ismailia.   Medal ; bronze star.

Macgregor, H. G., Major (Half-pay).
> D.A.A. and Q.M.G.   Base and lines of communication   Despatches "London Gazette," 2nd November, 1882.   Brevet of Lieutenant-Colonel.   4th class Osmanieh.   Medal and bronze star.

Mackenzie, C. J., Lieutenant, Seaforth Highlanders.
> Battle of Tel el-Kebir.   Medal with clasp ; bronze star.

Mackenzie, T. A., Lieutenant, Cameron Highlanders.
> Battle of Tel el-Kebir.   Medal with clasp ; bronze star.

Mackinnon, H. W. A., Surgeon-Major.
> Battle of Tel el-Kebir (slightly wounded).   Mentioned in despatches.   Medal with clasp ; bronze star.

Mackinnon, L. D., Lieutenant and Captain, Coldstream Guards.
> Battle of Tel el-Kebir.   Medal with clasp ; bronze star.

Mackinnon, W., now Quartermaster, 4th Battalion Highland Light Infantry.
> Medal ; bronze star.

Mackworth, Sir A. W., Bart., Major, Royal Engineers.
Action at Kassassin, 9th September; battle of Tel el-Kebir. Despatches "London Gazette," 2nd November, 1882. Brevet of Lieutenant-Colonel 3rd class Medjidie; medal with clasp; bronze star.

MacLaughlin, W., Lieutenant (Assistant Paymaster), Shropshire Light Infantry.
Defence of Alexandria; occupation of Kafr ed-Dauar; surrender of Damietta. Medal; bronze star.

Macleod, N., Lieutenant, Royal Highlanders.
Medal; bronze star.

Macleod, R. W., Lieutenant, Bengal Staff Corps.
Battle of Tel el-Kebir. Medal with clasp; bronze star.

Macmullen, F. R., Lieutenant, Duke of Wellington's Regiment.
Action of Kassassin and battle of Tel el-Kebir. Medal with clasp; bronze star.

Macnaghten, W. H., Colonel, Bengal Staff Corps.
Action of Kassassin, and battle of Tel el-Kebir. Despatches "London Gazette," 2nd November, 1882. 3rd class Osmanieh; C.B. Medal with clasp; bronze star.

Maconachie, J., Surgeon.
Medal; bronze star.

Macpherson, D., Colonel, Royal Highlanders.
Battle of Tel el-Kebir. Despatches "London Gazette," 2nd November, 1882. 3rd class Medjidie. Medal with clasp; bronze star.

Macpherson, D. II., Lieutenant, Seaforth Highlanders.
Battle of Tel el-Kebir. Medal with clasp; bronze star. 5th class Medjidie.

Macpherson, Sir H. T., Major-General, Bengal Staff Corps.
Commanded Indian Contingent. Battle of Tel el-Kebir, and subsequent pursuit to Zagazig. Despatches "London Gazette," 6th October and 2nd November, 1882. Thanked by Houses of Parliament. 2nd class Medjidie; K.C.S.I. Medal with clasp; bronze star. See General Orders, 28th August, 1882.

Macready, C. F. N., Lieutenant, Gordon Highlanders.
Battle of Tel el-Kebir. Medal with clasp; bronze star.

Mactaggart, Rev. J.
Battle of Tel-el-Kebir. Medal with clasp; bronze star.

Magrath, C. W. S., Surgeon.
Battle of Tel el-Kebir. Medal with clasp; bronze star.

Maitland, A. F., Lieutenant, Royal West Surrey Regiment.
Battle of Tel-el-Kebir. Medal with clasp; bronze star.

Maitland, C. B., Surgeon, Indian Medical Service.
Medal; bronze star.

Maitland, J. M. H., Lieutenant-Colonel, Royal Engineers.
Battle of Tel el-Kebir. Despatches "London Gazette," 2nd November, 1882. C.B.; 3rd class Medjidie. Medal with clasp; bronze star.

Malcolm, H. H. L., Lieutenant, Cameron Highlanders.
Battle of Tel-el-Kebir (wounded). Medal with clasp; bronze star.

Manley, F. C., Lieutenant, Coldstream Guards.
Action of Tel el-Maskhuta, and battle of Tel el-Kebir. Medal with clasp; bronze star.

Manley, W. G. N., Brigade Surgeon.
P.M.O. 2nd Division. Battle of Tel el-Kebir. Despatches "London Gazette," 2nd November, 1882. Promoted Deputy Surgeon-General. 3rd class Osmanieh. Medal with clasp; bronze star.

Mann, H. T. W, Lieutenant (Veterinary Surgeon).
Battle of Tel el-Kebir. Medal with clasp; bronze star.

Manningham-Buller, F. C., Major, Coldstream Guards
Action of Tel el-Maskhuta; and battle of Tel el-Kebir. Medal with clasp; bronze star.

Mantell, A. M., Lieutenant, Royal Engineers.
Medal and bronze star. See General Orders, 23rd August, 1882.

Marling, P. S., Lieutenant, King's Royal Rifle Corps.
Affair at Tel el-Maskhuta; action at Kassassin; battle of Tel el-Kebir. Medal with clasp; bronze star.

Marriot, R. A., Lieutenant, Royal Marines.
Bombardment of Forts of Alexandria; actions of Magfar, Mahsama, Kassassin; battle of Tel el-Kebir. 5th class Medjidie. Medal with two clasps; bronze star

Marryatt, H. C., Major, Manchester Regiment.
Medal; bronze star.

Marsh, H. C., Major, Bengal Staff Corps.
4th class Osmanieh. Medal; bronze star.

Marshall, J. D., Lieutenant of Orderlies.
Battle of Tel el-Kebir. Medal with clasp; bronze star.

Marston, J. A., Brigade Surgeon.
Sanitary Officer. Battle of Tel el-Kebir. Despatches "London Gazette," 2nd November, 1882. Promoted Deputy Surgeon-General. 3rd class Osmanieh. Medal with clasp; bronze star.

Martin, E. C., Captain, Royal Irish Fusiliers.
Battle of Tel el-Kebir. Medal with clasp; bronze star.

Martin, G. B. N., Captain, Royal Artillery.
A.D.C. to O.C. Royal Artillery. Despatches "London Gazette," 2nd November, 1882. Brevet of Major. 4th class Medjidie. Medal with clasp; bronze star.

Martin, J., Captain, Royal Highlanders.
Medal; bronze star.

Martin, J. H., now Lieutenant, 3rd Dragoon Guards.
Medal; bronze star.

Martin, M. K., Captain, Bengal Staff Corps.
Battle of Tel el-Kebir. Despatches "London Gazette," 2nd November, 1882. Medal with clasp; bronze star.

Martyr, C. G., Lieutenant, Duke of Cornwall's Light Infantry.
Reconnaissance in force on Kafr ed-Dauar; actions at Magfar, Tel el-Maskhuta, and Kassassin; battle of Tel el-Kebir. Medal with clasp; bronze star.

Mathias, V. D., Captain, Royal Marine Artillery.
Attack on the forts of Alexandria. Brevet of Lieutenant-Colonel. Medal with clasp; bronze star.

Mattei, A., Lieutenant, Malta Fencible Artillery.
Medal; bronze star.

Matthews, I., Veterinary Surgeon (Lieutenant).
Action of Tel-el Maskhuta; the two actions of Kassassin; battle of Tel el-Kebir; occupation of Cairo. Promoted Veterinary Surgeon 1st class. Medal with clasp; bronze star.

Maul, S. D., Lieutenant, York and Lancaster Regiment.
Battle of Tel el-Kebir. Medal with clasp; bronze star.

Maunsell, C. A., Surgeon-Major.
Medal; bronze star.

Maunsell, G. W., Lieutenant, Royal West Kent Regiment.
Battle of Tel el-Kebir. 5th class Medjidie. Medal with clasp; bronze star.

Maurice, J. F., Major, Royal Artillery.
D.A.A.G., Head-quarters. Actions of Magfar, Tel el-Maskhuta, Kassassin, 9th September; battle of Tel el-Kebir. Despatches "London Gazette," 2nd November, 1882. Brevet of Lieutenant-Colonel. 4th class Osmanieh; medal with clasp; bronze star.

Maxwell, A. B., Lieutenant, Manchester Regiment.
Medal; bronze star.

Maxwell, F., Lieutenant, Highland Light Infantry.
Battle of Tel el-Kebir. Medal with clasp; bronze star.

Maxwell, J. G., Lieutenant, Royal Highlanders.
Battle of Tel el-Kebir. Medal with clasp; bronze star.

Mayne, R. C. G., Lieutenant, Bombay Staff Corps.
Battle of Tel el-Kebir, forced march to and occupation of Zagazig, and occupation of Cairo. Medal with clasp; bronze star.

Meiklejohn, W. H.. Major, Royal Artillery.
Battle of Tel el-Kebir. Despatches "London Gazette," 17th November. 1882. 4th class Osmanieh. Medal with clasp; bronze star.

Melgund, J. G. (Viscount), Captain, Mounted Rifle Volunteers.
Attached to Mounted Infantry. Action at Tel el-Maskhuta (wounded). Despatches "London Gazette," 8th September and 2nd November, 1882. Granted honorary rank of Major (Auxiliary Forces). 4th class Medjidie. See General Orders, 26th August, 1882. Medal; bronze star.

Melliss, H., Major, Bombay Staff Corps.
As A.Q.M.G., Indian Contingent. Despatches "London Gazette," 2nd November, 1882. Brevet of Major. 4th class Medjidie. Medal with clasp; bronze star.

Melvill, C. G., Lieutenant, Manchester Regiment.
Medal; bronze star.

Menzies, J. J. B., Captain, Gordon Highlanders.
Battle of Tel el-Kebir. Medal with clasp; bronze star.

Merriman, C. M. H., Lieutenant, Shropshire Regiment.
Defence of Alexandria; occupation of Kafr ed-Dauar; surrender of Damietta. Medal; bronze star.

Methuen, Hon. P. S., Colonel, Scots Guards.
Commandant at Head-quarter Camp. Action of Tel el-Maskhuta, battle of Tel el-Kebir. 3rd class Osmanieh; C.B. Medal with clasp; bronze star.

Meyrick, J. J., Principal Veterinary Surgeon.
Despatches "London Gazette," 2nd November, 1882. 3rd class Osmanieh; C.B. Medal; bronze star.

Midwood, H., Lieutenant, Highland Light Infantry.
Battle of Tel el-Kebir (severely wounded). Medal with clasp; bronze star.

Milborne-Swinnerton-Pilkington, T. E.. Lieutenant, King's Royal Rifle Corps.
Battle of Tel el-Kebir. Medal with clasp; bronze star.

Mildmay, H. P. St. J.. Lieutenant, Grenadier Guards.
Action of Tel el-Maskhuta; battle of Tel el-Kebir. Medal with clasp; bronze star.

Miles, C. N., Lieutenant, 1st Life Guards.
Actions of Magfar, Mahsama, Kassassin; battle of Tel el-Kebir; march to and occupation of Cairo. Medal with clasp; bronze star.

Miller, W. B., Surgeon.
Action at Kassassin. Mentioned in despatches. Medal; bronze star.

Miller-Wallnutt, C. C, Lieutenant, Gordon Highlanders.
Battle of Tel el-Kebir. Medal with clasp; bronze star.

Mills, H. J., Major, Ordnance Store Department.
Despatches "London Gazette," 2nd November, 1882. Medal;
bronze star. 3rd class Medjidie.
Milward, C. H., Lieutenant, Royal Artillery.
Medal; bronze star.
Minchin, W. R., Lieutenant, Royal West Kent Regiment.
Medal; bronze star.
Mitchell, C. A. P., Surgeon.
Battle of Tel-el-Kebir. Medal with clasp; bronze star.
Mitchell, M. C., Surgeon.
Action of Tel el-Maskhuta, and battle of Tel el-Kebir. Medal with
clasp; bronze star.
Molloy, O. F., Surgeon.
Battle of Tel el-Kebir. Medal with clasp; bronze star.
Molyneux, W. C. F., Brevet Major, Cheshire Regiment.
D.A.A. and Q.M.G., 1st Division. Actions at Magfar and Tel
el-Maskhuta; both actions at Kassassin; and battle of Tel
el-Kebir. Despatches "London Gazette," 19th September and
2nd November, 1882. Brevet of Lieutenant-Colonel. 4th class
Osmanieh; medal with clasp; bronze star.
Monck, Hon. H. P. C. S., Lieutenant, Coldstream Guards.
Action of Tel el-Maskhuta; and battle of Tel el-Kebir. Medal with
clasp; bronze star.
Money, H. C., Lieutenant, Royal Marine Light Infantry.
Occupation of Port Saïd; actions of Tel el-Maskhuta, Kassassin;
and battle of Tel el-Kebir Mentioned in despatches. Medal
with clasp; bronze star.
Monro, S. C. H., Lieutenant, Seaforth Highlanders.
Engagement of Shaluf; seizure of Suez Canal east of Ismailia
battle of Tel el-Kebir; occupation of Zagazig and of Cairo.
Medal with clasp; bronze star.
Montagu, Hon. O. G. P., Major, Royal Horse Guards.
Brevet of Lieutenant-Colonel. Medal; bronze star.
Montagu, P., Lieutenant, 7th Dragoon Guards.
Actions of Magfar, Mahsama, Kassassin. Medal; bronze star.
Montagu-Stuart-Wortley, E. J., Lieutenant, King's Royal Rifle
Corps.
As Orderly Officer to Colonel on Staff, base and lines of commu-
nication; also to G.O.C. 1st Cavalry Brigade. Battle of Tel
el-Kebir. Medal with clasp; bronze star.
Montgomery, A. C. G., Lieutenant, 1st Battalion Highland Light
Infantry.
Battle of Tel el-Kebir. Medal with clasp; bronze star.
Montgomery, J. G. H. G., Lieutenant, Coldstream Guards.
Action of Tel el-Maskhuta; and battle of Tel el-Kebir. Medal with
clasp; bronze star.
Moore, H., Lieutenant-Colonel, Bombay Staff Corps.
Occupation of Suez and Ismaïlia, advance to Kassassin, battle of
Tel el-Kebir, pursuit to Zagazig, occupation of Cairo. Head of
Intelligence Department, Indian Contingent. 3rd class Osmanieh.
Medal with clasp; bronze star.
Moore, H. G., Major, Argyll and Sutherland Highlanders.
Provost-Marshal (A.A. and Q.M.G., Head-quarters). At second
action of Kassassin; and battle of Tel el-Kebir. Despatches
"London Gazette," 2nd November, 1882. C.B.; 3rd class Os-
manieh; medal with clasp; bronze star.

Moore, W., Captain, South Staffordshire Regiment.
Medal and bronze star.
Moores, S., Captain, Manchester Regiment.
Medal ; bronze star.
Morgan, A. B., Lieutenant-Colonel, Norfolk Regiment.
A.A.G., Indian Contingent. Despatches "London Gazette," 2nd
November, 1882. 3rd class Medjidie; C.B. Medal with clasp ;
bronze star.
Morgan, A. H., Surgeon.
Medal ; bronze star.
Morgan, Henry, Lieutenant-Colonel, Ordnance Store Department.
Despatches "London Gazette," 2nd November, 1882. Medal ;
bronze star. Promoted Assistant Commissary-General, with
relative rank of Lieutenant-Colonel.
Morris, Sir E., Major-General, Commissariat and Transport Staff.
Senior Commissariat Officer. Battle of Tel el-Kebir. Despatches
"London Gazette," 6th October and 2nd November, 1882. 2nd
class Medjidie ; K.C.B. ; medal with clasp ; bronze star.
Morris, H. G., Lieutenant, Duke of Cornwall's Light Infantry.
Actions at Magfar, Tel el-Maskhuta, and Kassassin ; battle of Tel
el-Kebir. Medal with clasp ; bronze star.
Morris, R., Major, Bengal Cavalry.
On transport duty. Battle of Tel el-Kebir. Medal with clasp ;
bronze star. See General Orders, 11th September, 1882.
Morris, W. B., Lieutenant, 7th Hussars.
Actions at Kassassin ; and battle of Tel el-Kebir. Medal with
clasp ; bronze star.
Morse, A. T., Lieutenant, Royal West Kent Regiment.
Medal ; bronze star.
Morse, R. E. R., Surgeon.
Medal ; bronze star.
Mortimer, W. H., Paymaster (Honorary Captain), Gordon Highlanders.
Battle of Tel el-Kebir. Medal with clasp ; bronze star.
Moss, W. A., Lieutenant of Orderlies.
Action of Kassassin. Medal and bronze star.
Mostyn, Hon. Montague, Paymaster.
See General Orders, 9th September, 1882.
Moynihan, T., Surgeon.
Medal ; bronze star.
Murdoch, C. H., Conductor of Supplies.
Medal ; bronze star.
Murphy, F. J., Lieutenant, 7th Dragoon Guards.
Actions of Magfar, Mahsama, Kassassin. Medal ; bronze star.
Murphy, P., Surgeon-Major, Indian Medical Service.
Battle of Tel el-Kebir. Medal with clasp ; bronze star.
Murray, Andrew, Major, Seaforth Highlanders.
Battle of Tel el-Kebir. Medal with clasp ; bronze star ; 4th class
Osmanieh.
Murray, C. W., Major, Gloucester Regiment.
As D.A.A. and Q.M.G., base and lines of communication. Battle
of Tel el-Kebir. Despatches "London Gazette," 2nd November,
1882. Brevet of Lieutenant-Colonel. 4th class Osmanieh. Medal
with clasp ; bronze star.
Murray, K. D., Major, Royal Irish Fusiliers.
D.A.A. and Q.M.G., 2nd Division. Battle of Tel el-Kebir. Despatches
"London Gazette," 2nd November, 1882. Brevet of Lieutenant-

Colonel. 4th class Osmanieh. Medal with clasp; bronze star.

Murray, P. H., Captain, Shropshire Light Infantry.
Defence of Alexandria, occupation of Kafr ed-Dauar, and surrender of Damietta. Medal; bronze star.

Murray, R. H., Brevet Major, Seaforth Highlanders.
As Brigade Major, Infantry Brigade, Indian Division. Battle of Tel el-Kebir; and occupation of Zagazig same night; and of Cairo. Medal with clasp; bronze star; 4th class Osmanieh. Brevet of Lieutenant-Colonel.

Murray-Dunlop, H. L., Lieutenant, Royal Artillery.
5th class Medjidie.

Maynors, W. B.
Capture of Mahsama; and battle of Tel-el-Kebir. Medal with clasp; bronze star.

Nairne, C. E., Lieutenant-Colonel, Royal Artillery.
Battle of Tel el-Kebir. Despatches "London Gazette," 2nd November, 1882. 3rd class Medjidie; C.B. Medal with clasp; bronze star.

Nash, W., Surgeon.
Medal; bronze star.

Nash. W. P., Captain, Manchester Regiment.
Medal; bronze star.

Needham, C., Major, 1st Life Guards.
Actions of Magfar, Mahsama, Kassassin, 28th August; battle of Tel el-Kebir; march to and occupation of Cairo. Brevet of Lieutenant-Colonel. Medal with clasp; bronze star.

Nesfield, Henry W.
See General Orders, 3rd September, 1882.

Newcombe, H. G., Captain, Royal Artillery.
4th class Medjidie. Medal; bronze star.

Newman, W., Lieutenant, Royal Artillery.
3rd class Medjidie. Medal; bronze star.

Nichols, R., Quartermaster, Commissariat and Transport Staff.
Medal; bronze star.

Nicholls, A., Lieutenant, Berkshire Regiment.
Surrender of Kafr ed-Dauar. Medal; bronze star.

Nicholson, W. G., Captain, Royal Engineers.
Battle of Tel el-Kebir. 4th class Osmanieh Medal with clasp; bronze star.

Noble, E. J. W., Captain, Royal Marine Artillery.
Actions at Mallaha, Magfar, Tel el-Maskhuta, Kassassin (horse killed); and battle of Tel-Kebir. Despatches "London Gazette," 19th September, 1882. Brevet of Major. 4th class Medjidie. Medal with clasp; bronze star.

Noding, T. E., Surgeon.
Medal; bronze star.

Norris, S. L., Lieutenant, Royal Engineers.
Action of Magfar. Medal; bronze star.

Norton, G. F. A., Lieutenant, Royal Artillery.
Battle of Tel el-Kebir. Medal with clasp.

Noyes, G. A., Major, Royal Artillery.
Medal; bronze star.

Nugent, C. B. P. N. H., Royal Engineers, Brigadier-General on Staff.
Commanding Royal Engineer in command of the left at Kassassin

during battle of Tel el-Kebir. Despatches "London Gazette," 6th October and 2nd November, 1882. 2nd class Medjidie; K.C.B. Medal; bronze star.

Nugent, R. A., Captain, Commissariat and Transport Staff.
Battle of Tel el-Kebir. 4th class Medjidie Medal with clasp; bronze star.

O'Brien, D. J. T., Lieutenant, Manchester Regiment.
Medal; bronze star.
O'Connor, D., Lieutenant of Orderlies.
Medal and bronze star.
O'Connor, P. F., Surgeon, Bengal Staff Corps.
Battle of Tel el-Kebir. Medal with clasp; bronze star.
O'Donnell, T. J., Surgeon.
Medal; bronze star.
O'Dwyer, T. F., Surgeon-Major.
In command of a bearer company. Action at Kassassin; and battle of Tel el-Kebir. Despatches "London Gazette," 2nd November, 1882. Promoted Surgeon-Major, with relative rank of Lieutenant-Colonel. Medal with clasp; bronze star.
Ogilvy, W. L. K., Lieutenant-Colonel, King's Royal Rifle Corps.
Reconnaissance at Ramleh; affair at Tel el-Maskhuta; actions at Kassassin; and battle of Tel el-Kebir. Medal with clasp; bronze star; 4th class Osmanieh.
Ogle, F. A., Major, Royal Marines.
Reconnaissance of 5th August; and actions at Magfar (slightly wounded), Tel el-Maskhuta, Kassassin; and battle of Tel el-Kebir. Despatches "London Gazette," 19th September, 1882. Brevet of Lieutenant-Colonel. 4th class Osmanieh. Medal with clasp; bronze star.
O'Keeffe, M. W., Surgeon.
Battle of Tel el-Kebir. Medal with clasp; bronze star.
Oldfield, J. R. H., Lieutenant, Royal Marines.
Medal; bronze star.
O'Leary, E. F., Brigade Surgeon.
Medal; bronze star. See General Orders, 27th August, 1882.
Olivey, W. R., Lieutenant-Colonel.
Chief Paymaster. 3rd class Osmanich; C.B. (civil). Medal; bronze star. See General Orders, 4th September, 1882.
O'Neill, Rev. O. A. W., Chaplain to the Forces.
Medal; bronze star.
O'Neill, W. H., Lieutenant, Royal Artillery.
Battle of Tel el-Kebir.
Orange, J. E, Lieutenant, King's Royal Rifle Corps.
Medal; bronze star.
Orford, A., Lieutenant.
Actions of Magfar, Kassassin, and battle of Tel el-Kebir. Medal with clasp; bronze star.
Orr, A. S., Lieutenant, Royal Irish Regiment.
Battle of Tel el-Kebir. Medal with clasp; bronze star.
Orr-Ewing, J., Lieutenant, 4th Dragoon Guards.
Action at Tel el-Maskhuta; capture of Mahsama; first action at Kassassin; battle of Tel el-Kebir; subsequent pursuit to Belbeis; surrender and occupation of Cairo. Medal with clasp; bronze star.

Osborne, R. T., Captain of Orderlies
  Battle of Tel el-Kebir. Mentioned in despatches. Granted hono-
    rary rank of Captain. Medal with clasp; bronze star.
Osburne, J., Surgeon.
  Battle of Tel el-Kebir. Medal with clasp; bronze star.
Overton, E. F., now Quartermaster, King's Royal Rifle Corps.
  Reconnaissance of 5th August, affair at Tel el-Maskhuta, action at
    Kassassin, and battle of Tel el-Kebir. Medal with clasp; bronze
    star.
Owen, C. W., Surgeon, Indian Medical Service.
  Battle of Tel el-Kebir. Medal with clasp; bronze star.
Ozanne, H. W., Lieutenant, Royal West Kent Regiment.
  Action at Kassassin.

Pagan, G. A., Lieutenant, Highland Light Infantry.
  Battle of Tel el-Kebir. Medal with clasp; bronze star.
Pain, A. H., Brevet Major, Gordon Highlanders.
  Battle of Tel el-Kebir. Medal with clasp; bronze star.
Pallin, S. L., Veterinary Surgeon (Captain).
  Battle of Tel el-Kebir. Medal with clasp; bronze star.
Palmer, F. C., Captain, 7th Dragoon Guards.
  Actions of Magfar, Mahsama, Kassassin; battle of Tel el-Kebir,
    and forced march to Cairo. Medal with clasp; bronze star.
Palmer, W. H., Lieutenant, Royal Marines.
  Actions of Tel el-Maskhuta, Kassassin, 9th September; and battle
    of Tel el-Kebir. Medal with clasp; bronze star.
Park, J. A., Lieutenant, Black Watch.
  Died of wounds received in action at Tel el-Kebir.
Parke, T. H., Surgeon.
  Medal; bronze star.
Parker, H., Lieutenant, Liverpool Regiment.
  Battle of Tel el-Kebir. Medal with clasp; bronze star.
Parr, H. H., Major, Somersetshire Light Infantry.
  Commanded Mounted Infantry from 2nd August to 5th October
    and present at action of Tel el-Maskhuta, 24th August (severely
    wounded). Despatches "London Gazette," 8th September and
    2nd November, 1882. Brevet of Major. 4th class Medjidie
    Medal; bronze star. See General Orders, 26th August, 1882.
Parsons, C. S. B., Lieutenant, Royal Horse Artillery.
  Actions at Mahsama and Kassassin (horse shot); and battle of
    Tel el-Kebir. Despatches "London Gazette," 2nd November, 1882.
    Medal with clasp; bronze star; and 5th class Medjidie. Brevet
    of Major.
Parsons, F., Surgeon-Major, Indian Medical Service.
  Battle of Tel el-Kebir. Medal with clasp; bronze star.
Parsons, W., Quartermaster, Commissariat and Transport Corps.
  Medal; bronze star.
Patton-Bethune, H. B., Lieutenant, 3rd Hussars.
  Battle of Tel-el-Kebir. Medal with clasp; bronze star.
Paul, E. T., Lieutenant, Bengal Staff Corps.
  Battle of Tel-el-Kebir, and subsequent pursuit to Zagazig. Medal
    with clasp; bronze star.
Payne, C. H., Lieutenant, Gordon Highlanders.
  Battle of Tel el-Kebir. Medal with clasp; bronze star.
Pearce, G. R., Lieutenant, Manchester Regiment.
  Medal; bronze star

Pearse, J. L., Lieutenant, Shropshire Regiment.
Defence of Alexandria, occupation of Kafr ed-Dauar, and surrender of Damietta. Medal; bronze star.
Pearse, N. L., Lieutenant, Derbyshire Regiment.
Action at Kassassin on 9th September, and battle of Tel el-Kebir. Medal with clasp; bronze star.
Peckitt, R. W., Captain, York and Lancaster Regiment.
Actions at Kassassin and Magfar. Mentioned in despatches. Brevet of Major. Medal; bronze star.
Peile, S. P., Lieutenant, Royal Marines.
Occupation of Ismailia; actions of Magfar and Tel el-Maskhuta. Medal; bronze star.
Pelly, H. G., Lieutenant, Royal Artillery.
Battle of Tel el-Kebir. Medal with clasp; bronze star.
Pemberton, E. St. C., Lieutenant, Royal Engineers.
Battle of Tel el-Kebir. Medal with clasp; bronze star.
Pengree, H. H., Captain, Royal Artillery.
Battle of Tel el-Kebir. 4th class Medjidie. Medal with clasp; bronze star.
Pennington, C. R., Major and Lieutenant-Colonel, Bengal Staff Corps.
Action at Kassassin; battle of Tel el-Kebir. Despatches "London Gazette," 17th November, 1882. 4th class Osmanieh. Medal with clasp; bronze star.
Pennington, F., Major, Royal Artillery.
Medal; bronze star.
Perkins, H. C., Lieutenant, Duke of Cornwall's Light Infantry.
Reconnaissance in force at Kafr ed-Dauar; actions at Magfar, Tel el-Maskhuta, and Kassassin; battle of Tel-el-Kebir. Medal with clasp; bronze star.
Perry, G., Surgeon-Major, Coldstream Guards.
Action of Tel el-Maskhuta and battle of Tel el-Kebir. Medal with clasp; bronze star.
Perry, L. F., Major, Royal Artillery.
Battle of Tel el-Kebir. Despatches "London Gazette," 2nd November, 1882. Brevet of Lieutenant-Colonel. 3rd class Medjidie. Medal with clasp; bronze star.
Peyton, W. R. B., Lieutenant, Shropshire Regiment.
Defence of Alexandria, occupation of Kafr ed-Dauar, and surrender of Damietta. Medal; bronze star.
Philips, Joseph, Major, Royal Marines.
Mentioned in despatches. Brevet of Lieutenant-Colonel. 4th class Osmanieh. Medal and bronze star.
Phillips, E. P., Surgeon, Welsh Regiment.
Medal; bronze star.
Phillips, E., Quartermaster, Commissariat and Transport Corps.
Medal; bronze star.
Phillips, T., Lieutenant-Colonel, 18th Hussars.
Medal and bronze star.
Philpot, F., Captain of Orderlies.
Medal and bronze star.
Pierson, A. H., Surgeon, Indian Medical Service.
Battle of Tel el-Kebir. Medal with clasp; bronze star.
Pierson, J. E., Lieutenant, Royal Sussex Regiment.
Defence of Alexandria; surrender of Kafr ed-Dauar; occupation of Damanhur; and surrender of Damietta. Medal and bronze star.

Pigott, C. B., Lieutenant, King's Royal Rifle Corps.
Served with the Mounted Infantry at reconnaissance at Ramleh, action of Magfar, affair at Tel el-Maskhuta, and action at Kassassin (dangerously wounded). Despatches "London Gazette," 8th September and 19th September, 1882. Promoted Captain for distinguished service. 5th class Medjidie ; medal ; bronze star. See General Orders, 26th August, 1882.

Pilkington, Milborne Swinnerton.
See General Orders, 16th August, 1882.

Pipe-Wolferstan, E. S., Lieutenant, South Staffordshire Regiment.
Medal and bronze star.

Pirie, A. G., Lieutenant, Gordon Highlanders.
Died of wounds received in action at Tel el-Kebir. 5th Class Medjidie.

Pirie, D. V., Lieutenant, 4th Royal Irish Dragoons.
Extra A.D.C. to Major-General Graham. Actions of Magfar Mahsama, Kassassin. Despatches "London Gazette," 19th September and 2nd November, 1882. Medal ; bronze star.

Pleydell-Bouverie, G., Lieutenant, Coldstream Guards.
Action of Tel el-Maskhuta and battle of Tel-el-Kebir. Medal with clasp ; bronze star.

Poingdestre, A., Lieutenant, South Staffordshire Regiment.
Reconnaissance of 5th August. Medal and bronze star.

Polden, R. J., Surgeon, Indian Medical Service.
Medal ; bronze star.

Pole-Carew, R., Lieutenant, Coldstream Guards.
Action at Tel el-Maskhuta and battle of Tel el-Kebir. Medal with clasp ; bronze star.

Pollen, W. H., Lieutenant, Royal Engineers.
Medal and bronze star.

Pollock, C. F., Surgeon-Major.
Battle of Tel el-Kebir. Medal with clasp ; bronze star.

Pope, P. E., Lieutenant-Colonel, 4th Dragoon Guards.
Actions at Magfar and Tel el-Maskhuta ; capture of Mahsama ; first action at Kassassin. Medal ; bronze star.

Pope, W. W., Surgeon.
Battle of Tel el-Kebir. Medal with clasp ; bronze star.

Portelli, A. M., Captain, Malta Fencible Artillery.
Mentioned in despatches. Brevet of Lieutenant-Colonel. C.M.G. Medal ; bronze star.

Potter, H., Surgeon-Major, Indian Medical Service.
Medal ; bronze star.

Power, E. R., Surgeon.
Medal ; bronze star.

Power, J. L., Captain, York and Lancaster Regiment.
Battle of Tel el-Kebir. Mentioned in despatches. Medal with clasp ; bronze star.

Powles, T. W., Lieutenant, Royal Artillery.
Battle of Tel el-Kebir. Medal with clasp ; bronze star.

Prendergast, J., Surgeon.
Battle of Tel el-Kebir. Medal with clasp ; bronze star.

Pressey, A., Lieutenant, Royal West Kent Regiment.
Medal ; bronze star

Prince, R., Major, Shropshire Light Infantry.
Defence of Alexandria, occupation of Kafr ed-Dauar, surrender of Damietta. Medal ; bronze star.

Pringle, D., Captain of Orderlies.
Battle of Tel el-Kebir. Granted honorary rank of Captain. Medal with clasp; bronze star.

Pringle, Sir N. W. D., Bart., Major, Staffordshire Regiment.
Medal and bronze star.

Priolean, L. H., Lieutenant, Manchester Regiment.
Medal; bronze star.

Pulteney, W. P., Lieutenant, Scots Guards.
Actions of Magfar, Tel el-Maskhuta, and battle of Tel el-Kebir. Medal with clasp; bronze star.

Puzey, A. R., Captain, Royal Engineers.
Despatches "London Gazette," 2nd November, 1882 Brevet of Major. Medal and bronze star.

Pym, H. R. L., Lieutenant, Royal Marine Artillery.
Action at Mallaha, Kassassin, battle of Tel el-Kebir. Despatches "London Gazette," 19th September, 1882. Medal with clasp; bronze star.

Pyne, J., Paymaster (Honorary Captain).
Medal; bronze star.

Quill, B. C., Captain, York and Lancaster Regiment.
Battle of Tel el-Kebir. Medal with clasp; bronze star.

Quinn, T., Lieutenant, Manchester Regiment.
Medal; bronze star.

Rainsford, M. E. R., Captain, Commissariat and Transport Staff.
Medal; bronze star.

Rainsford, W. J. R., Surgeon.
Medal; bronze star.

Raitt, F. J., Lieutenant, Royal Marine Light Infantry.
Reconnaissance of 6th August; action at Kassassin, 9th September. Medal; bronze star.

Raitt, G. D. C., Lieutenant, Royal Marine Artillery.
Bombardment of Alexandria. Medal with clasp; bronze star.

Ramsay, T., Surgeon-Major.
Medal; bronze star.

Ramsbotham, W. B., Surgeon-Major.
Medal; bronze star.

Ramsden, W. J. F., Captain, Coldstream Guards.
Action of Tel el-Maskhuta and battle of Tel el-Kebir. Medal with clasp; bronze star.

Randall, J. H., Lieutenant-Colonel, Commissariat and Transport Staff.
Despatches "London Gazette," 2nd November, 1882; C.B.; 3rd class Medjidie. Medal; bronze star.

Rathborne, St. G. J., Captain, Berkshire Regiment.
Surrender of Kafr ed-Dauar. Medal; bronze star.

Ratigan, A. H., Surgeon.
Medal; bronze star.

Rawlins, G. W., Lieutenant, Loyal North Lancashire Regiment.
Medal; bronze star.

Rawstorne, G. A. L., Captain, Royal Marine Artillery.
Actions at Magfar, Tel el-Maskhuta, Kassassin; battle of Tel el-Kebir. Despatches "London Gazette," 19th September, 1882. Medal with clasp; bronze star.

Ray, S. K., Surgeon-Major.
Battle of Tel el-Kebir. Medal with clasp; bronze star.

Rayment, G. J. R., Veterinary Surgeon (Lieutenant).
   Action of Mahsama. Medal; bronze star. Promoted Veterinary
      Surgeon 1st class.
Reay, C. T., Lieutenant, Manchester Regiment.
   Medal; bronze star.
Reed, E. M., Lieutenant, Royal Sussex Regiment.
   Medal and bronze star.
Reeves, H. S. E., Major, Commissariat and Transport Staff.
   As Director of Transport. Despatches "London Gazette," 2nd
      November, 1882. Promoted Assistant Commissary-General with
      relative rank of Lieutenant-Colonel. 3rd class Medjidie; medal;
      bronze star.
Reeves, J., Captain, South Staffordshire Regiment.
   Medal; bronze star.
Reilly, B. L. P., Captain, Bombay Staff Corps.
   Medal; bronze star.
Remmington, S. L. M., Captain, Berkshire Regiment.
   Medal; bronze star.
Reynardson, C. B., Captain, Grenadier Guards.
   Action of Tel el-Maskhuta. Medal; bronze star.
Reynolds, E. O., Surgeon, Army Medical Department.
   Battle of Tel el-Kebir. Medal with clasp; bronze star.
Reynolds, J. H., Lieutenant, Grenadier Guards.
   Action of Tel el-Maskhuta and battle of Tel el-Kebir. Medal with
      clasp; bronze star.
Reynolds, T., Quartermaster, Commissariat and Transport Corps.
   Medal; bronze star.
Rhodes, E., Lieutenant, Berkshire Regiment.
   Surrender of Kafr ed-Dauar. Medal; bronze star.
Rich, H. B., Captain, Royal Engineers.
   Medal and bronze star.
Richardson, R. M., Lieutenant, Seaforth Highlanders.
   Engagement of Shaluf; seizure of Suez Canal east of Ismailia;
      battle of Tel el-Kebir; occupation of Zagazig and of Cairo.
      Medal with clasp; bronze star.
Richardson, W. D., Major, Commissariat and Transport Staff.
   Medal; bronze star.
Richardson, W. S., Lieutenant-Colonel, Duke of Cornwall's Light
      Infantry.
   Actions at Magfar, Kassassin; battle of Tel el-Kebir (severely
      wounded). Despatches "London Gazette," 19th September and
      2nd November, 1882. 3rd class Medjidie; C.B. Medal with
      clasp; bronze star.
Ridley, C. P., Captain, Manchester Regiment.
   Medal; bronze star.
Ridley, H. M., Lieutenant, 7th Hussars.
   Battle of Tel el-Kebir. Medal with clasp; bronze star.
Rind, A. T. S. A., Brevet Major, Bengal Staff Corps.
   Medal; bronze star.
Riordan, R. De B., Surgeon-Major.
   Senior Medical Officer with the advance force which landed at
      Alexandria in July 1882. Medal; bronze star.
Riordan, W. E., Surgeon-Major.
   Medal; bronze star.
Risk, E. J. E., Surgeon-Major.
   Medal; bronze star.

Ritchie, James, Captain, Corps of Signallers.
Battle of Tel el-Kebir. 4th class Medjidie. Medal with clasp; bronze star. See General Orders, 30th August, 1882.

Rivett-Carnac, E. H, Lieutenant, Bengal Staff Corps.
Action of Kassassin; battle of Tel el-Kebir. 5th class Medjidie. Medal with clasp; bronze star.

Robarts, C. J., Lieutenant, Bengal Staff Corps.
Action of Kassassin; battle of Tel el-Kebir. Medal with clasp; bronze star.

Robinson, J., Surgeon-Major.
Battle of Tel el-Kebir. Medal with clasp; bronze star.

Robinson, P. A., Paymaster, Royal Irish Regiment.
Medal; bronze star.

Robinson. R. H., Surgeon.
Medal; bronze star.

Robinson, W. G. W., Colonel, Commissariat and Transport Staff.
Senior Commissariat Officer, base and lines of communication. Despatches "London Gazette," 2nd November, 1882. Promoted Deputy Commissary-General; C.B.; 3rd class Osmanieh. Medal; bronze star.

Roche, R. J., Lieutenant, Royal West Kent Regiment.
Medal; bronze star.

Roche, T. H. de M., Lieutenant, Royal Marines.
Actions at Mallaha, Tel el-Maskhuta, Kassassin; battle of Tel el-Kebir, and occupation of Cairo. Medal with clasp; bronze star.

Rochfort-Boyd, C. A., Captain, Royal Engineers.
Despatches "London Gazette," 2nd November, 1882. Brevet of Major. Medal and bronze star.

Rochfort-Boyd, G. W. W., Captain and Adjutant, 2nd Battalion Manchester Regiment.
Medal; bronze star.

Rocke, J. H., Colonel (Half-pay), Deputy Judge Advocate.
As Deputy Judge Advocate-General. Despatches "London Gazette," 2nd November, 1882. C.B.; 2nd class Medjidie; medal with clasp; bronze star.

Rodney, G. B. H. D., Lord, Lieutenant, 1st Life Guards.
Actions of Magfar, Mahsama, Kassassin; battle of Tel el-Kebir; march to and occupation of Cairo. Medal with clasp; bronze star.

Rogers, G. W. N., Major, Royal Irish Regiment.
Battle of Tel el-Kebir. Despatches "London Gazette," 2nd November, 1882. Brevet of Lieutenant-Colonel. 4th class Osmanieh. Medal with clasp; bronze star.

Rogers, H. H., Lieutenant, Royal Artillery.
Battle of Tel el-Kebir. Medal with clasp; bronze star.

Rogers, J., Captain, Commissariat and Transport Staff.
Medal; bronze star.

Rogers, J. G., Surgeon.
In medical charge of 19th Hussars. Action of Kassassin; and battle of Tel el-Kebir. Mentioned in despatches. Promoted Surgeon-Major. Medal with clasp; bronze star.

Rogers, R. G., Lieutenant-Colonel, Bengal Staff Corps.
Battle of Tel el-Kebir. Despatches "London Gazette," 2nd November, 1882. A.D.C. to the Queen. 3rd class Medjidie. Medal with clasp; bronze star.

Rogerson, W., Major, Shropshire Regiment.
> Defence of Alexandria; occupation of Kafr ed-Dauar, and surrender of Damietta. Medal; bronze star.

Romilly, F. W., Lieutenant, Scots Guards.
> Actions of Magfar, Tel el-Maskhuta, and battle of Tel el-Kebir. Medal with clasp; bronze star.

Ronald-Taylor, N., Lieutenant-Colonel, Commissariat and Transport Corps.
> 3rd class Medjidie. Medal; bronze star.

Rooke, H. D., Major, Shropshire Regiment.
> Defence of Alexandria; occupation of Kafr ed-Dauar, and surrender of Damietta. Medal; bronze star.

Rose, A. S., Surgeon.
> Medal; bronze star.

Rose, J., York and Lancaster Regiment.
> Battle of Tel el-Kebir. Medal with clasp; bronze star.

Rostron, J. A., Veterinary Surgeon, 2nd Life Guards.
> Actions of Magfar, Mahsama, Kassassin, and battle of Tel el-Kebir. Medal with clasp; bronze star.

Rough, W. E. M., Lieutenant-Colonel, 7th Dragoon Guards.
> Actions of Magfar, Mahsama, Kassassin; battle of Tel el-Kebir, and forced march to Cairo. Medal with clasp; bronze star.

Rouse, R. S., Staff Paymaster (Major).
> Medal; bronze star.

Rowe, O., Lieutenant, Royal Artillery.
> Medal; bronze star.

Rowe, W. E., Lieutenant, Royal West Kent Regiment.
> Medal; bronze star.

Rowlandson, M. A., Major, Madras Staff Corps.
> Battle of Tel el-Kebir. Medal with clasp; bronze star.   4th class Osmanieh.

Rowney, W., Surgeon.
> Medal; bronze star.

Rundle, H. M. L., Lieutenant, Royal Artillery.
> Battle of Tel-el-Kebir. Medal with clasp; bronze star.

Russell, Sir B. C., Colonel, 13th Hussars.
> Commanded 1st Cavalry Brigade. Capture of Mahsama. Led the cavalry charge at action of Kassassin; battle of Tel el-Kebir. Despatches "London Gazette," 8th September, 19th September, and 6th October, 1882. March to and occupation of Cairo. K.C.B.; 2nd class Medjidie; medal with clasp; bronze star.

Russell, Lord H. A., Lieutenant-General.
> Action of Tel el-Maskhuta and battle of Tel el-Kebir.   Medal with clasp; bronze star.

Russell, H. A., Commissary-General of Ordnance.
> Senior Ordnance Store Officer. Despatches "London Gazette," 2nd November, 1882; C.B.; 2nd class Medjidie. Medal; bronze star. See General Orders, 9th September, 1882.

Ryan, C. A., Captain, Royal Artillery.
> Medal; bronze star.

Ryan, C. J., Major, Manchester Regiment.
> Medal; bronze star.

Ryan, M. R., Surgeon.
> Battle of Tel el-Kebir. Medal with clasp; bronze star

Ryder, D. G. R., Lieutenant, King's Royal Rifle Corps.
> Affair at Tel el-Maskhuta; action at Kassassin; and battle of Tel el-Kebir. Medal with clasp; bronze star.

Ryres, H. E., Major, Bengal Staff Corps.
Actions of Kassassin, and battle of Tel el-Kebir. Despatches "London Gazette," 2nd November, 1882. Brevet of Lieutenant-Colonel. Medal with clasp; bronze star.

St. Aubyn, E. S., Lieutenant, King's Royal Rifle Corps.
Reconnaissance at Ramleh; affair at Tel el-Maskhuta; action at Kassassin; battle of Tel el-Kebir. Medal with clasp; bronze star.

St. Clair, J. L. C., Captain, Argyll and Sutherland Highlanders.
Medal; bronze star.

St. Clair, T. S., Major, Berkshire Regiment.
Reconnaissance at Ramleh, and operations near Alexandria; surrender of Kafr ed-Dauar. Medal; bronze star.

St. Lawrence, Hon. K. D., Lieutenant, 5th Dragoon Guards.
Battle of Tel el-Kebir. Medal with clasp; bronze star.

St. Leger, H. H., Lieutenant-Colonel, Cameron Highlanders.
Battle of Tel el-Kebir. Medal with clasp; bronze star.

St. Vincent, J. E. L., Viscount, Lieutenant-Colonel, 16th Lancers.
Despatches "London Gazette," 2nd November, 1882. 4th class Medjidie; medal with clasp; bronze star.

Salkeld, C. E., Major, Bengal Staff Corps.
Action of Kassassin; battle of Tel el-Kebir. Medal with clasp; bronze star.

Salmond, W., Major, Royal Engineers.
Employed as Commanding Royal Engineer at base of operations. Despatches "London Gazette," 2nd November, 1882. Brevet of Lieutenant-Colonel. 4th class Osmanieh; medal and bronze star. See General Orders, 23rd August, 1882.

Sandbach, A. E., Lieutenant, Royal Engineers.
Battle of Tel el-Kebir. Medal with clasp; bronze star.

Sandford, F. M. H., Lieutenant, Grenadier Guards.
Action at Tel el-Maskhuta and battle of Tel el-Kebir. Medal with clasp; bronze star.

Sandwith, J. H., Captain, Royal Marine Light Infantry.
Despatches "London Gazette," 2nd November, 1882. Brevet of Major; 4th class Medjidie. See General Orders, 18th August, 1882.

Sandys, A. A., Captain, 4th Dragoon Guards.
Action at Tel el-Maskhuta; capture of Mahsama; first action at Kassassin; battle of Tel el-Kebir; pursuit to Belbeis; surrender and occupation of Cairo. Medal with clasp; bronze star.

Sangster, T. A. G., Lieutenant, Royal West Kent Regiment.
Medal; bronze star.

Saportas, A. D., Major, Manchester Regiment.
Medal; bronze star.

Sapte, H. L., Captain and Adjutant, Royal Sussex Regiment.
Medal and bronze star.

Sartin, S. R., Veterinary Surgeon (Captain).
Medal; bronze star.

Sartorius, E. H., Major, East Lancashire Regiment.
D.A.A. and Q.M.G., base and lines of communication. Despatches "London Gazette," 17th November, 1882. Brevet of Lieutenant-Colonel. 4th class Osmanieh. Medal; bronze star.

Sartorius, G. C., Major, Bombay Staff Corps.
Medal; bronze star.

Saunder, E. C., Lieutenant-Colonel.
As Senior Commissariat Officer, 1st Division. Battle of Tel el-Kebir. Promoted Deputy Commissary-General. 3rd class Medjidie. Medal with clasp; bronze star.

Savage, J. B., Veterinary Surgeon (Lieutenant).
Medal; bronze star.

Scaife, H. B., Lieutenant, Royal Sussex Regiment.
Defence of Alexandria; surrender of Kafr ed-Dauar; and occupation of Damanhur. Medal and bronze star.

Scholes, H. S., Lieutenant, York and Lancaster Regiment.
Battle of Tel-el-Kebir. Medal with clasp; bronze star.

Schomberg, H. St. G., Captain, Royal Marines.
Bombardment and occupation of Alexandria; occupation of Port Said; operations in the Suez Canal. Brevet of Major. Medal with clasp; bronze star.

Schreiber, B. F., Lieutenant-Colonel, Royal Artillery.
Commanded Royal Artillery, 1st Division. Action at Tel el-Maskhuta; capture of Mahsama; action at Kassassin on 9th September; and battle of Tel el-Kebir. Despatches "London Gazette," 2nd and 17th November, 1882. C.B.; 3rd class Medjidie; medal with clasp; bronze star.

Scott, D. A., Lieutenant, Royal Engineers.
Despatches "London Gazette," 2nd November, 1882. Brevet of Major. Medal and bronze star.

Scott, F. B., Surgeon-Major, Army Medical Department.
Battle of Tel el-Kebir. C.M.G.; medal with clasp; bronze star.

Scott, J. S. R., Lieutenant, 3rd Hussars.
Medal; bronze star.

Scott, J. W., Major, Royal Marines.
Commanded Royal Marines at occupation of Port Saïd. Present at actions of Tel el-Maskhuta, Kassassin Lock, Kassassin, and battle of Tel el-Kebir. Despatches "London Gazette," 8th September, 1882. Brevet of Lieutenant-Colonel. Medal with clasp; 4th class Osmanieh; bronze star.

Scott-Elliot, A., Lieutenant, Queen's Own Cameron Highlanders.
Battle of Tel el-Kebir. Medal with clasp; bronze star.

Serase-Dickins, S. W., Lieutenant, Highland Light Infantry.
Battle of Tel el-Kebir. Medal with clasp; bronze star.

Scudamore-Stanhope, Hon. E. T.
Reconnaissance at Ramleh; affair at Tel el-Maskhuta; action at Kassassin; and battle of Tel el-Kebir. Medal with clasp; bronze star.

Sears, J. W., Lieutenant, South Staffordshire Regiment.
Reconnaissance of 5th August. Medal and bronze star.

Selwyn, C. W., Lieutenant, Royal Horse Guards Blue.
Medal; bronze star.

Seymour, Lord W. F. E., Major, Coldstream Guards.
Action of Tel el-Maskhuta; and battle of Tel el-Kebir. 3rd class Osmanieh; medal with clasp; bronze star.

Sharp, R. G. A., Lieutenant, Royal Sussex Regiment.
Operations at Ramleh; surrender of Kafr ed-Dauar; occupation of Damanhur; and surrender of Damietta. Medal; bronze star.

Sharpe, F. J., Lieutenant, Middlesex Regiment.
March from Ismailia to Cairo, and occupation of latter town. Medal; bronze star.

Shaw, F. C., Lieutenant, Derbyshire Regiment.
Medal ; bronze star.
Shaw, G., Surgeon-Major, Army Medical Department.
Killed in action at Kassassin, 28th August, 1882.
Shaw, J. A., Surgeon-Major, Army Medical Department.
Battle of Tel el-Kebir. Mentioned in despatches. Medal with
clasp; bronze star.
Shaw-Hellier, T. B., Lieutenant-Colonel, 4th Dragoon Guards.
Commanded 4th Dragoon Guards. Action at Tel el-Maskhuta ;
capture of Mahsama ; first action at Kassassin. Medal; bronze star.
Sheppard, C. L., Conductor of Stores.
Medal ; bronze star.
Shewan, G., Surgeon, Bengal Medical Service.
Battle of Tel el-Kebir. Medal with clasp ; bronze star.
Shute, H. G. D., Lieutenant, Coldstream Guards.
Action of Tel el-Maskhuta ; and battle of Tel el-Kebir. Medal with
clasp ; bronze star.
Simpson, A. E., Captain, Manchester Regiment.
Medal ; bronze star.
Simpson, J. M. T., Lieutenant-Colonel, York and Lancaster Regiment.
Battle of Tel el-Kebir. Medal with clasp ; bronze star.
Sinclair, C., now Lieutenant, Black Watch (Royal Highlanders).
Battle of Tel el-Kebir. Medal with clasp ; bronze star.
Sinclair, W., Major, South Staffordshire Regiment.
Reconnaissance of 5th August. Medal and bronze star.
Singer, G. H., Paymaster (Honorary Captain), Manchester Regiment.
Medal ; bronze star.
Sitwell, C. G. H., Lieutenant, Shropshire Light Infantry.
Defence of Alexandria ; occupation of Kafr ed-Dauar ; surrender of
Damietta. Medal ; bronze star.
Skinner, E. G., Captain, Ordnance Store Department.
Action of Kassassin. Despatches " London Gazette," 2nd Novem-
ber, 1882. Promoted Assistant Commissary-General of Ordnance.
4th class Medjidie. Medal ; bronze star.
Skirving, D. S., Captain, Commissariat and Transport Staff.
Medal ; bronze star.
Slade, F. G., Captain, Royal Artillery.
4th class Medjidie. Medal and bronze star.
Smith, Clement, Paymaster, Seaforth Highlanders.
Battle of Tel el-Kebir. Medal with clasp ; bronze star.
Smith, C., Surgeon-General (Madras).
P.M.O., Indian Contingent. Battle of Tel el-Kebir ; forced march
to and occupation of Zagazig. Despatches " London Gazette,"
17th November, 1882. 3rd class Osmanieh ; C.B. Medal with
clasp ; bronze star.
Smith, C. Holled, Captain, King's Royal Rifle Corps.
Reconnaissance at Ramleh ; affair at Tel el-Maskhuta ; action at
Kassassin ; battle of Tel el-Kebir. Despatches "London Gazette,"
2nd November, 1882. Brevet of Major. Medal with clasp ;
bronze star.
Smith, Rev. George, Chaplain, 4th class.
Medal ; bronze star.
Smith, H. S., Lieutenant, Manchester Regiment.
Medal ; bronze star.
Smith, J. Adolphus, Lieutenant-Colonel, 1st West India Regiment.
Medal ; bronze star.

Smith, P., Lieutenant-Colonel, Grenadier Guards.
    Action of Tel el-Maskhuta. Battle of Tel el Kebir. Despatches
    "London Gazette," 2nd November, 1882. 3rd class Medjidie;
    C.B. Medal with clasp; bronze star.
Smith, Peter, now Quartermaster, Scots Guards.
    Battle of Tel el-Kebir. Medal with clasp; bronze star.
Smith, S., Captain, Royal Engineers.
    Battle of Tel el-Kebir. Despatches "London Gazette," 2nd No-
    vember, 1882. Brevet of Major. Medal with clasp; bronze
    star.
Smith, S. M., Veterinary Surgeon (Lieutenant).
    Actions of Tel el-Maskhuta and Mahsama. Medal; bronze star.
Smith, W. A., Lieutenant, Royal Artillery.
    Despatches "London Gazette," 2nd November, 1882. 5th class
    Medjidie. Medal; bronze star.
Smith-Cuninghame, J. A., Lieutenant, 2nd Life Guards.
    Two actions at Kassa-sin, and battle of Tel el-Kebir. Medal with
    clasp; bronze star.
Smith-Dorrien, H. L., Captain, 2nd Battalion Derbyshire Regiment.
    Raised and commanded Corps of Mounted Infantry. Medal; bronze
    star.
Smyth, H. F., Major, Royal Artillery (Half-pay).
Solbé, Rev. C. A., Chaplain, 3rd class.
    Medal; bronze star.
Somerset, Lord H. E. B., Lieutenant, Royal Horse Guards.
    Two actions at Kassassin, and battle of Tel el-Kebir. Medal with
    clasp; bronze star.
Somervell, L., Lieutenant, Highland Light Infantry.
    Killed in action at Tel el-Kebir.
Souter, T., now Lieutenant, Black Watch (Royal Highlanders).
    Battle of Tel el-Kebir. Despatches "London Gazette," 2nd No-
    vember, 1882. Promoted Lieutenant for distinguished service.
Sparkes, J. G., Captain, Derbyshire Regiment.
    Medal; bronze star.
Speid, F. L., Lieutenant, Royal Highlanders.
    Battle of Tel-el-Kebir (wounded). Medal with clasp; bronze
    star.
Spence, E. K. E., Lieutenant, Bengal Staff Corps.
    Battle of Tel el-Kebir. Medal with clasp; bronze star.
Spiller, D. C. O., Staff Paymaster (Major).
    Medal; bronze star.
Spooner, W. B., Veterinary Surgeon (Lieutenant).
    Medal; bronze star.
Spottiswoode, A. A., Lieutenant, Seaforth Highlanders.
    Engagement of Shaluf; seizure of Suez Canal east of Ismailia;
    battle of Tel el-Kebir; occupation of Zagazig and of Cairo.
    Medal with clasp; bronze star.
Starkey, L. E., Lieutenant, 4th Hussars.
    Battle of Tel el-Kebir. Medal with clasp; bronze star.
Steele, F. W., Lieutenant, Duke of Cornwall's Light Infantry.
    Reconnaissance in force on Kafr ed-Dauar. Actions at Magfar,
    Tel el-Maskhuta, and Kassassin; battle of Tel el-Kebir. Medal
    with clasp; bronze star.
Steele, St. G. L., Lieutenant, Bengal Staff Corps.
    Action of Kassassin, and battle of Tel-el-Kebir. Medal with clasp;
    bronze star

Steevens, J., Captain, Ordnance Store Department.
Senior Ordnance Store Officer, 2nd Division. Battle of Tel el-Kebir. Despatches "London Gazette," 2nd November, 1882. Promoted Assistant Commissary-General of Ordnance. 4th class Medjidie; medal with clasp; bronze star.

Sterling, J. B., Major, Coldstream Guards.
Action of Tel el-Maskhuta; and battle of Tel el-Kebir (wounded). 4th class Osmanieh. Medal with clasp; bronze star

Stevens, G. S., Lieutenant-Colonel, Bombay Staff Corps.
Medal; bronze star.

Stevenson, T. R., Lieutenant-Colonel, Royal Irish Fusiliers.
Battle of Tel el-Kebir. Despatches "London Gazette," 17th November, 1882; C.B. Medal with clasp; bronze star.

Stevenson, W. H., Lieutenant, Highland Light Infantry.
Battle of Tel el-Kebir. Medal with clasp; bronze star.

Stewart, H. K., Lieutenant, Gordon Highlanders.
Battle of Tel el-Kebir. Medal with clasp; bronze star.

Stewart, H., Brevet Lieutenant-Colonel, 3rd Dragoon Guards.
A.A. and Q.M.G., Cavalry Division. Action of Tel el-Maskhuta. Capture of Mahsama; battle of Tel el-Kebir; and surrender and occupation of Cairo. Despatches "London Gazette," 8th September, 6th October, and 2nd November, 1882. A.D.C. to the Queen; C.B.; 3rd class Osmanieh. Medal with clasp; bronze star.

Stockley, V. M., Lieutenant, Bengal Staff Corps.
Action of Kassassin, battle of Tel el-Kebir, and occupation of Cairo. Medal with clasp; bronze star.

Stockwell, C. M., Lieutenant-Colonel, Seaforth Highlanders.
Commanded 1st Battalion Seaforth Highlanders. Seizure of Suez Canal cast of Ismailia; battle of Tel el-Kebir; occupation of Zagazig and of Cairo. Despatches "London Gazette," 8th September and 2nd November, 1882. 3rd class Medjidie. Medal with clasp; bronze star. Distinguished service reward.

Stokes, F. O. L., Lieutenant, Derbyshire Regiment.
Medal; bronze star.

Stoneman, J., Captain, Commissariat and Transport Staff.
Medal; bronze star.

Stopford, Hon. E. B. L. H., Lieutenant, Royal Irish Fusiliers.
Battle of Tel el-Kebir. Medal with clasp; bronze star.

Stopford, Hon. F. W., Lieutenant, Grenadier Guards.
A.D.C. to Chief of Staff. Despatches "London Gazette," 2nd November, 1882. 5th class Medjidie. Medal with clasp; bronze star.

Stopford, L. A. M., Lieutenant, Derbyshire Regiment.
Medal; bronze star.

Stracey, C. E., Lieutenant, Manchester Regiment.
Medal; bronze star.

Stracey, J. B., Lieutenant, Scots Guards.
Actions of Magfar and Tel el-Maskhuta; battle of Tel el-Kebir. Medal with clasp; bronze star.

Straghan, A., Lieutenant-Colonel, Highland Light Infantry.
Battle of Tel el-Kebir. Despatches "London Gazette," 2nd November, 1882; C.B.; 3rd class Medjidie. Medal with clasp; bronze star.

Strange, R. G., Lieutenant, Royal Artillery.
Medal; bronze star.

Strong, H. H., Major, Royal Marine Light Infantry.
Killed in action at Tel el-Kebir.

Stubbs, A. G. B., Lieutenant, Manchester Regiment.
Medal; bronze star.

Studdy, R. W., Major, Manchester Regiment.
Medal; bronze star.

Sturgeon, G. C., Major, 24th Middlesex Rifle Volunteer Corps.
Head of Military Postal Department. Despatches "London Gazette," 2nd November, 1882. Medal and bronze star.

Swabey, L. W., Surgeon.
Medal; bronze star.

Swaine, C. E., Captain, 11th Hussars.
A.D.C. to Brigadier-General, Cavalry Brigade. Action of Tel el-Maskhuta; capture of Mahsama; both actions at Kassassin; battle of Tel el-Kebir; pursuit to Belbeis; surrender and occupation of Cairo. Despatches "London Gazette," 2nd November, 1882. Brevet of Major. 4th class Medjidie. Medal with clasp: bronze star.

Swaine, L. V., Major, Rifle Brigade.
Military Secretary to G.O.C. Battle of Tel el-Kebir. Despatches "London Gazette," 2nd November, 1882. Brevet of Lieutenant-Colonel. 3rd class Medjidie; C.B.; medal with clasp; bronze star.

Swanton, J. H., Lieutenant, Royal Marine Light Infantry.
Bombardment of forts of Alexandria, occupation of lines of Alexandria and of forts in Abukir Bay. Medal with clasp; bronze star.

Swinburne, T. R., Lieutenant, Royal Marine Artillery.
Despatches "London Gazette," 8th September. Medal; bronze star.

Swinton, G. S., Lieutenant, Berkshire Regiment.
Surrender of Kafr ed-Dauar. Medal; bronze star.

Swinton, R. R., Lieutenant, Derbyshire Regiment.
Medal; bronze star.

Sykes, J., Surgeon, Bengal Medical Service.
Battle of Tel el-Kebir. Medal with clasp; bronze star.

Symonds, G. H., Lieutenant, Royal Irish Regiment.
Battle of Tel el-Kebir. Medal with clasp; bronze star.

Synge, R. F. M. F. M., Lieutenant, Highland Light Infantry.
Battle of Tel el-Kebir (wounded). Medal with clasp; bronze star.

Tabor, J. M., Captain, Royal Horse Artillery.
Battle of Tel el-Kebir. Medal with clasp; bronze star.

Talbot, H. L., Lieutenant, Royal Engineers.
Bombardment of Forts of Alexandria; reconnaissance of 5th August; actions of Magfar, Tel el-Maskhuta, Kassassin; and battle of Tel el-Kebir. Despatches "London Gazette," 19th September, 1882. 5th class Medjidie. Medal with two clasps; bronze star.

Talbot, Hon. R. A. J., Lieutenant and Captain, 1st Life Guards.
Actions of Magfar, Mahsama, Kassassin, and battle of Tel el-Kebir; march to and occupation of Cairo. Despatches "London Gazette," 2nd November, 1882. 4th class Osmanieh.

Tanner, O. V., Brigadier-General.
Commanded Infantry Brigade, Indian Contingent. Affair at Shaluf; and battle of Tel el-Kebir. Despatches "London Gazette," 8th September, 6th October, and 2nd November, 1882. 2nd class Medjidie; K.C.B.; medal with clasp; bronze star.

Tanner, W., Surgeon-Major.
Medal; bronze star.

Tatham, A. G., Lieutenant, Royal Marines.
Bombardment of forts of Alexandria. Medal with clasp; bronze star.
Tattersall, J. C. de V., Lieutenant, 2nd Dragoon Guards.
5th class Medjidie; medal and bronze star. See General Orders, 30th August, 1882.
Taylor, A. M., Major, 19th Hussars.
Battle of Tel el-Kebir. Brevet of Lieutenant-Colonel. 4th class Osmanieh. Medal with clasp; bronze star.
Taylor, F. E. V., Captain, Derbyshire Regiment.
Medal ; bronze star.
Taylor, P. T. H., Major, Royal Artillery.
Battle of Tel el-Kebir. Despatches "London Gazette," 2nd November, 1882. Medal with clasp; bronze star. Brevet of Lieutenant-Colonel. 3rd class Medjidie.
Taylor, W., Surgeon-Major.
Battle of Tel el-Kebir. Medal with clasp; bronze star. 4th class Medjidie.
Taylor, William Western, Lieutenant, Bengal Staff Corps.
Battle of Tel el-Kebir. Brevet of Lieutenant-Colonel. Medal with clasp; bronze star.
Teck, His Serene Highness F. P. C. L. A., Duke of.
As a Volunteer. Action at Tel el-Maskhuta ; and battle of Tel el-Kebir. Colonel in army. Medal with clasp; bronze star.
Temple, G. E., Lieutenant, Derbyshire Regiment.
Medal ; bronze star.
Templer, J. G. E., Lieutenant, Highland Light Infantry.
Battle of Tel el-Kebir. Medal with clasp; bronze star.
Templer, J. L. B., Captain, King's Royal Rifle Corps.
Medal ; bronze star.
Tenison, W., Lieutenant, Manchester Regiment.
Medal ; bronze star.
Tennant, C. R., Captain, 2nd Life Guards.
Actions of Magfar, Mahsama, Kassassin, and battle of Tel el-Kebir. Medal with clasp ; bronze star.
Tennyson-D'Eyncourt, A. L., Lieutenant, Berkshire Regiment.
Surrender of Kafr ed-Dauar. Medal; bronze star.
Ternan, R. R. B., Captain (Paymaster), Manchester Regiment.
Medal ; bronze star.
Ternan, T. P. B., Lieutenant, Manchester Regiment.
Medal ; bronze star.
Terrot, C. E., Major, Shropshire Regiment.
Defence of Alexandria; surrender of Kafr ed-Dauar. Medal; bronze star.
Terry, Arthur F., Lieutenant-Colonel, King's Royal Rifle Corps.
Battle of Tel el-Kebir. Medal with clasp ; bronze star.
Terry, W. G., Lieutenant, Royal Artillery.
Medal ; bronze star.
Terry, W. S., Captain, Royal Irish Fusiliers.
Battle of Tel el-Kebir. Medal with clasp; bronze star.
Thackeray, M., Lieutenant, South Staffordshire Regiment.
Medal and bronze star.
Thackwell, W. de W. R., Lieutenant-Colonel, South Staffordshire Regiment.
Acted as Brigadier-General in command of the Ramleh field force ; commanded left column at reconnaissance of 5th August. Mentioned in despatches. 3rd class Medjidie. Medal ; bronze star.

Thatcher, H. W., Lieutenant, King's Shropshire Light Infantry.
Defence of Alexandria; occupation of Kafr ed-Dauar; surrender of
Damietta. Medal; bronze star.

Thomas, E. A., Major, 7th Dragoon Guards.
Actions of Mahsama, Kassassin, battle of Tel el-Kebir, and forced
march to Cairo. Medal; bronze star.

Thomas, Fredk. Wm., Lieutenant, Manchester Regiment.
Medal; bronze star.

Thomas, Sir G. V., Lieutenant, Royal Horse Artillery.
Action at Kassassin, 9th September; battle of Tel el-Kebir; forced
march to Cairo. Medal with clasp; bronze star.

Thompson, C. E., Captain, Derbyshire Regiment.
Medal; bronze star

Thompson, C. W.. Captain, Royal Artillery.
Actions of Kassassin, battle of Tel-el-Kebir, and forced march to
Cairo. Medal with clasp; bronze star.

Thompson, D. H., Major, Bengal Staff Corps.
Battle of Tel el-Kebir. Medal with clasp; bronze star.

Thomsett, R. G., Surgeon.
Medal; bronze star.

Thomson, A. G., Lieutenant, Royal Artillery.
Battle of Tel el-Kebir. Medal with clasp; bronze star.

Thomson, H., Veterinary Surgeon (Lieutenant).
Action of Kassassin; battle of Tel el-Kebir. Medal with clasp;
bronze star. Promoted Veterinary Surgeon 1st class.

Thornhill, W. R., Lieutenant, Royal Highlanders.
Medal; bronze star.

Thornton, J. H., Brigade Surgeon.
Medal; bronze star.

Thring, W. P., Captain, Royal Artillery.
Second action at Kassassin and battle of Tel el-Kebir. Medal with
clasp; bronze star.

Thynne, R. T., Major and Lieutenant-Colonel, Grenadier Guards.
4th class Osmanieh. Medal; bronze star.

Tidbury, J., Surgeon.
Reconnaissance of 5th August; battle of Tel el-Kebir. Medal with
clasp; bronze star.

Tighe, W. F., Lieutenant, Grenadier Guards.
Action of Tel el-Maskhuta and battle of Tel el-Kebir. Medal with
clasp; bronze star.

Tighe, F., Lieutenant of Orderlies.
Action at Kassassin; battle of Tel el-Kebir. Medal with clasp;
bronze star.

Timbrell, T., Staff Paymaster.
Medal; bronze star.

Tims, F., Quartermaster, Ordnance Store Department.
Medal; bronze star.

Tod, G. R., Lieutenant, Seaforth Highlanders.
Seizure of Suez Canal east of Ismailia; battle of Tel el-Kebir;
occupation of Zagazig and of Cairo Medal with clasp; bronze star.

Todd, F. J., Major, Royal Irish Fusiliers.
Battle of Tel el-Kebir. 4th class Osmanieh. Medal with clasp;
bronze star.

Todd-Thornton, F. G., Lieutenant, Royal Sussex Regiment.
Operations at Ramleh; surrender of Kafr ed-Dauar; and occupation
of Damanhur. Medal; bronze star.

Toker, A. C., Major, Bengal Staff Corps.
   D.A.A.G., Indian Contingent. Battle of Tel el-Kebir. Despatches
"London Gazette," 2nd November, 1882. Brevet of Lieutenant-
Colonel. 4th class Osmanieh. Medal with clasp; bronze star.

Tolmie, T. C., Surgeon-Major.
   Battle of Tel el-Kebir. Medal with clasp; bronze star.

Tolson, W., Major, Royal Sussex Regiment.
   Medal and bronze star.

Tombe, H. E., Lieutenant, Suffolk Regiment.
   Medal; bronze star.

Tomlinson, W. W., Surgeon-Major.
   Battle of Tel el-Kebir. Medal with clasp; bronze star.

Toms, F. B. R., Lieutenant, Royal Artillery.
   Battle of Tel el-Kebir. Medal with clasp; bronze star.

Toppin, J. M., Major, Royal Irish Fusiliers.
   Medal; bronze star.

Tower, A., Major, Derbyshire Regiment.
   Acting Brigade Major to Commandant of Alexandria. Medal;
bronze star.

Tower, E. A., Lieutenant, Derbyshire Regiment.
   Medal; bronze star.

Townsend, E., Surgeon-Major.
   Battle of Tel el-Kebir. Medal with clasp; bronze star.

Townshend, F. T., Major, 2nd Life Guards.
   Actions at Magfar, Mahsama, and Kassassin (wounded).
Brevet of Lieutenant-Colonel. 4th class Osmanieh. Medal;
bronze star.

Trafford, L. J., Lieutenant, Royal Sussex Regiment.
   Defence of Alexandria. Medal and bronze star.

Trapani, A., Lieutenant, Malta Fencible Artillery.
   Medal; bronze star.

Trapani, C., Lieutenant, Malta Fencible Artillery.
   Medal; bronze star

Trevor, G. A., Lieutenant, Royal Sussex Regiment.
   Defence of Alexandria; surrender of Kafr ed-Dauar; occupation
of Damanhur; and surrender of Damietta. Medal and bronze star.

Trotter, Warren F., Lieutenant, Royal Marine Artillery.
   Bombardment of forts of Alexandria. Medal with clasp; bronze
star.

Troup, J. I., Major, Commissariat and Transport Staff.
   Medal; bronze star.

Troup, R. W., Surgeon-Major.
   Action at Kassassin, 28th August, and battle of Tel el-Kebir. Medal
with clasp; bronze star.

Truell, R. H., Lieutenant-Colonel, Shropshire Regiment.
   Defence of Alexandria, occupation of Kafr ed-Dauar, and surrender
of Damietta. Medal; bronze star.

Tucker, W. G., Captain, Royal Marine Artillery.
   Reconnaissance of 5th August; actions at Magfar, Tel el Mas-
khuta, Kassassin; and battle of Tel el-Kebir. Despatches "London
Gazette," 19th September and 2nd November, 1882. Brevet of
Major. 4th class Medjidie. Medal with clasp; bronze star.

Tuckey, T. B. A., Surgeon.
   Medal; bronze star.

Tuke, M. L., Lieutenant, Royal Engineers.
   Action at Kassassin on 9th September. Medal and bronze star.

Tulloch, A. B., Major Welsh Regiment.
Was Military Staff Officer to Admiral Commanding-in-chief at bombardment of the forts of Alexandria; afterwards in charge of Intelligence Department; and as A.A.G. to advance force under Major-General Graham. Occupation of Port Said; second action at Kassassin; and battle of Tel el-Kebir. Despatches "London Gazette," 29th July, 8th September, and 2nd November, 1882. Brevet of Lieutenant-Colonel. C.B.; 3rd class Medjidie; medal with two clasps; bronze star.
Turner, C., Lieutenant, Berkshire Regiment.
Surrender of Kafr ed-Dauar Medal; bronze star.
Turner, C. P., Surgeon.
Battle of Tel el-Kebir. Medal with clasp; bronze star.
Tuson, H. B., Lieutenant-Colonel, Royal Marines.
Commanded Royal Marine Artillery battalion at reconnaissance of 5th August. Commanded right column. Actions of Magfar, Mahsama, Kassassin, and battle of Tel el-Kebir. Despatches "London Gazette," 19th September and 2nd November, 1882. A.D.C. to the Queen. 3rd class Medjidie; C.B. Medal with clasp; bronze star.
Twiss, G. E., Surgeon.
Surrender of Kafr ed-Dauar. Medal; bronze star.
Twynam, P. A. A., Colonel (Half-pay).
A.A. and Q.M.G., 2nd Division. Battle of Tel el-Kebir. Despatches "London Gazette," 2nd November, 1882. C.B.; 3rd class Osmanieh; medal with clasp; bronze star.
Tyler, J. C., Lieutenant, Royal Engineers.
Action at Kassassin, 9th September. Medal and bronze star.
Tyrwhitt-Walker, J., Lieutenant, Royal Irish Fusiliers.
Battle of Tel-el-Kebir. Medal with clasp; bronze star.

Upperton, J., Colonel, Bengal Staff Corps.
Action at Kassassin, battle of Tel el-Kebir, and occupation of Cairo. Despatches "London Gazette," 2nd November, 1882. 3rd class Medjidie; C.B. Medal with clasp; bronze star.
Urquhart, B. C, Lieutenant, Cameron Highlanders.
Battle of Tel-el-Kebir. Medal with clasp; bronze star.
Utermarck, R. J. G., Lieutenant, Manchester Regiment.
Medal; bronze star.

Vance, E. J., Lieutenant, Suffolk Regiment.
Medal; bronze star.
Vandeleur, John O., Lieutenant-Colonel, Royal Sussex Regiment.
Defence of Alexandria; operations at Ramleh; surrender of Kafr ed-Dauar; occupation of Damanhur; and surrender of Damietta. Medal and bronze star.
Vander-Meulen, J. H. (Honorary Captain), Paymaster, Royal West Kent Regiment.
Medal; bronze star.
Vanneck, Hon. J. C., Lieutenant-Colonel, Scots Guards.
Actions of Magfar, Tel ci-Mashkhuta; battle of Tel el-Kebir. Medal with clasp; bronze star.
Van Straubenzee, T., Lieutenant-Colonel, Royal Artillery.
Commanded Royal Artillery, Indian Contingent. Battle of Tel el-Kebir. Despatches "London Gazette," 17th November, 1882. 3rd class Medjidie; C.B. Medal with clasp; bronze star.

189

Vaughan, H. B., Lieutenant, Bengal Staff Corps.
 Medal and bronze star.
Vaughan-Hughes, E., Lieutenant, Royal Artillery.
 As Orderly Officer to Lieutenant-Colonel T. Van Straubenzee.
 Battle of Tel el-Kebir. Medal with clasp; bronze star.
Veale. H. R. L., Brigade Surgeon.
 Medal; bronze star.
Verschoyle, J. H, Lieutenant, Duke of Cornwall's Light Infantry.
 Battle of Tel-el-Kebir. Medal with clasp; bronze star.
Vesey, G. C., Lieutenant, Shropshire Light Infantry.
 Defence of Alexandria; occupation of Kafr ed-Dauar; surrender of
 Damietta. Medal; bronze star.
Viall, T., Captain, Postal Department.
 Served with Army Post Office Corps. Medal; bronze star.
Vidal, W. S., Lieutenant, Royal Engineers.
 Action at Kassassin on 9th September; and battle of Tel el-Kebir.
 Medal with clasp; bronze star.
Vigor, F. G., Captain, Duke of Cornwall's Light Infantry.
 Medal; bronze star.
Vivian, Ralph, Captain, Scots Guards.
 Actions of Magfar, Tel el-Maskhuta, and battle of Tel el-Kebir
 Medal with clasp; bronze star
Vizard, R. D., Lieutenant, Manchester Regiment.
 Medal; bronze star.
Vores, C. H. S., Lieutenant, Royal Artillery.
 Battle of Tel-el-Kebir. Medal with clasp; bronze star.
Vyryan, B. G., Major, Indian Local Force, Bengal.
 Commanded outpost at Serapeum. Medal and bronze star.

Waiford, N. L., Captain, Royal Artillery.
 Medal: bronze star.
Walker, E. H., Captain, Royal Artillery.
 Battle of Tel el-Kebir. Medal with clasp; bronze star. 4th class
 Medjidie. See General Orders, 3rd September, 1882.
Walker, F., Veterinary Surgeon, 1st Life Guards (Captain).
 Actions of Magfar, Mahsama, Kassassin; battle of Tel el-Kebir;
 march to and occupation of Cairo. Medal with clasp; bronze star.
Walker, J., Surgeon-Major.
 Medal; bronze star.
Walker, John Selby, Major, Black Watch (Royal Highlanders).
 Battle of Tel el-Kebir. Medal with clasp; bronze star
Wallace, C. T., Major, Highland Light Infantry.
 Battle of Tel el-Kebir. 4th class Osmanieh. Medal with clasp;
 bronze star.
Wallace, James, Captain, Seaforth Highlanders.
 Seizure of Suez Canal east of Ismailia; battle of Tel el-Kebir;
 occupation of Zagazig and of Cairo. Medal with clasp; bronze
 star.
Wallace, W. A. J., Major, Royal Engineers.
 In charge of the railway arrangements. Battle of Tel el-Kebir.
 Despatches "London Gazette," 2nd November, 1882. Brevet
 of Lieutenant-Colonel. 4th class Osmanieh; medal with clasp;
 bronze star. See General Orders, 31st August, 1882.
Wallace, W. F. A., Lieutenant, Shropshire Light Infantry.
 Defence of Alexandria, occupation of Kafr ed-Dauar, and surrender
 of Damietta. Medal; bronze star.

Waller, S., Captain, Royal Engineers.
Action at Tel el-Maskhuta; and battle of Tel el-Kebir. Despatches "London Gazette," 2nd November, 1882. Brevet of Major 4th class Medjidie; medal with clasp; bronze star.

Walsh, John, Quartermaster, Seaforth Highlanders.
Seizure of Suez Canal east of Ismailia; battle of Tel el-Kebir; occupation of Cairo. Medal with clasp; bronze star. Honorary rank of Major.

Walsh, T., Surgeon-Major.
Battle of Tel-el-Kebir. Medal with clasp; bronze star.

Walton, H E. B., Captain, 4th Dragoon Guards.
Action at Tel el-Maskhuta, capture of Mahsama, first action at Kassassin; battle of Tel-el-Kebir, and subsequent pursuit to Belbeis, and surrender and occupation of Cairo. Medal with clasp; bronze star.

Walton, W. M. B., Major, Royal Artillery.
Battle of Tel el-Kebir. Despatches "London Gazette," 2nd November, 1882. 3rd class Medjidie; C.B. Medal with clasp; bronze star.

Ward, H. A. H., Major, King's Royal Rifle Corps.
Reconnaissance at Ramleh; affair at Tel el-Maskhuta; action at Kassassin; and battle of Tel el-Kebir. Medal with clasp; bronze star.

Ward, A. T., Lieutenant, Royal Irish Regiment.
Battle of Tel el-Kebir. Medal with clasp; bronze star.

Ward, W., Major, Royal Artillery.
Battle of Tel el-Kebir. Despatches "London Gazette," 2nd November, 1882. Brevet of Lieutenant-Colonel. 3rd class Medjidie. Medal with clasp; bronze star.

Warde, H. M. A., Captain, 19th Hussars.
Medal; bronze star.

Wardell, J., Captain, Royal Marine Light Infantry.
Killed in action at Tel el-Kebir.

Wardrop, F. M., Captain, 3rd Dragoon Guards.
A.D.C. to G.O.C. Battle of Tel el-Kebir. Despatches "London Gazette," 2nd November, 1882. Brevet of Major. 4th class Medjidie; medal with clasp; bronze star.

Waring, W. W., Lieutenant, 11th Hussars.
Medal; bronze star.

Warrand, A. R. B., Lieutenant, Seaforth Highlanders.
Engagement of Shaluf; seizure of Suez Canal east of Ismailia; battle of Tel el-Kebir; occupation of Zagazig and of Cairo. Medal with clasp; bronze star.

Warren, C., Brevet Lieutenant-Colonel, Royal Engineers.
Employed on special service under the Admiralty in connection with the murder of Professor Palmer and his party, August 1882 to March 1883. Medal and bronze star. 3rd class Medjidie; K.C.M.G.

Warren, J., Surgeon-Major.
Medal; bronze star.

Watson, C. M., Captain, Royal Engineers.
Actions at Tel el-Maskhuta and Kassassin; and battle of Tel el-Kebir; surrender and occupation of Cairo. Brevet of Major. 4th class Medjidie. Medal with clasp; bronze star.

Watson, John Edward, Lieutenant, Manchester Regiment
Medal; bronze star.

Wauchope, A. G., Captain, Royal Highlanders.
Battle of Tel el-Kebir. Medal with clasp; bronze star.
Webb, W. E., Surgeon.
Battle of Tel el-Kebir. Medal with clasp; bronze star.
Webber, C E., Lieutenant-Colonel, Royal Engineers.
A.A. and Q.M.G., Head-quarters. Battle of Tel el-Kebir.
Despatches "London Gazette," 2nd November, 1882. C.B.;
3rd class Medjidie; medal with clasp; bronze star. See General
Orders, 31st August, 1882; ditto, 11th September, 1882.
Webster, A. G., Lieutenant-Colonel, 19th Hussars.
Battle of Tel el-Kebir. Despatches "London Gazette," 2nd No-
vember, 1882. 4th class Osmanieh. Medal with clasp; bronze star.
Webster, W., Quartermaster, Coldstream Guards.
Action of Tel el-Maskhuta; and battle of Tel el-Kebir. Medal with
clasp; bronze star.
Wedderburn, A. S., Lieutenant, Royal Artillery.
Battle of Tel el-Kebir (horse shot). Medal with clasp; bronze star.
Weir, R., Riding Master, Royal Horse Guards.
Despatches "London Gazette," 2nd November, 1882. Promoted
Quartermaster, Ordnance Store Department. Medal; bronze star.
Wellings, B. W., Surgeon.
Battle of Tel el-Kebir. Medal with clasp; bronze star.
Weston, G. E., Surgeon.
Medal; bronze star.
Whately, R. P., Lieutenant, Royal Sussex Regiment.
Defence of Alexandria. Medal and bronze star.
Wheble, J. St. L., Lieutenant, Royal Horse Artillery.
Battle of Tel el-Kebir. Medal with clasp; bronze star.
Wheble, W. F., Paymaster (Honorary Major), 7th Dragoon Guards.
Medal; bronze star.
Wheeler, E., Captain, Royal Marine Artillery.
Actions of Magfar and Tel el-Maskhuta, both actions at Kassassin,
battle of Tel el-Kebir. Medal with clasp; bronze star.
Wheler, C. S., Lieutenant, Bengal Staff Corps.
Battle of Tel el-Kebir. Medal with clasp; bronze star.
Whipple, J. H. C., Surgeon, Coldstream Guards.
Action of Tel el-Maskhuta; and battle of Tel el-Kebir. Medal with
clasp; bronze star.
Whistler, A. E., Lieutenant, Wiltshire Regiment (prob. Indian Staff Corps).
Medal; bronze star.
White, D., Quartermaster, Manchester Regiment.
Medal; bronze star.
White, Fredk., Lieutenant, 14th Middlesex Rifle Volunteers.
Bombardment of Alexandria, occupation of the lines of the town,
occupation of Port Said. Medal with clasp; bronze star.
White, John, Quartermaster, 19th Hussars.
Medal; bronze star.
White, Hon. Locke, Lieutenant, Scots Guards.
Actions of Magfar, Tel el-Maskhuta, and battle of Tel el-Kebir.
Medal with clasp; bronze star.
Whitfield, G. D., Veterinary Surgeon.
Medal; bronze star.
Whitmore, M. D., Captain, Royal Engineers.
Medal and bronze star.
Whittington, G. J. C., Paymaster (Captain).
Medal; bronze star.

Wickham, G. L., Captain, Royal Horse Guards.
  Battle of Tel el-Kebir. Despatches "London Gazette," 2nd November, 1882. Brevet of Major. 4th class Medjidie. Medal with clasp; bronze star.

Wickham, H., Lieutenant, Scots Guards.
  Actions of Magfar, Tel el-Maskhuta, and battle of Tel el-Kebir Medal with clasp; bronze star.

Wigram, G. J., Lieutenant-Colonel, Coldstream Guards.
  Action of Tel el-Maskhuta; and battle of Tel el-Kebir. Despatches "London Gazette," 2nd November, 1882. C.B.; 3rd class Medjidie; medal with clasp: bronze star.

Wilbraham, L. B., Lieutenant, Royal Irish Fusiliers.
  Battle of Tel el-Kebir. Medal with clasp; bronze star.

Wildman, C. W., Captain, Royal Irish Fusiliers.
  Battle of Tel el-Kebir. Medal with clasp; bronze star.

Wilkins, J., Quartermaster, King's Royal Rifle Corps.
  Action at Kassassin; and battle of Tel el-Kebir. Medal with clasp; bronze star.

Wilkinson, H. C., Brigadier-General (Half-pay).
  Commanded 2nd Cavalry Brigade. Operations at Kassassin; reconnaissances before Tel el-Kebir; battle of Tel el-Kebir and subsequent pursuit; and occupation of Cairo. Despatches "London Gazette," 2nd and 17th November, 1882. C.B.; 2nd class Medjidie; medal with clasp; bronze star.

Will, G. E., Surgeon-Major.
  Battle of Tel el-Kebir. Medal with clasp; bronze star

Williams, Solomon, Quartermaster (Honorary Captain), 4th Dragoon Guards.
  Battle of Tel el-Kebir, subsequent pursuit to Belbeis, surrender and occupation of Cairo. Medal with clasp; bronze star.

Williams-Freeman, G. C. P., Lieutenant, Royal Sussex Regiment.
  Defence of Alexandria; surrender of Kafr ed-Dauar, occupation of Damanhur, and surrender of Damietta. Medal and bronze star.

Williamson, J. F., Surgeon.
  Battle of Tel el-Kebir. Medal with clasp; bronze star.

Willis, C. F., Surgeon, Bombay Medical Service.
  Battle of Tel el-Kebir. Medal with clasp; bronze star.

Willis, C. H., Lieutenant, Royal Marine Light Infantry.
  Occupation of Alexandria, occupation and defence of El-Meks fort. Medal; bronze star.

Willis, G. H. S., Lieutenant-General.
  Commanded 1st Division. Commanded the troops at actions of Magfar, Tel el-Maskhuta, and capture of Mahsama, and at action at Kassassin, 9th September; and the 1st Division at battle of Tel el-Kebir (wounded). Despatches "London Gazette," 8th and 26th September, 6th October, and 2nd November, 1882, Thanked by both Houses of Parliament. K.C.B.; 2nd class Osmanieh; medal with clasp; bronze star.

Willock, H. B., Lieutenant, Royal Engineers.
  Medal and bronze star.

Willoughby, Sir J. C., Lieutenant, Royal Horse Guards.
  Battle of Tel el-Kebir. Medal with clasp; bronze star.

Willoughby, R. Le M., Lieutenant, 4th Dragoon Guards.
  Action at Tel el-Maskhuta, capture of Mahsama, first action at Kassassin. Medal; bronze star.

Willshire, Sir R. T., Bart., Lieutenant, Scots Guards.
  Actions of Magfar, Tel el-Maskhuta, and battle of Tel el-Kebir.
  Medal with clasp; bronze star.
Wilson, Aristos, Lieutenant, Manchester Regiment.
  Medal ; bronze star.
Wilsm, B. R., Lieutenant, 4th Dragoon Guards.
  Battle of Tel el-Kebir. Medal with clasp; bronze star ; 5th class
  Medjidie.
Wilson, Sir C. W., Lieutenant-Colonel, Royal Engineers.
  Medal with clasp; bronze star.
Wilson, F. E. E., Lieutenant-Colonel, York and Lancaster Regiment.
  Action at Kassassin. Battle of Tel el-Kebir. Despatches " London
  Gazette," 19th September and 2nd November, 1882. 3rd class
  Medjidie ; C.B. Medal with clasp; bronze star.
Wilson, James, Surgeon-Major, Medical Staff Corps.
  Medal ; bronze star.
Wilson, W. D., Surgeon-Major.
  Medal; bronze star.
Wiltshire, H., Major, 2nd Gloucester Engineer Volunteers.
  Battle of Tel el-Kebir. Medal with clasp; bronze star.
Wingate, G. M., Lieutenant, Royal Artillery.
  Battle of Tel el-Kebir. Medal with clasp; bronze star.
Winn, J., Lieutenant, Royal Engineers.
  Medal and bronze star.
Wintour, F., Lieutenant, Royal West Kent Regiment.
  Medal ; bronze star.
Wolfe, G., Lieutenant, Royal Irish Fusiliers.
  Battle of Tel el-Kebir. Medal with clasp ; bronze star.
Wolseley, G. B., Brevet Lieutenant-Colonel, York and Lancaster Regiment.
  As A.A.G. Battle of Tel el-Kebir. Despatches "London Gazette,"
  2nd November, 1882. A.D.C. to the Queen. 3rd class Medjidie.
  Medal with clasp; bronze star. See General Orders, 13th Sep-
  tember, 1882.
Wolseley, Sir G. J., Lieutenant-General.
  Commanded in Chief the Army. Capture of Mahsama; action at
  Tel el-Maskhuta; and battle of Tel el-Kebir. Thanked by both
  Houses of Parliament, and raised to the Peerage. Promoted
  General for distinguished service. 1st class Osmanieh ; medal
  with clasp ; bronze star.
Wood, E., Captain, Royal Engineers.
  Reconnaissance of 5th August at Ramleh ; and battle of Tel el-
  Kebir. Despatches "London Gazette," 2nd November, 1882.
  Brevet of Major. 4th class Medjidie ; medal with clasp ; bronze
  star.
Wood, Sir H. E, Major-General.
  Commanded 4th Brigade, 2nd Division. Operations near Alex-
  andria ; and surrender of Kafr ed-Dauar and Damietta. Despatches
  "London Gazette," 2nd November, 1882. Thanked by both
  Houses of Parliament. 2nd class Medjidie ; medal and bronze
  star.
Wood, O. G., Surgeon, Army Medical Department.
  Battle of Tel el-Kebir. Medal with clasp ; bronze star.
Woodford, E. F., Lieutenant, York and Lancaster Regiment.
  Battle of Tel el-Kebir. Medal with clasp; bronze star.
Woods, H. C. M., Captain, Royal Artillery.
  Battle of Tel el-Kebir. Medal with clasp; bronze star.

Worlledge, J. F., Lieutenant, Bengal Staff Corps.
    Battle of Tel el-Kebir. Medal with clasp; bronze star.
Worsley, H. R. B., Lieutenant-Colonel, Bengal Staff Corps.
    Battle of Tel el-Kebir. Despatches "London Gazette," 2nd November, 1882. Medal with clasp; 3rd class of Medjidie; bronze star; C.B.
Wylly, C. H., Lieutenant, South Staffordshire Regiment.
    Medal and bronze star.
Wylly, H. C., Lieutenant, Derbyshire Regiment.
    Medal; bronze star.
Wynyard, M., Captain, Royal West Kent Regiment.
    Medal; bronze star.

Yeatman-Biggs, A. G., Major, Royal Artillery.
    Brigade Major, Royal Artillery. Despatches "London Gazette," 2nd November, 1882. Brevet of Lieutenant-Colonel. 4th class Osmanieh; medal; bronze star.
Young, J., now Lieutenant, Liverpool Regiment.
    Battle of Tel el-Kebir. Despatches "London Gazette," 2nd November, 1882. Medal with clasp; bronze star.
Young, J. C., Lieutenant, Royal Sussex Regiment.
    Medal and bronze star.
Yourdi, J. R., Surgeon.
    Medal; bronze star.

APPENDIX V.

TABLE showing the Number of Rounds expended by R.A.

Date and Place of Action.	N–A.	G–B.	A–1.	D–1.	I–2.	N–2.	C–3.	J–3.	H–1.	7–1 N.D.	Total No. of Rounds.
24th August— Magfar	280	...	...	...	...	...	...	...	...	...	280
25th August— Mahsama	196	24	30	...	...	...	...	...	...	...	250
28th August— Kassassin	117	37	...	...	...	...	...	...	...	...	154
9th September – Kassassin	138	30	40	30	...	...	...	...	...	40	278
13th September— Tel-el-Kebir	88	36	84	63	30	68	33	7	24	43	475
Total in campaign .	819	127	154	93	30	68	33	7	24	82	1,437

APPENDIX VI.

LIST of Ordnance captured at Tel el-Kebir, 13th September, 1882.

Nature of Gun.		Number captured.	Calibre.	Number of Grooves.	Weight of Shell.
			Centimetres.		Lb. oz.
Bronze, R.M.L. La Hitte	..	7	9	6	8 6
Steel, R.B.L. Krupp Essen, 1871	..	47	9	16	14 10
Steel, R.B.L. Krupp Essen, 1871	..	10	8	12	9 14
Total ..	..	58	..	..	..

APPENDIX VII.

LISTS of Killed and Wounded in the several Actions of the Campaign.

1. *During the Action of Magfar and Capture of Mahsama, 24th and 25th August.*

Corps.	Killed.			Wounded.			Sunstroke.	
	Officers.	Men.	Horses.	Officers.	Men.	Horses.	Admissions.	Deaths.
Household Cavalry ..	..	1	11	..	12	..	16	..
4th Dragoon Guards ..	..	..	..	..	..	..	..	..
7th Dragoon Guards ..	..	..	3	1	5	6	..	..
Mounted Infantry ..	..	..	..	2	1	..	..	..
N Battery A Brigade Royal Horse Artillery	..	3	7	..	1	..	..	..
2nd York and Lancaster Regiment	..	1	..	..	6	..	25	..
3rd King's Royal Rifle Corps	..	..	..	..	..	..	..	1
	..	5	21	3	25	6	41	1

2. *At Kassassin on 28th August (General Graham's Force).*

Corps.	Killed.		Wounded.	
	Officers.	Non-commissioned Officers and Men.	Officers.	Non-commissioned Officers and Men.
4th Dragoon Guards	..	..	..	1
Mounted Infantry	..	..	2	5
Royal Marine Artillery ..	..	6	3	21
Duke of Cornwall's Light Infantry..	..	..	4	14
3rd Battalion King's Royal Rifle Corps	..	..	1	..
2nd Battalion York and Lancaster..	..	1	..	9
Army Medical Department ..	1*	..	..	..
Army Hospital Corps	..	..	..	1
	1	7	10	51

* Surgeon-Major G. Shaw.

At Kassassin on 28th August (Mahsama Force).

Corps.	Killed.		Wounded.		Horses.	
	Officers.	Non-commissioned Officers and Men.	Officers.	Non-commissioned Officers and Men.	Killed.	Wounded.
1st Life Guards	..	6	..	5	9	11
2nd Life Guards	..	..	1	1	..	6
Royal Horse Guards	..	1	..	7	11	6
7th Dragoon Guards	1*	1	..	3	..	..
Commissariat and Transport Corps	..	..	..	1	..	..
	..	8	1	17	20	21

* Lieutenant H. C. Gribble, 3rd Dragoon Guards (attached).

3. *Action at Kassassin on 9th September.*

Corps.	Killed.		Wounded.		Horses.	
	Officers.	Men.	Officers.	Men.	Killed.	Wounded.
G Battery, B Brigade, Royal Horse Artillery	..	..	..	1	..	1*
2nd Bengal Cavalry	..	..	..	2	..	..
13th Lancers	..	1	..	1	1	3
N Battery, A Brigade, Royal Horse Artillery	..	..	..	2	..	..
2nd Royal Irish Regiment	..	..	..	2	..	..
Royal Marine Light Infantry	..	..	..	25	..	..
2nd York and Lancaster Regiment	..	..	..	6	..	..
Staff, Royal Artillery	..	..	..	..	1	..
A Battery, 1st Brigade, Royal Artillery	..	..	..	3	2	3
D Battery, 1st Brigade, Royal Artillery	..	..	..	5	1	3
3rd King's Royal Rifles	..	2	..	28	..	..
Staff	..	..	1	..	..	..
Royal Navy	..	..	1	..	..	..
	..	3	2	75	5	10

* Mule.

4. In the Action at Tel-el-Kebir on 13th September, 1882.

Corps.	Killed.		Wounded.		Missing.	
	Officers.	Men.	Officers.	Men.	Officers.	Men.
Staff	..	..	2	..	..	..
19th Hussars	..	..	1	..	..	..
Royal Artillery	..	..	2	17	..	..
Grenadier Guards	..	1	1¶	9	..	..
Coldstream Guards.. ..	..	..	1	7	..	..
Scots Guards	..	..	..	4	..	..
Royal Highlanders.. ..	2*	7	6**	39	..	2
Gordon Highlanders ..	1†	5	1††	29	..	4
Cameron Highlanders	..	13	3	45	..	..
Highland Light Infantry ..	3‡	14	5	52	..	..
2nd Royal Irish	1§	1	2	17	..	..
York and Lancaster ..	..	..	..	12	..	..
1st Royal Irish Fusiliers ..	..	2	..	34	..	3
Royal Marine Light Infantry..	2‖	3	1	53	..	21
Duke of Cornwall's Light Infantry ..	..	..	1	5	..	..
King's Royal Rifle Corps	..	..	..	20	..	..
Indian Contingent	..	1	..	9	..	..
Seaforth Highlanders ..	..	1	..	3	..	..
Chaplains..	..	..	1	..	..	..
	9	48	27	355	..	30

* Lieutenants T. J. Graham-Stirling and J. G. McNeill.
† Lieutenant H. G. Brooks.
‡ Major T. Colville, Lieutenants D. S. Kays and L. Somervell.
§ Captain C. M. Jones, Connaught Rangers (attached).
‖ Major H. H. Strong and Captain J. Wardell.
¶ Major and Lieutenant-Colonel R. F. Balfour (died of wounds).
** Including Lieutenant J. A. Park (died of wounds).
†† Lieutenant A. G. Pirie (died of wounds).

The Nominal Role of Casualties at "Tel-El-Kebir" appears on Appendix viii on page 217 after the Index.

INDEX.

A.

B.

C.

D.

E.

205

H.

CE-N

K.

L.

M.

N.

O.

P.

R.

213

T.

Page

Tel el-Maskhuta. Action of.

Tel el-Maskhuta. Action of ..

Page

Tel el-Maskhuta. Action of .. — 50
Dam and embankment at — 50
Dam at. Removal of, and steps necessitated by till removed.. — 55
Embankment at, and removal of ditto — 55
Tel el-Kebir. Fight at anticipated, 3rd July, 1882 — 5
Reasons of Cairo Council for occupying — 41
Motives for selecting the mode of attack and rejecting turning movements — 71-73
Absolute falsehood of statement that any Egyptian in Tel el-Kebir was bribed. "The gilded bayonets of" a sheer invention of jealous fancy — 75
Orders for attack, rations, transport, &c... — 78
Force available for storming — 85
The strange streak of light. The two men first on the parapet — 85
Tents. Provision of — 6
Tents and camp equipage. Want of — 57
Thackwell, Colonel, commands force which seized the ridge at Ramleh, 24th July — 13
Commands left column of reconnaissance — 17 et seq.
"Thalia" in the Canal — 35
Thewfik. Appointment of as Khedive . — 1
Loss of power — 1
Receives dual note — 1
In Cairo during Alexandria riots — 2
Supplies horses for mounted infantry — 12
Dismisses Arabi from Ministry of War. Is denounced by Arabi — 16
Mandate to Admiral Hoskins for seizing Suez Canal — 29
Submission to of Cairo authorities, 13th September . — 101
Enters Cairo in triumph — 104
Parade of troops before — 105
Thompson, Commander, R.N., at Ismailia — 66
Thomson, Lieutenant, R.N., at Ismailia — 66
Thornycroft torpedo-boats. Services of to expedition — 24
Timsa Lake. Convenient basin for transports — 9
Toulba Pasha surrenders — 100
"Tower Hill" in the Canal — 35
Towing-cutters placed on Canal — 55
Trains, armoured. Construction of — 14
First employment of — 14
Trains, use of at Zagazig to secure hold of station — 101
Transport in Egypt. Nature of — 7
Absence of peace organization in England adds importance to seizure of railways and canals — 9
Regimental. See Regimental Transport.
Tucker, Captain, Royal Marine Artillery. At Kassassin — 61
At Kassassin, 9th September — 69
Tug, with railway staff, in Canal — 35
Tulloch, Major (afterwards Lieutenant-Colonel), sent to report on Ismailia route — 7
Collects information — 21
Surprises sentries, Port Said — 31
His reports on ground at Tel el-Kebir — 72
His observation of the outwork at Tel el-Kebir, not recognizing it as such — 75
Turkey. See Sultan.
Twynam, Colonel, brings up Royal Rifles — 89

V.

Valises, soldiers'. Sent to Tel el-Maskhuta — 57
Vote of Credit — 15

215

W.

Page

Wagons, Artillery. Delay of .. 59
Water. Arrangements for .. 6
 Boiling and filtering. Necessity for .. 57
 Risk to supply of causes movement on Magfar .. 37
 Carts. Arrangements for .. 5
 Carts. How sent Tel el-Kebir .. 78
Watson, Captain, R.E. At Belbeis .. 97
 At Cairo .. 98
 At the Citadel .. 99
Wellesley, Sir Arthur. His view of English "public opinion" on military
 expeditions .. 53
West Kent Regiment. Wing moves to Ismailia .. 34
 Occupy Nefisha .. 35
 At Kassassin, second action .. 68
 At Kassassin and with column .. 78, 79
Wheeled transport. Absence of roads for .. 7
Wilkinson, General. At Shaluf .. 54
 At Kassassin, 9th September .. 69
 Leads night march out of camp.. 84
 Moves on Aabasa Lock and Belbeis .. 97
 Leaves Sir Drury Lowe's force, reaches Cairo, and enters it by mistake 102
Willis, General, Leaves England .. 20
 Assumes command at Alexandria .. 20
 Accompanies cavalry to Magfar .. 44
 Is given command of the troops at Magfar .. 46
 Sends support to General Graham .. 60
 Sends Brigade of Guards towards Kassassin .. 65
 Moved up to Kassassin 7th September .. 67
 Orders General Graham's brigade to turn out .. 68
 Telegraphs for Brigade of Guards .. 69
 Orders general advance .. 69
 Halts troops during action of 9th September. Reasons for this .. 70
 His selection of a point in Tel el-Kebir lines to march on .. 76
 His guiding of his own division.. 82
 His view of the cause of the late arrival of his division 82 (note)
 His reason for changing the formation of his division .. 82
 Orders "attack formation" for 2nd Brigade .. 85
 Sends Colonel Gillespie to ask for help of guns .. 89
 Joins Lieutenant-Colonel Brancker's battery .. 93
 Tel el-Kebir after 13th September .. 102
Wolseley, Sir G. As Adjutant-General orders various steps to be taken in
 preparation for possible expedition .. 4
 His Memorandum of 3rd July, 1882, giving scheme of expedition .. 4
 Prostrated with erysipelas .. 20
 Perfectly recovered. Telegraphs from Gibraltar .. 20
 Reaches Alexandria .. 22
 Accepts proposal to prepare 3rd Division.. 28
 Arranges with Sir B. Seymour for seizing Suez Canal .. 29
 In the Canal .. 35
 Letter to Sir E. Hamley .. 38
 Goes with cavalry to Magfar .. 44
 His decision to fight an action at Magfar. Grounds for it .. 44, 45
 At Tel el-Maskhuta .. 50, 51
 Decides to bring round 2nd Division (part) from Alexandria. Reasons
 for selecting time for this .. 57
 Orders forces at Alexandria to remain on defensive.. 58
 His action in arranging for prompt pursuit affected by knowing Arabi's
 intention to burn Cairo .. 70
 His observation of enemy's outpost system determines his choice of a
 night attack .. 71
 His motives for selecting this mode of attack on Tel el-Kebir .. 71–73
 Nearly shot by men at bivouac .. 83
 In night march .. 84

Casualties at "Tel-El-Kebir" 13th September, 1882
(Extracted from contemporary issues of the London Gazette)

2nd Grenadier Guards

5969	Pte. Birtles, P.	(Wnd)	3167	Pte. Parker, H.	(Wnd)
	Cpl. Churchhouse	,,		Cpl. Shepherd	,,
	Pte. Collett, W.	,,	6967	Pte. Smith, S.	,,
	C/Sgt. Holmes..	(K/A)	6771	,, Welsh, J.	,,
7101	Pte. Kearns, M.	(Wnd)	3994	,, Winnett, T.	,,

2nd Coldstream Guards

2820	Pte. Barrett, A.	(Wnd)	4460	Pte. Savin, G.	(Wnd)
3797	,, Canning, J.	,,	4037	Cpl. Smith, C.	,,
4291	,, Cochran, C.	,,		A/Sgt. Snelling	,,
	,, Hatchett	,,			

1st Scots Guards

	Pte. Gaw	(Wnd)	3655	Pte. Proctor, J.	(Wnd)
	Cpl. Geddes	,,	5045	Cpl. Webster, W.	,,

2nd Royal Irish Regiment

489	Pte. Cannon, J.	(Wnd)	991	Pte. Maher, P.	(Wnd)
395	,, Connolly, P.	,,	337	,, Malone, P.	,,
2082	Sgt. Darmody, M.	,,	933	,, Neill, P.	,,
503	L/Cpl. Devine, F. S.	(K/A)	1489	,, Ryan, P.	,,
97	Pte. Fleming, M..	(Wnd)	2148	C/Sgt. Savage, W. J.	,,
542	,, Golding, J.	,,	1875	Pte. Sexton, J.	,,
2209	,, Gough, P.	,,	2330	,, Shea, J.	,,
	,, Guy, A.	,,	2255	,, Stars, P. .. .. .. (D/Wds)
375	,, Lines, H.	,,	118	,, Woodall, J.	,,
2384	,, Looby, C.	,,			

2nd Yorks & Lancs Regiment

210	Pte. Ball, J.	(Wnd)	2055	Pte. Narey, L.	(Wnd)
1762	,, Brown, T.	,,	865	,, Sharpe, J.	,,
2510	,, Feeney, J.	,,	2301	,, Skelly, M.	,,
472	C/Sgt. Flynn, T.	,,	1920	,, Spinks, R.	,,
389	Pte. Grantham, W.	,,	2147	,, Vaughan, A.	,,
168	,, Howe	,,	2378	,, Wilson, G.	,,

K/A — Killed in Action
Wnd — Wounded in Action
Pres.K — Presumably Killed
D/Wds — Died of Wounds
Msg — Missing

2nd Duke of Cornwall's Light Infantry

	Cpl.	Clarke, W.	(Wnd)	48	Sgt.	Pearce, F.	(Wnd)
	Pte.	Gilroy, H.	,,	118	Bmn.	Robinson, W.	,,
	,,	O'Shea, M.	,,				

1st Royal Irish Fusiliers

	Cpl.	Anderson, J.	(Wnd)	1104	Pte.	Ingram, J.	(Wnd)
3	Sgt.	Brown, J. G.	,,		Sgt.	King	(K/A)
2386	Cpl.	Butler, T.	,,		Pte.	Keany, P.	(Wnd)
2589	L/Cpl.	Byrne, F.	,,	70	,,	Keating, J.	,,
2550	Pte.	Brady, M.	,,	48	,,	Kelly, J.	,,
2260	,,	Brady, P.	,,	386	,,	King, W.	,,
9	,,	Byrne, P.	,,		,,	Langan, T.	,,
	Cpl.	Cavanagh, J.	,,		,,	Loughran, T.	,,
	,,	Crompton, T.	,,		,,	McCaul	(K/A)
6084	L/Cpl.	Connolly, J...	,,		Sgt.	McGrath, P. J.	(Wnd)
	Pte.	Chambers, J.	,,		Cpl.	McAdary, J.	,,
	,,	Connors, M.	,,	571	Pte.	Mahoney, J.	,,
	,,	Conway, P...	,,	634	,,	Murphy, J...	,,
2563	,,	Cox, W.	,,	2402	Cpl.	O'Brien, J...	,,
	Sgt.	Doyle, J. M.	,,		Pte.	Reily, W.	,,
1401	Cpl.	Foley, J. C.	,,	2591	,,	Reynolds, G.	,,
2696	Pte.	Fahey, T.	,,	251	,,	Ryan, E.	,,
38	,,	Fitzgerald, J.	,,		,,	Stewart, J...	,,
1351	,,	Head, J.	,,		,,	Tyrell, J.	,,
1663	Sgt.	Johnston, J.	,,				

1st Royal Highlanders

1808	Pte.	Arthur, J.	(Wnd)	1294	S/Maj.	McNeil, J.	(K)
1629	L/Cpl.	Bannigan, J.	(K/A)	1434	Pte.	Michie, A.	,,
1247	Pte.	Bedson, G.	(Wnd.)	1685	C/Sgt.	McDonald, J.	(Wnd)
2668	,,	Bell, P...	,,	1416/2416			
263	,,	Boardman, J.	,,		L/Cpl.	McIntosh, J.	,,
2683	,,	Borland, W.	,,	1528	Pte.	McEwen, F...	,,
1724	Dmr.	Clark, W.	,,	2716	,,	McGeoch, D.	,,
1661	Sgt.	Campbell, W.	,,	697	,,	McLucas, A.	,,
114	Pte.	Cairns, P.	,,	1111	,,	Meek, J.	,,
172	,,	Cameron, D.	,,	768	,,	Murphy, M.	(Pres.K)
1688	,,	Slack, T.	,,	2641	,,	Payne, A.	(Wnd)
792	,,	Clark, T. M.	(Pres.K)	2485	,,	Robertson, G.	(K)
2699	,,	Constable, J.	(Wnd)	16	,,	Russell, M.	(D/Wds)
1192	,,	Cunningham, J...	,,	1454	,,	Smith, A.	(K)
68	,,	Dempsey, M.	,,	300	,,	Stevenson, R.	,,
194	,,	Dow, H.	,,	1449	L/Cpl.	Smith, A.	(Wnd)
1196	,,	Duff, H.	(D/Wds)	224	Pte.	Simpson, W. J.	(Msg)
2628	Cpl.	Falconer, J.	(Wnd)	165	,,	Steel, P.	(Wnd)
1100/11	Pte.	Fryer, C.	,,	1103	,,	Turnbull, G.	,,
1662	,,	Hargreaves, J.	(K/A)	1806	Sgt.	Walker, P.	(D/Wds)
238	,,	Holdsworth, E.	(Wnd)	688	Pte.	Walker, W...	(Wnd)
2466	,,	Hollingham, J.	,,	417	,,	Wassell, J...	,,
675	,,	Inkson, W.	,,	1244	,,	Wilson, J.	,,
198	L/Cpl.	Johnston, J.	,,	1089	,,	Young, H.	(D/Wds)
1494	Pte.	Kenny, J.	,,				

1st Gordon Highlanders

1558	Pte.	Anderson, F. C.	(Wnd)	1928	,,	Bartlett, T.	(Wnd)
264	,,	Baker, W.	(Msg)	2012	Cpl.	Costello, J.	,,

519	Pte.	Connor, M. ..	.. ..	(Wnd)	2087	,, Martin, W.	(Msg)
1902	L/Cpl.	Durrant, J. ..	.. ..	,,	402	,, Matchett, W.	,,
956	L/Sgt.	Fitzgerald, P.	.. ..	(K/A)	81	,, Melvin, J.	(Wnd)
1294	Pte.	Gallagher, J.	.. ..	(Wnd)	200	,, Money, H.	,,
1813	,,	Hedger, E. ..	.. ..	,,	266	Cpl. Ryan, M.	,,
571	,,	Hinkman, M.	.. ..	,,	1581	Pte. Reid, W.	,,
428	,,	Hodges, H. ..	.. ..	,,	1638	,, Smith, T.	(K/A)
531	,,	Johnson, M.	.. ..	,,	331	,, Smith, J.	(Wnd)
1714	,,	Lyon, S. ..	.. ..	,,	560	Sgt. Tattersall, H.	(Msg)
49	L/Cpl.	Munro, W. ..	.. ..	(K/A)	1835	L/Cpl. Thompson, J.	(Wnd)
1340	Sgt.	Marsh, W. ..	.. ..	(Wnd)	1941	Pte. Vincent, J.	,,
13	Dmr.	McIntosh, C.	.. ..	,,	2047	,, Welsford, G.	(K/A)
179	Pte.	McDonald, C.	.. ..	,,	554	,, Wilson, W.	,,
287	,,	McDonald, W.	.. ..	,,	1321	L/Cpl. Willis, J. H.	(Wnd)
95	,,	McGill, J. ..	.. ..	,,	1475	Pte. Wallace, J.	,,
577	Pte.	McGrath, J...	.. ..	(Wnd)	1883	,, Warren, J.	,,
1477	,,	Marrett, J. ..	.. ..	,,	555	,, Wood, W.	,,

Cameron Highlanders

2299	Pte.	Alexander, D.	.. ..	(Wnd)	1424	Pte. McAlister, A.	.. .. (Wnd)
2049	,,	Bodel, W. ..	.. ..	(K/A)	1500	,, McAlister, J.	.. .. ,,
2304	,,	Brown, R. ..	.. ..	,,	1472	,, McRae, T. ..	.. .. ,,
1536	,,	Bell, D. ..	.. ..	(Wnd)	446	,, McKale, J. ..	.. .. ,,
1261	,,	Bottomley, T.	.. ..	,,	908	,, McKenzie, W.	.. .. ,,
1055	,,	Brown, T. ..	.. ..	,,	376	,, Meers, T. ..	.. .. ,,
83	,,	Burns, M. ..	.. ..	,,	1461	,, Murray, A. ..	.. .. ,,
1455	,,	Cameron, D.	.. ..	(K/A)	1565	,, Murray, D. ..	.. .. ,,
127	,,	Crawford, G.	.. ..	,,	2197	,, Nelson, D. ..	.. .. ,,
1912	C/Sgt.	Chapman, F.	.. ..	(Wnd)	1483	,, Patterson, A.	.. .. (K/A)
2099	Cpl.	Cattanach, W.	.. ..	,,	2156	,, Pollock, J. ..	.. .. ,,
1448	L/Cpl.	Cumming, J.	.. ..	,,	901	,, Page, J. ..	.. .. (Wnd)
2247	Pte.	Chapman, W.	.. ..	,,	68	,, Quinty, G. ..	.. .. ,,
455	,,	Charsels, J. ..	.. ..	,,	2087	,, Rugg, G. ..	.. .. (K/A)
84	,,	Cockcroft, W.	.. ..	,,	146	,, Robertson, R.	.. .. (Wnd)
117	,,	Dumiston, A.	.. ..	(K/A)	550	,, Rogers, J. ..	.. .. ,,
2175	,,	Dick, J. ..	.. ..	(Wnd)	2354	,, Simon, W. ..	.. .. (K/A)
124	,,	Drummond, C.	.. ..	,,	299	,, Smith, W. ..	.. .. ,,
2192	,,	Duff, J. ..	.. ..	,,	2062	L/Cpl. Sillie, F. ..	.. .. (Wnd)
2125	Sgt.	Gunn, D. ..	.. ..	,,	426	Pte. Sheppard, J.	.. .. ,,
2051	Pte.	Hyslop, J. ..	.. ..	(K/A)	2266	,, Smith, J. C...	.. .. ,,
1406	,,	Hart, J. ..	.. ..	(Wnd)	1026	,, Spens, R. ..	.. .. ,,
2338	,,	Head, H. ..	.. ..	,,	215	,, Telford, A. ..	.. .. ,,
909	,,	Hewitt, K. H.	.. ..	,,	2343	,, Walker, J. ..	.. .. ,,
80	,,	Kenny, P. ..	.. ..	(K/A)	302	,, White, M. ..	.. .. ,,
2300	,,	King, T. ..	.. ..	,,	1662	,, Witherspoon, W.	.. .. ,,
292	,,	Kynoch, P...	.. ..	(Wnd)	1439	,, Wilson or Woolson, W.	(Wnd)
1378	Sgt.	McKenzie, A.	.. ..	,,	108	,, Young, L. ..	.. .. ,,
1873	Cpl.	McKay, J. ..	.. ..	,,			

2nd Highland Light Infantry

344	Pte.	Allen, J.	.. ..	(K/A)	82	Sgt. Dempster, W.	.. .. (K/A)
1532	,,	Amer, A.	.. ..	,,	858	,, Davis, S.	.. .. (Wnd)
2714	,,	Ambrose, W.	.. ..	(Wnd)	2552	Pte. Dixon, J. ..	.. .. ,,
2693	Cpl.	Buchán, W.	.. ..	,,	304	,, Dogherty, J.	.. .. ,,
2580	Pte.	Baird, W. ..	.. ..	,,	291	,, Duncan, G. ..	.. .. ,,
2223	,,	Braslin, P. ..	.. ..	,,	2269	L/Cpl. England, R. ..	.. .. (Msg)
1561	,,	Crawley, C. ..	.. ..	(K/A)	104	Pte. Ellis, E. ..	.. .. (Wnd)
1703	Sgt.	Cousins, H. ..	.. ..	(Wnd)	1419	., Fraser, A. ..	.. ., ,,
756	Pte.	Campbell, T.	.. ..	,,	512	,, Finnegan, M.	.. .. ,,
658	,,	Crancy, H. ..	.. ..	,,	166	,, Geraghty, T.	.. :. ,,
656	,,	Cranmer, W.	.. ..	,,	70	Cpl. Hill, J. ..	.. .. ,,

610	Pte.	Hayes, J.	(Wnd)		83	„	Moodie, J.	(Wnd)
689	„	Hunt, S.	„		381	„	Moran, E.	„
2357	„	Johnston, W.	(K/A)		229	„	Morrison, J.	(Msg)
411	„	Jarvis, R.	(Wnd)		2322	„	O'Neil, W.	„
564	Cpl.	Kellie, J.	„		2481	„	Porteous, J.	(K/A)
206	Pte.	Jordon, J.	„		2691	„	Porter, J.	(Wnd)
2313	„	Kelman, W.	„		1089	Dmr.	Rennie, P.	„
625	„	Kemody, R.	(Msg)		2290	Pte.	Rees, J.	„
1734	„	Kerrigan, C.	(Wnd)		101	„	Roche, J.	„
?	L/Cpl.	Livingston, A.	„		621	„	Rodgers, F.	„
1418	Pte.	Laing, R.	„		289	„	Roome, W.	„
563	„	Linbow, J.	„		1139	„	Ross, J.	„
1802	„	Livingstone, W.	„		2801	Sgt.	Scott, J.	(K/A)
1313	„	Lockwood, J.	„		647	Pte.	Sheen, S.	„
2783	L/Sgt.	McAlister, J.	(K/A)		1812	C/Sgt.	Stewart, A.	„
2786	Pte.	McLean, W.	„		201	Sgt.	Spiers, H.	(Wnd)
364	Pte.	Montgomery, J.	(K/A)		263	Pte.	Stapleton, J.	(Msg)
766	Sgt.	McLaren, J.	(Wnd)		2216	„	Stapleton, J.	(Wnd)
1611	Cpl.	McMillen, T.	„		2530	„	Sutherland, T.	„
293	Pte.	McAtear, W.	„		8	„	Taylor, W.	(Msg)
754	„	McCahon, E.	„		1837	„	Thompson, W.	(Wnd)
223	„	McDermott, J.	„		480	„	Tweedie, J.	(Msg)
431	„	Makin, W.	„		666	Cpl.	Ward, W.	(Wnd)
2633	„	Malloy, H.	(Msg)		162	Pte.	Wallace, G.	„
2558	„	Manning, M.	„		527	„	Whitehouse, A.	„
482	„	Martin, D.	„		811	„	Williamson, T.	„
839	„	Metcalf, J.	„					

3rd King's Royal Rifle Corps

421	Sgt.	Bell, W.	(Wnd)		3586	Pte.	Holden, J.	(Wnd)
2269	Pte.	Cooper, G.	„		1493	„	Hurley, M.	„
	„	Coleman	„			„	Mansbridge	„
	„	Dalton	„			„	Moore, J.	„
2299	„	Dowling, J.	„			„	Nunn	„
	„	Fidler	„			„	Palmer	„
4194	„	Garrett, E.	„			„	Riley	„
	„	Grey	„			„	Spearing	„
3455	„	Harwood, T.	„		3826	„	Stockhill, J.	„
	„	Hawkins	„			„	Wells	„

1st Seaforth Highlanders

1068	Pte.	Grant, A.	(Wnd)		1415	C/Sgt.	McDonald, W.	(Wnd)
1881	„	Higgs, C.	(K/A)		1216	Cpl.	Ross, D.	„

Royal Marine Light Infantry

9/Co.	Pte.	Armstrong, J.	(Wnd)		17/Co.	Bgr.	Gunn, F. A.	(Wnd)
27/Co.	„	Bathe, C. F.	(D/Wds)		20/Co.	Pte.	Gee, J.	„
33/Co.	„	Baxter, A. J.	(Wnd)		2/Co.	„	Godfrey, J.	„
17/Co.	„	Beldham, H.	(D/Wds)		12/Co.	„	Granger, J. S.	„
19/Co.	„	Buckley, D.	(Wnd)		38/Co.	„	Harrison, T.	„
38/Co.	„	Burbidge, D.	„		18/Co.	„	Hawes, J.	„
13/Co.	„	Burke, M.	„		10/Co.	„	Heap, J.	„
2/Co.	„	Burke, M.	„		15/Co.	„	Heathwaite, J.	„
30/Co.	„	Burrows, J.	„		5/Co.	„	House, S.	„
14/Co.	„	Castle, A.	(K/A)		34/Co.	„	Hutton, H.	„
30/Co.	Bgr.	Challenor, G. W.	(Wnd)		14/Co.	Sgt.	Jarvis, E. A.	(K/A)
10/Co.	Pte.	Cullin, J.	„		?	Pte.	Jenkins, W.	(Wnd)
16/Co.	„	Day, G.	„		40/Co.	„	Jordan, E. J.	„
18/Co.	„	Ellis, H.	(K/A)		44/Co.	„	Kennedy, W.	„

42/Co.	Pte.	Kitlow, J.	(Wnd)	37/Co.	..	Rutler, H. G.	,,
6/Co.	,,	Lee, T.	,,	28/Co.	,,	Salvage, C.	,,
22/Co.	,,	Lloyd, E.	,,	8/Co.	,,	Seine, W.	,,
14/Co.	Sgt.	McKenzie, J.	,,	2/Co.	,,	Sheen, T.	,,
1/Co.	,,	Moore, G.	,,	1/Co.	,,	Smith, Chas.	,,
22/Co.	Pte.	McCarthy, P.	,,	1/Co.	,,	Thirhiet, J.	,,
25/Co.	,,	Medley, H.	,,	12/Co.	,,	Warren, J.	,,
22/Co.	,,	Murray, R.	(D/Wds)	29/Co.	,,	Webster, J.	,,
21/Co.	,,	Nicholson, L.	(Wnd)	34/Co.	,,	Wilkins, E.	,,
33/Co.	,,	Power, W.	,,	20/Co.	,,	Williams, D.	,,
1/Co.	,,	Parker, B.	,,	2/Co.	,,	Wilson, W.	(D/Wds)
41/Co.	,,	Richards, E. A.	,,	38/Co.	,,	Wragg, S.	(Wnd)
31/Co.	,,	Roberts, A.	,,	25/Co.	,,	Wright, G.	,,
5/Co.	,,	Rogers, J.	,,				

Royal Artillery

1/2 Bty.	13515	Sgt. Barrett, W. T.	(Wnd)	1/2	,,		Dvr. Hurley .. .. -	,,
D/1 ,,	4135	Gnr. Beel, D. ..	,,	A/1	,,		,, Joyce, T. ..	,,
C/3 ,,		Gnr. Britain	,,	D/1	,,	8813	,, Kelsey, W. ..	,,
D/1 ,,		Sgt. Cook, A.	,,	N/2	,,	10065	,, Madigan, J...	,,
1/2 ,,		Cpl. Cormack ..	,,	1/2	,,	12250	Sgt. McCartney ..	,,
N/2 ,,	12831	Gnr. Cowell, B. ..	,,	A/1	,,	13779	Dvr. Taggart, J. ..	,,
A/1 ,,		Dvr. Cresswell J...	,,	A/1	,,		,, White, W. ..	,,
A/1 ,,	13705	Gnr. Dowman, B.	,,	A/1	,,	32187	Gnr. Watson, W...	,,
D/1 ,,		Flatt, G. ..	,,					

Officers

Lt.-Colonel	Balfour, R.	2/Grenadier Guards	(Wnd)
Reverend	Bellord, J.	Chaplain	,,
Lieutenant	Barclay, D.	19/Hussars	,,
,,	Brooks, H. G.	1/Gordons	(K/A)
,,	Blackburn, A. G.	1/Camerons	(Wnd)
Lt.-Adjutant	Cowan, H. V.	Staff (R.A.)	,,
Lieutenant	Chicester, A. G.	2/R. Irish R.	,,
Captain	Coveney, R. C.	1/R. Highlanders	,,
,,	Cumberland, G. B.	,, ,, ...	,,
Major	Colville	2/H.L.I.	(K/A)
Lieutenant	Carey, G. T. J.	,, ...	(Wnd)
Captain	Dalbiac, H. S.	F/1 Battery (R.A.)	,,
Lieutenant	Drummond-Woolf, H. H. ..	2/R. Fusiliers (att. R. Irish R.)	,,
,,	Edwards, W. M. M.	2/H.L.I.	,,
Captain	Fox, G. M.	1/R. Highlanders	,,
Lieutenant	Heneage, A. R.	2/H.L.I.	,,
Captain	Jones, C. N.	2/Conn. Rangers (att. R. Irish R.) ..	(K/A)
Lieutenant	Kays, D. S.	2/H.L.I.	,,
,,	Livingstone	1/R. Highlanders	(Wnd)
,,	Macdougall, S.	2/A. & S. Highlanders (att. Camerons)	,,
,,	McCausland, E.	R.M.L.I.	,,
,,	McNeill, J. G.	1/R. Highlanders	(K/A)
,,	Midwood, H.	2/H.L.I.	(Wnd)
,,	Malcolm, H. H. L.	1/Camerons	,,
,,	Park, J. A.	1/R. Highlanders	,,
,,	Pirie, A. G.	1/Gordons	,,
,,	Rawson, Wyatt	H.Q. Staff (R.N.)	,,
Lt.-Colonel	Richardson, W. S...	2/D.C.L.I.	,,
,,	Sterling, J. B.	2/Coldstream Guards	,,
Major	Strong, H. H.	R.M.L.I.	(K/A
Captain	Speid, F. L.	1/R. Highlanders	(Wnd)
Lieutenant	Sterling, Graham	,, ,, ...	(K/A)
,,	Somervell, L.	2/H.L.I.	,,
,,	Synge, R. F. M.	,, ...	(Wnd)
Lt.-General	Willis, G. H. S., C.B.	Staff (1st Division)	,,
Captain	Wardell, J. C.	R.M.L.I.	(K/A)

Lightning Source UK Ltd.
Milton Keynes UK
UKOW04f1412071117
312330UK00001B/81/P